3/00

A PILGRIM POPE

A PILGRIM POPE

Messages for the World

POPE JOHN PAUL II

EDITED BY **Cardinal Achille Silvestrini**
WITH THE ASSISTANCE OF **Jerome M. Vereb**, C.P.
FOREWORD BY **Cardinal Pio Laghi**

A Giniger Book
PUBLISHED IN ASSOCIATION WITH

**Andrews McMeel
Publishing**

Kansas City

www.andrewsmcmeel.com

99 00 01 02 03 RDH 10 9 8 7 6 5 4 3 2 1

Library of Congress Cataloging-in-Publication Data

John Paul II, Pope, 1920–
   A pilgrim Pope : messages for the world / edited by Cardinal Achille Silvestrini, with the assistance of Jerome M. Vereb.
       p.   cm.
   "A Giniger book."
   ISBN 0-7407-0045-6 (hardcover)
   1. Catholic Church—Doctrines Papal documents. I. Silvestrini, Achille, 1923–   . II. Vereb, Jerome M. III. Title.
   BX870   1978c Oct.
   230'.2—dc21
                                                        99-33238
                                                            CIP

Attention Schools and Businesses

Andrews McMeel books are available at quantity discounts with bulk purchase for educational, business, or sales promotional use. For information, please write to: Special Sales Department, Andrews McMeel Publishing, 4520 Main Street, Kansas City, Missouri 64111.

CONTENTS

PART I

PART II

PART III

$\mathcal{F}$OREWORD

THIS COMPENDIUM OF THE PILGRIM JOURNEYS of Pope John Paul II bespeaks his innovative ministry in the history of the Popes. Never before has one Pontiff traveled so extensively in the service of the Gospel. This Pope has occupied the Chair of Peter longer than any other in this century. He has also lived and ministered in a time of rapid social change, during which communications are more immediate and long-distance travel is more efficient.

The fundamental character of Karol Wojtyla was revealed on that October Sunday in 1978 when his pontificate as Pope John Paul II was formally inaugurated. At the end of the ceremony, after greeting the world in a variety of languages, he went forward to meet the crowd of some 250,000 by waving his crosier before him in St. Peter's Square. This symbol of the episcopacy had already been restyled into a crucifix by his predecessor, Pope Paul VI. By this gesture, the newly elected Pope deferred the crowd's applause directed at him to the image of Jesus on the Cross. The new Pope did not want a popular cult directed at him, but a clear prominence to the person of the Son of God, Jesus Christ.

Pope John Paul II soon followed up the great innovations of his election and installation, all focused on ethnic and global inferences by the press, with his encyclical *Redemptor Hominis*. The central theme of the Pope's first encyclical is that Jesus is at the heart of human history. "The Church wishes to serve this single end: that each person may be able to find Christ, in order that Christ may walk with each person the path of life, with the power of the truth about man and the world that is contained in the mystery of the incarnation and the redemption and with the power of the love that is radiated by that truth" (*R.H.* 13).

Right from the start, Pope John Paul II defined himself as a person with a mission—to carry Jesus Christ to the world, to all its many countries, to the variety of expressions of culture, to each person, to every expression of need. From his first encyclical, he also emphasized that the years of his pontificate might run concurrently with the preparations for the new millennium. He wrote, "For the Church, the People of God, spread, although unevenly, to the most distant limits of the earth, it will be a year of a great Jubilee" (*R.H.*).

Now that we are on the threshold of that Jubilee and the start of a new millennium, the many pastoral journeys of Pope John Paul II have very much helped the entire world raise its consciousness to the new age about to dawn and to the presence of grace in the midst of many transitions which accompany the events we prepare to celebrate.

Cardinal Achille Silvestrini has organized passages from the papal addresses delivered on these many trips from Rome to various nations. They reveal the complexities of our era with its many challenges, but they also reveal the faith of one who is secure in a simple answer to life's challenges: "All things in Christ."

CARDINAL PIO LAGHI
Prefect
Congregation for Catholic Education

*P*REFACE

Il Cardinale Achille Silvestrini

POPE JOHN PAUL II's regular travels are one of the most striking and original aspects of his pontificate. Pastoral visits and pilgrimages are cardinal elements in his service to the Church Universal and have become a means of communication with the entire world.

The Bishop of Rome travels in order to encounter the Catholic community. But he also uses these occasions to reach out to other Christians, thereby giving his ministry an extraordinary ecumenical dimension. In addition, he is always desirous of meeting with representatives of the Jewish community and other believers in God, including those from other religious confessions. His pastoral visits, in fact, show his willingness to neglect no avenue in his quest to reach all men and women of goodwill. By addressing them sincerely and intimately, he strives to show that in every person there are deep, shared values and that, under the Fatherhood of God, humanity is a single family called to dialogue and collaboration regarding justice and freedom for everyone.

The Pope, as Successor of Peter, is sent to confirm his brothers in the Episcopate in their mandate to shepherd the ecclesial community and help it grow in faith. This is a service of charity that continually opens to an ever-wider horizon, as the call to faith is addressed to all people. In harmony with the bishops, the Pope confirms all of his brothers and sisters in their commitment to faith in Christ. In this way, they become close to every person, beginning with the "last" because of material or spiritual poverty. Wherever the Pope visits, he remembers above all that Christ has already preceded him. The joyful reception reserved for him everywhere by persons of all faiths—and by those burdened by doubt, and even those who fail to recognize themselves in the vision of man and history which arises from the Gospel— is a sign of hopeful expectation for him—whom the Pope represents and by whom he is sent: Christ the Redeemer of man. The profound fraternity which an encounter with the Pope engenders is none other than the reawakening of an awareness of a presence, that of Christ.

Since the Pope intends to guide the Church, which is everywhere, deeper into the mystery of Christ, he also encounters on that same road the men and women of our time. With respect and veneration, this voyager traverses the different regions of the globe and encounters Christians and non-Christians alike, with their unique histories, cultures, and, most important, with their religious journeys. He seeks an encounter with people from every corner of the globe, from every age group and personal and social condition, with the man or woman who lives, works, loves, and hopes, with those who suffer under life's burdens. Having dedicated his entire existence to the one who said "I am the way" (Jn 14:6), the Holy Father was able to write in his first encyclical—the prelude to his pontificate—"the way of the Church is man" (*R.H.* 14).

From the moment of his first discourse in October 1978, Pope John Paul II's intentions have been clear. His ministry would be one of going in search of the men and women of our time to announce to them the Gospel, that is, the person of Jesus, Son of God, our brother who "knows what is in the heart of man" and who can thus address the heart's deepest questions. Each person is a person who awaits, in the depths of his being and from Christ alone, the gift of "the Spirit without measure" (see Jn 3:34).

The Pope's entire ministry draws motivation and strength from this decision to lead all people either onto or farther along the path to Christ. The pages of this book seek to give due recognition to this pilgrimage of faith as well as to the importance of not turning one's back on the path—the "Way"—once it has been taken.

John Paul II will clearly emerge in these pages as *"pastor"* and *"pilgrim."*

The Papal visits of John Paul II have occurred largely in response to invitations extended from Bishops Conferences around the world, from international organizations such as the United Nations, or from government leaders. In many instances, the invitations for a visit have come from all three sources combined. The focus of each journey is pastoral in nature and is directly connected to the contemporary proclamation of the Gospel. Often the Pontiff has been present to some critical need, as in the instance of his journey to war-torn Sarajevo, in Bosnia. He also speaks to the many issues of our era, an era characterized by rapid change, exposure to mass media, and an overall shift in personal and social morality.

All too often, the visits of the Pope have been viewed by the popular press strictly from a moral perspective, but as Pope John Paul himself said in an address at Trinity College in Washington, D.C., in 1979, "The moral life and life of faith are so intimately associated that it is impossible to separate them." Underlying the ethical statements for which he has become renowned are his deep personal convictions of the abiding presence of God, the centrality of the mystery of the Redemption, the Church as a communion of believers, and the power of the Sacrament of the Holy Eucharist. For this reason, many of the addresses included in this volume are homilies delivered in the context of the celebration of the Mass.

As we can see, the Pope comes as a Shepherd to bring sustenance to people today, his message is drawn from the Word of God and the Church's tradition, piety, and practice. It is always a message of joy, hope, and comfort. Hence the texts of papal messages are carefully prepared to be long-lasting in their effect.

Another note about Pope John Paul II is that he has always traveled as a pilgrim, a point he made poignantly by kissing the ground of each country visited for the first time, and by his many references to local places of faith and spirituality in his discourses.

He is *the* pilgrim of our time, who knows how to encounter Christ in the people around him, in their challenges and poverty, in their great aspirations and realizations, in the struggles that humanity endures to guarantee truth, justice, and peace for everyone. And this pilgrim knows well that man can truly discover himself in an encounter with Christ. With his words and the eloquent content of his gestures he helps people to recognize their weakness and their sin, so that they can draw near to the Lord Jesus and his Church and receive the embrace of pardon.

This Pontiff is a pastor and pilgrim in the footsteps of Paul VI. It was Paul VI, in fact, who had earlier expressed his conviction regarding the usefulness of the direct presence of the Pontiff on the world scene in order to facilitate the spread of the Christian message. His courageous and unheard-of idea found realization in a few trips of enormous symbolic significance.

Throughout the modern era, in fact, the Popes traveled outside of Rome. Pius VI and Pius VII in the Napoleonic era, for reasons of forced exile, as well as Pius IX who attempted to prevent the collapse of the Papal States. After the resolution of the "Roman problem" with the signing of the Lateran Pacts between Italy and the Holy See in 1929, the Popes—Ratti and Pacelli—began once more to travel outside the Vatican. John XXIII went to Loreto and Assisi on the vigil of the opening of the Second Vatican Council. Paul VI "invented," however, the contemporary sense of apostolic voyages when he went to the Holy Land, the United Nations, Istanbul, Geneva, and later Africa, India, Latin America, the Philippines, Australia, and Fatima. His visits had an underlying logic. He traveled to the land of the Church's origins, to areas of division to show his desire for unity, and to the great frontiers of the Church's future missionary endeavors on every continent. He concluded with the trip to Fatima as if imploring the breath of the Holy Spirit to touch the lands of the East, then under anti-Christian regimes.

John Paul II is not an ordinary world traveler. His pastoral visits are part of his vocation and require a clear method. He tries to reach all of the local churches to reawaken a systematic missionary action in the Catholic community and to encourage fraternal openness throughout the world. This is his way of exercising his Petrine office and promoting the new evangelization. His eagerness to promote the spreading of the Gospel to those who have not yet had the opportunity to hear it is tied closely to his concern about reevangelizing the churches of ancient Christian tradition. These churches are going through a grave crisis of identity notwithstanding promising signs of the Spirit's vitality. John Paul II, like his predecessor, confirms during his apostolic visits that the Church's best response to her internal difficulties rests firmly with a decisive effort of evangelization.

This is how he has transformed his pontificate into a semi-itinerant service, accomplishing his voyages always as pastor and pilgrim. When he travels in the context of civil communities and international organizations, he always strives to bring the Church's dealings with states beyond the traditional dimensions of relations between institutions to one of civil discourse with peoples, nations, and individuals. In his view, diplomatic emissaries must be representations of peoples more than governments. But in his discourses to various state leaders he strives constantly to underscore that man's ties to God demand that the international community construct its life on binding ethical norms. Only in this way can peaceful and just coexistence be preserved among peoples, and the dignity of man created in the image and likeness of the Creator be safeguarded.

In conclusion, I would like to cite a few enlightening words of John Paul II that affirm his decisive convictions as traveler and apostle: "God willing, I will go to the many places where I have been invited. . . . The more difficult the path of people in general, of families, of the community and the world, the more it becomes necessary that the Good Shepherd be seen as one who lays down his life for his flock. . . . It seems to me that even the post-Conciliar life of the Church has changed this need into an imperative, on the level of a commandment and an obligation in conscience" (André Frossard, *Non Abbiate Paura,* Rome 1983, pp. 246 ff). The Pope finds in his visits the very reasons underlying their necessity. In an effort to describe the "theological" and "apostolic" root of his travels, he had the following to say during a trip to Africa: "Some people in Europe think that the Pope should not travel, that he should stay in Rome, as it has always been. . . . Instead, I want to say here that it is a grace of God that I have come, because in this way I can get to know you . . . and this strengthens me in the conviction that the time has come in which the Bishops of Rome—that is, the Popes—must not consider themselves only Successors of Peter, but also heirs of Paul as well who, we know well, was never at rest: He was always on the move" (M. Malinski, *Le radici di Papa Wojtyla,* Rome 1979, p. 168).

It is hoped that this book will convey something of the words and message of Pope John Paul II as an incentive that demonstrates the dynamism of a Shepherd whose care for his flock has been consistently global, individual, and meaningful. It is all the more significant when one considers the obstacles of illness, distance, geography, and climate he has had to surmount in his undertakings. Yet the spirit which he sought to convey has also sustained him and made clear the authenticity of his message and the sincerity of his efforts.

CARDINAL ACHILLE SILVESTRINI
Prefect
Congregation for Oriental Churches

INTRODUCTION

THE MANY JOURNEYS OF POPE JOHN PAUL II tell a story. That story in turn discloses the irrevocable effect this man has had on the latter part of the twentieth century. He embraced the world and formed it into his own parish. He was the pastor of that parish. Never again could someone claim that the papacy remains aloof, out of touch with problems and with persons. Endowed with tireless stamina, versatile linguistic skills, and a thirst to experience the many expressions of life, he reached beyond Italy's boundaries and eventually circled the globe in some eighty-five trips.

In the course of his pontificate, Pope John Paul addressed the United Nations, the International Labor Organization, the European Parliament, and the World Council of Churches. To all of these postwar institutions of international collaboration, he stressed the message of unity. The frontiers of nationalism and ideology were no longer an impediment to that deep quest for human communion which is a part of everybody's inner hunger. Instead, those boundaries invited that creative response which was soon to be forthcoming. This is the genius of Pope John Paul. His message is delivered on the social and on the personal level at the same time!

Very often, while visiting another country, he beatified or canonized heroes and heroines of the faith; many of these were, dramatically, martyrs of the twentieth century. These events underscore the depth of commitment to the will of God that is asked of each of us. At the same time the ceremonies with their liturgies—no longer confined to Rome—contribute to a sense of religious culture which the Pontiff was anxious to develop and support. Building upon the example of his predecessor, Pope Paul VI, he often used the expression "the civilization of love." John Paul also had phrases of his own which he used to support family life. He spoke of a "culture of life," as opposed to a "culture of death." Both of these, of course, define the fundamental issues of family life, the theme that he consistently reiterated in national visits and in every conceivable circumstance.

Essentially, the entire history of the papal pilgrimages to date can be defined in three phases. The first phase runs from 1979 to 1981, when the theme of "evangelization" predominated, especially as outlined in Pope Paul VI's document *Evangelii Nuntiandi* (1975). Pope John Paul addressed this theme to the hierarchy of each nation he visited. In 1981, the same year that the attempt was made on his life, he also actively took up the theme of "solidarity," especially as it became a buzzword of the labor and political struggles of Eastern Europe. That term has never left his vocabulary. It signifies so much more than politics or the jargon of ideology. The time from 1981 to 1989 constitutes Part II of this book. The third part, from 1989 to the present, outlines the dangers of succumbing to materialism and fads, as well as the anticipation of the jubilee year of Jesus' birth, the millennium theme, as it were. It rejoices in liberation from the quest for consumption and threats of the Cold War.

Most important, in 1983-84, the Pope took up the theme of the "new evangelization": This phrase, coined in Haiti and developed a year later in the Dominican Republic, is a clarion call for a vigorous and all-inclusive attempt to communicate the Gospel. According to Father Avery Dulles, the invitation to the new evangelization has four notes: the participation of every Christian; its distinction from foreign missions; its direction to cultures; its comprehensiveness, that is, the process involves cathechesis, moral instruction, and social doctrine. The vision of the Pope embraces a world transformed by the "glory of the Lord" (see Avery Dulles, S.J., "John Paul II and the New Evangelization—What Does It Mean?" in Ralph Martin and Peter Williamson, *Pope John Paul II and the New Evangelization* [Ignatius Press, 1995, pp. 29-32]).

Toward that end, the Pontiff is a missionary, a teacher, an ambassador, a shepherd, a pilgrim, and, above all, an exemplar of his own message. The image of himself wearing a straw hat and holding a little girl from Cuilapan, Mexico, during his first apostolic journey in 1979 will forever be the icon of his pontificate. The artifacts in that photograph tell the whole story. His travels make him unique among all his predecessors. As the pastor of a global parish, he made house calls. The effect of his presence in so many diverse cultures has literally changed the world and indeed transformed human history.

PART I

*E*VANGELIZATION
AND
GLOBAL POLITICS

ᴅOMINICAN REPUBLIC 1979

THE FIRST APOSTOLIC VISIT of Pope John Paul II was to Santo Domingo in the Dominican Republic. As he left the plane, the Pope knelt and kissed the ground as Columbus had done more than 480 years before. While this visit was a stopover on his way to Mexico and the Puebla Conference, the homily at the public Mass was indeed significant. For it provided continuity between the policy of his predecessor, Pope Paul VI, and the development of his own phraseology, the "new evangelization" which he would coin some four years later. Further, in the context of the New World, the Americas, the Pope styled himself as a missionary. The following text is from the Mass of 25 January 1979.

I come to these American lands as a pilgrim of peace and hope, to take part in an ecclesial event of evangelization, urged in my turn by the words of the Apostle Paul: "If I preach the gospel, that gives me no ground for boasting. For necessity is laid upon me. Woe to me if I do not preach the gospel!" [1 Cor 9:16].

The present period of the history of humanity calls for a renewed transmission of faith, to communicate to modern man the perennial message of Christ adapted to his concrete conditions of life.

This evangelization is a constant and an essential exigency of ecclesial dynamics. In his encyclical *Evangelii Nuntiandi,* Paul VI affirmed: "Evangelizing is in fact the grace and vocation proper to the Church, her deepest identity. She exists in order to evangelize" [n. 14].

And the same Pontiff states that "as an evangelizer, Christ first of all proclaims a kingdom, the kingdom of God." "As the kernel and center of his good news, Christ proclaims salvation. This great gift which is, above all, liberation from everything that oppresses man but which is, above all, liberation from sin and the evil one" [ibid., nn. 8–9].

The Church, faithful to her mission, continues to present to the men of every age, with the help of the Holy Spirit and under the Pope's guidance, the message of salvation of her divine founder.

This Dominican land was once the first to receive, and then to give impetus to, a grand enterprise of evangelization which deserves great admiration and gratitude. From the end of the fifteenth century, this beloved nation opens us to the faith of Jesus Christ: to this it has remained faithful up to the present. The Holy See, on its side, created the first Episcopal Sees of America precisely in this island, and subsequently the archiepiscopal and primatial see of Santo Domingo.

In a comparatively short period, the paths of faith crossed the Dominican land and the continent in all directions, laying the foundations of the heritage, become life, that we contemplate today in what was called the New World.

The fact is that the proclamation of the Gospel and human advancement cannot be dissociated—this is the great lesson, valid also today. But for the Church, the former cannot be confused or exhausted, as some people claim, in the latter. That would be to close to man infinite spaces that God has opened to him and it would be to distort the deep and complete meaning of evangelization, which is above all the proclamation of the good news of Christ the Savior.

Jesus Christ manifested this love above all in his hidden life—"He has done all things well" [Mk 7:37]—and by proclaiming the Gospel: then, by his death and resurrection, the paschal ministry in which man meets with his definitive vocation to eternal life, to union with God. This is the eschatological dimension of love. ✠

*M*EXICO 1979

ON 27 JANUARY 1979, Pope John Paul visited the Shrine of Our Lady of Guadalupe outside Mexico City. Under this title, Mary is known as Patroness of the Americas. In a discourse that is as much a prayer as a homily, Pope John Paul reveals his personal piety and devotion to Mary, the Mother of Jesus.

H ail Mary!
It is with immense love and reverence that I utter these words, words so simple and at the same time so marvelous. No one will ever be able to greet you in a more wonderful way than the way in which the Archangel once greeted you at the moment of the Annunciation. "Hail Mary, full of grace, the Lord is with thee." I repeat these words, words that so many hearts ponder upon and so many lips utter throughout the world. We here present utter them together, and we are aware that these are the words with which God himself, through his messenger, greeted you, the woman promised in the Garden of Eden, chosen from eternity as the Mother of the Word, the Mother of Divine Wisdom, the Mother of the Son of God.

In fact, when the first missionaries who reached America from lands of eminent Marian tradition taught the rudiments of Christian faith, they also taught love for you, the Mother of Jesus and of all people. And ever since the time that the Indian Juan Diego spoke of the sweet Lady of Tepeyac, you, Mother of Guadalupe, have entered decisively into the Christian life of the people of Mexico. No less has been your presence in other places where your children invoke you with tender names, as Our Lady of Alta Gracia, of the Apareciada, of Lujan, and with many other no less affectionate names, not to give an unending list—names by which in each nation and even in each region the peoples of Latin America express their most profound devotion to you and under which you protect them in their pilgrimage of faith.

The Pope—who comes from a country in which your images, especially one, that of Jasna Góra, are also a sign of your presence in the nation's life and its hazardous history—is particularly sensitive to this sign of your presence here in the life of the People of God in Mexico, in its history, a history which has also been not easy and at times even dramatic. But you are also equally present in the life of the many other peoples of Latin America, presiding over and guiding not only their past, whether remote or recent, but also the present moment, with its uncertainties and shadows. The Pope perceives in the depths of his heart the special bonds that link you with his people and his people with you. This people, that gives you the affectionate name of La Morenita, this people and indirectly the whole of this vast continent, lives its spiritual unity thanks to the fact that you are its Mother who, through her love, creates, preserves, and increases closeness between her children.

Hail Mother of Mexico!
Mother of Latin America!

IN 1968 the Latin American Episcopal Conference met at Medellín, Colombia, where they declared the Catholic Church in that region to be the "Church of the Poor." Ten years later, amid great political unrest, the bishops invited Pope Paul VI to return to celebrate an anniversary and to address the political, social, economic, and above all theological issues of the day. Ten years later, Pope Paul VI and his successor, Pope John Paul I, died suddenly, within two months of each other. Pope John Paul II accepted the invitation and addressed the CELAM Conference, the Third General Assembly of the Latin American Episcopal Conference, on January 28 in Puebla de los Angeles in Mexico.

His address was the first real challenge to his pontificate. Conservative elements hoped the Pontiff would censure progressive liberation theologians who seemed to come close to Marxism in addressing the social challenges in Latin America. More liberal observers wanted the Church to continue the direction set at the previous meeting of Medellín, in which the members championed the rights of the poor and allied themselves with the promotion of social justice and human rights. In his ground-breaking speech Pope John Paul assumed a third position: Recalling the teaching of his predecessor, Pope Paul VI, he reaffirmed the essential role of the Church to be that of evangelization. Without denying the reality of politics, he called for an attitude that was above politics. He encouraged the clergy to reinforce their spiritual ministry and he strengthened the laity in tasks of political and social responsibility. Moving from the Gospels, he addressed the nature of the Church and the truth about the redemptive mission of Jesus. He spoke about the nature of men and women as being both human and divine in Christ. Then, he addressed the duties of the bishops themselves in promoting unity, promoting human dignity, in supporting the family, in fostering vocations to the priesthood and religious life, and in the formation of youth. His strongest words took into account the tragedy of the Latin American situation in the various forms in which it expressed itself in that day.

In the face of what has been said hitherto, the Church sees with deep sorrow "the sometimes massive increase of human rights violations in all parts of society and of the world. . . . Who can deny that today individual persons and civil powers violate basic rights of the human person with impunity: rights such as the right to be born, the right to life, the right to responsible procreation, to work, to peace, to freedom and social justice, the right to participate in the decisions that affect people and nations? And what can be said when we face the various forms of collective violence like discrimination against individuals and groups, the use of physical and psychological torture perpetrated against prisoners or political dissenters? The list grows when we turn to the instances of the abduction of persons for political reasons and look at the acts of kidnapping for material gain which attacks so dramatically family life and the social fabric. [Message of John Paul II to the Secretary-General of the United Nations Organization on 2 December 1978: Thirtieth Anniversary of the Declaration of Human Rights].

We cry out once more: Respect man! He is the image of God! Evangelize, so that this may become a reality; so that the Lord may transform hearts and human eyes, the political and economic systems, with man's responsible commitment as the starting point! Pastoral commitments in this field must be encouraged through a correct idea of liberation. "Liberation from everything that oppresses man but which is above all, liberation from sin and the evil one, in the joy of knowing God and being known by him" [*Evangelii Nuntiandi,* 9]. Liberation made up of reconciliation and forgiveness. Liberation springing from the reality of being children of God, whom we are able to call Abba, Father [Rom 8:15]; a reality which makes us recognize in every man a brother of ours, capable of being transformed in his heart through God's mercy. Liberation that, with the energy of love, urges us toward fellowship, the summit and fullness of which we find in the Lord. Liberation as the overcoming of the various forms of slavery and man-made idols and as the growth of the new man. Liberation that in the framework of the Church's proper mission is not reduced to the simple and narrow economic, political, social, or culture dimension, and is not sacrificed to the demands of any strategy, practice, or short-term solution [see *Evangelii Nuntiandi, 33*]. ✠

BAHAMAS 1979

ON 31 JANUARY 1979, Pope John Paul departed the American hemisphere. He made a brief stopover at Nassau in the Bahamas.

B eing here this evening in your midst, I have the opportunity to formulate my best wishes for the entire population of the Bahamas. My hope for everyone is that there may be constant progress along the path of authentic and integral human advancement. With the profound conviction of the surpassing dignity of the human person, may all the people of these islands make their individual and unique contributions to the common good of all—a common good that takes into account the personal rights and duties of all citizens.

God bless the Bahamas, today and forever! ✠

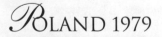POLAND 1979

ON 2 JUNE 1979, Pope John Paul II made his first apostolic visitation to Poland, returning as a native son. Historians now recall that journey as a milestone; many view this as the symbolic beginning of the end of the Cold War in the twentieth century. The visit is characterized by the Pope's pride in the religious history of his own nation. Citing the Venerable Hedwig (or Jadwiga), the queen of Poland and heroine of the nation to whose memory he was devoted, the Pope spoke to the need for reconciliation among all the nations of Europe as a visible sign of Christendom and as a mark of communion, which is a fruit of the Church's apostolic activity. He also commemorated Saint Stanislaus of Kraków, whose jubilee year it was.

The saints whom we are commemorating here today before Our Lady of Jasna Góra offer us across the centuries a witness of unity between fellow countrymen and of reconciliation between nations. I want to express my good wishes for this unity and reconciliation; for this I pray ardently. Unity strikes root in the life of the nation, as in the difficult historical period for Poland it struck root through Saint Stanislaus, when human life at the various levels responds to the demands of justice and love. The family constitutes the first of these levels. And I wish to pray today with all of you, dear fellow countrymen, for the unity of all the families of Poland. This unity has its origin in the sacrament of Marriage, in the solemn promises with which a man and a woman become united with each other for the whole of life, repeating the sacramental "till death do us part." This unity comes from love and mutual trust, and bears fruit in the love and trust of the children toward the parents. What a misfortune it would be if love and trust between husband and wife or between parents and children should weaken or crumble. Aware as we are of the evil brought by the falling apart of the family, let us today pray that nothing may happen which can destroy its unity, so that the family may continue to be truly the "seat of justice and love."

Similar justice and love are needed by the nation if it is to be inwardly united, if it is to constitute an unbreakable unity. Although it is impossible to compare the nation—that society composed of many millions of people—with the family—the smallest community, as we know of, human society—nevertheless unity depends on justice, a justice that satisfies the needs and guarantees the rights and duties of each member of the nation, so as not to give rise to disharmony and opposition because of the differences brought by evident privileges for some and discrimination against others. From our country's history we know how difficult this task is: all the same we cannot exempt ourselves from the great effort aimed at building up just unity between the children of the same country. This must be accompanied by love for this country, love for its culture and history, love for its specific values that determine its place in the great family of nations, love, finally, for our fellow countrymen, people who speak the same language and have responsibility for the common cause to which we give the name of "our country." As I pray today together with you for the internal unity of the nation of which Saint Stanislaus became patron, especially in the thirteenth and fourteenth centuries, I wish to recommend to the Mother of God in Jasna Góra reconciliation between the nations, of which reconciliation we see one mediating in the figure of Saint Hedwig.

THAT SAME EVENING, Pope John Paul II spoke of his intention to consecrate his pontificate to the Madonna of Jasna Góra:

Mary, Queen of Poland, I am close to you, I remember you." Within a short time we shall repeat these words which, from the time of the Great Novena in preparation for the Millennium of the Baptism, have become the call of Jasna Góra and of the Church in Poland. I shall repeat them today with you as the pilgrim Pope in his native land.

How greatly these words correspond to the invitation which we hear so often in the Gospel: "Be watchful"! By answering this invitation of Christ himself we desire today as every evening at the hour of the call of Jasna Góra to say to Mary: "Mary, Queen of Poland, I am close to you, I remember you, I watch."

These words, simple yet forceful, express what it means to be a Christian in Poland at all times, but in a special way during this decisive millenary period of the history of the Church and of the nation. To be a Christian is to be watchful, as the soldier is watchful, as a mother is with her child.

To be watchful means to protect something of great value.

To be watchful and to remember in this way is to stand next to

Mary. I am close to you! I cannot be close to you, to Our Lady of Jasna Góra, unless I am watchful and I remember in this way. If I watch and I remember, then I am close to her. And because she has so penetrated into our hearts it is easier for us to be watchful and remember what is our heritage and our duty, standing next to Mary. "I am near you."

AMONG THE POLISH SAINTS REMEMBERED by Pope John Paul II was a Polish priest named Maximilian Kolbe, who died on 14 August 1941 in Auschwitz. During his visit to Auschwitz the Pope remembered the heroism of Maximilian Kolbe and the tragic death of Edith Stein, a Carmelite nun known as Sister Teresa Benedicta of the Cross.

I have come and I kneel on this Golgotha of the modern world, on these tombs, largely nameless, like the great tomb of the Unknown Soldier. I kneel before all the inscriptions that come one after another bearing the memory of the victims of Auschwitz. In the languages: Polish, English, Bulgarian, Romany, Czech, Danish, French, Greek, Hebrew, Yiddish, Spanish, Flemish, Serbo-Croatian, German, Norwegian, Romanian, Hungarian, and Italian.

In particular I pause with you, dear participants in this encounter, before the inscription in Hebrew. This inscription awakens the memory of the people whose sons and daughters were intended for total extermination. This people draws its origin from Abraham, our father in faith [Rom 4:12], as was expressed by Paul of Tarsus. The very people that received from God the commandment "Thou shalt not kill," itself experienced in a special measure what is meant by killing. It is not permissible for anyone to pass by this inscription with indifference. Finally, the last inscription: that in Poland six million Poles lost their lives during the Second World War: a fifth of the nation. Yet another stage in the centuries-old fight of this nation, my nation, for its fundamental rights among the peoples of Europe. Yet another loud cry for the right to a place of its own on the map of Europe. Yet another painful reckoning with the conscience of mankind.

Auschwitz is such a reckoning. It is impossible merely to visit it. It is necessary on this occasion to think with fear of how far hatred can go, how far man's destruction of man can go, how far cruelty can go.

Auschwitz is a testimony of war. War brings with it a dispropor-
tionate growth of hate, destruction, and cruelty. It cannot be denied
that it also manifests new capabilities of human courage, heroism,
and patriotism. But the fact remains that it is the reckoning of the
losses that prevails. That reckoning prevails more and more, since
each day sees an increase in the destructive capacity of the weapons
invented by modern technology. Not only those who directly bring
about wars are responsible for them, but also those who fail to do all
they can to prevent them. Therefore I would like to repeat in this
place the words that Pope Paul VI pronounced before the United Nations Organization:

"It is enough to remember that the blood of millions of men,
numberless and unprecedented sufferings, useless slaughter and
frightful ruin, are the sanction of the covenant which unites you in a
solemn pledge which must change the future history of the world: no
more war, war never again. It is peace, peace which must guide the
destinies of peoples and of all mankind."

AS HE LEFT POLAND ON 10 JULY, Pope John Paul turned and spoke
warm words of thanks to representatives of the media for having
brought Poland closer to the world and for having made Poland the
site of an international pilgrimage.

D ear friends, we have already met in other places far from
here, but even though the successor of Peter is at home in
any part of the world—since his commission is to "all nations" [Mt 28:19]—it gives me very special satisfaction and pleasure
to meet you and open my arms to you here on the soil of the beloved
land of my birth. I pray that a great new enrichment of the spirit and
a profound inner peace may have been granted to you in the shrines
and holy places where the faith of the Polish people finds intense expression. Making pilgrimages is a very traditional practice among us
Christians. Particular places are regarded as specially sacred because
of the holiness and virtue achieved by individuals who live there, and
their sacredness increases with the passage of time through the
prayers and the sacrifices of the pilgrim multitudes who visit them.
And now, at the moment of my departure, I thank you, my

friends of the media, for having been with me on my pilgrimage. I thank you and the various agencies of communication which you represent for having—I think I can say—brought the whole world to Poland, to be by my side and share with me these precious days of prayer—and homecoming. ✠

$\mathcal{I}$RELAND 1979

IN AUGUST OF 1879, an apparition was reported in Knock, Ireland, by the members of several Irish farm families. In the mist from a rainy summer's evening, the vision of Mary, the child Jesus, and Saint John the Evangelist appeared. In the history of popular piety and Marian apparitions, this particular encounter is most unusual. There is no message delivered and there was no ensuing series of visions. Irish Catholic tradition imputes the meaning to be the abiding maternal protection of Mary with her people.

The Pope's third pastoral visit of his pontificate coincides with the centenary of the Shrine of Our Lady of Knock. John Paul's message characterizes the faith of the Irish. His remarks express not history, but instead they offer a challenge. The Pope arrived in Ireland on 29 September 1979.

The present time is an important moment in the history of the universal Church and, in particular, of the Church in Ireland. So many things have changed. So many valuable new insights have been gained in what it means to be Christian. So many new problems have to be faced by the faithful, either because of the increased pace of change in society, or because of the new demands that are made on the People of God—demands to live to the fullest, the mission of evangelization. The Second Vatican Council and the Synod of Bishops have brought new pastoral vitality to the whole Church. My revered predecessor Paul VI taught the Church to be open to the needs of humanity and at the same time to be unfailingly faithful to the unchanging message of Christ. Loyal to the teaching of the College of Bishops together with the Pope, the Church in Ireland has gratefully accepted the riches of the Council and the Synods.

The Irish Catholic people have clung faithfully, sometimes in spite of pressures to the contrary, to the rich expressions of faith, to the fervent sacramental practices, and to that dedication to charity, which have always been a special mark of your Church. But the task of renewal in Christ is never finished. Every generation, with its own mentality and characteristics, is like a new continent to be won for Christ. The Church must constantly look for new ways that will enable her to understand more profoundly and to carry out with renewed vigor the mission received from her Founder. In this arduous task, like so many times before when the Church was faced with a new challenge, we turn to Mary, the Mother of God and the Seat of Wisdom, trusting that she will show us again the way to her Son. ✠

UNITED STATES 1979

On 1 October 1979, Pope John Paul arrived in Boston, Massachusetts, where he was greeted by Mrs. Rosalynn Carter, First Lady of the United States. On that occasion, as throughout most of the visit, Pope John Paul delivered his public discourse in the rain. The stops on his visit included not only Boston, but also New York, Philadelphia, Washington, D.C., Chicago, and Des Moines. While in New York on 2 October, the Pope delivered a major address at the United Nations, thus continuing the tradition of his predecessor Pope Paul VI who visited the United Nations first, in 1965.

You will forgive me, ladies and gentlemen, for evoking this memory. But I would be untrue to the history of this century, I would be dishonest with regard to the great cause of man, which we all wish to serve, if I should keep silent, I who come from the country on whose living body Oświęcim [Auschwitz] was at one time constructed. But my purpose in evoking this memory is above all to show what painful experiences and sufferings by millions of people gave rise to the Universal Declaration of Human Rights, which has been placed as the basic inspiration and *cornerstone* of the United Nations Organization. This Declaration was paid for by millions of our brothers and sisters at the cost of their suffering and sacrifice, brought out by the brutalization that darkened and made insensitive the human consciences of their oppressors and of those who carried out a real genocide. This price cannot have been paid in vain! The Universal Declaration of Human Rights—with its train of many declarations and conventions on highly important aspects of human rights, in favor of children, of women, of equality between races, and especially the two international covenants on economic, social, and cultural rights and on civil and political rights—must remain the basic value in the United Nations Organization with which the consciences of its members must be confronted and from which they must draw continual inspiration.

LATER THAT SAME DAY in an address to the Archdiocese of New York, he combined the personalist character of his philosophy with the evangelical character of the Beatitudes [Mt 5:1–11].

Social thinking and social practice inspired by the Gospel must always be marked by a special sensitivity toward those who are most in distress, those who are extremely poor, those suffering from all the physical, mental, and moral ills that afflict humanity, including hunger, neglect, unemployment, and despair. There are many poor people of this sort around the world. There are many in your own midst. On many occasions, your nation has gained a well-deserved reputation for generosity, both public and private. Be faithful to that tradition, in keeping with your vast possibilities and present responsibilities. The network of charitable works of each kind that the Church has succeeded in creating here is a valuable means for effectively mobilizing generous undertakings aimed at relieving the situations of distress that continually arise both at home and elsewhere in the world. Make an effort to ensure that this form of aid keeps its irreplaceable character as a fraternal and personal encounter with those who are in distress: if necessary, reestablish this very character against all the elements that work in the opposite direction. Let this sort of aid be respectful of the freedom and dignity of those being helped, and let it be a means of forming the conscience of the givers. ✠

$\mathcal{T}$URKEY 1979

On 29 November 1979, Pope John Paul made an innovatively ecumenical gesture by his visit to the Ecumenical Patriarchate in Turkey. The purpose of the trip was to celebrate with the ecumenical patriarch, his Holiness, Dimitrios I, the Feast of Saint Andrew. The Pope dramatically underscored the theological concept of "communion" enjoyed between Roman Catholics and Orthodox Christians. This visit was the first of many dramatic ecumenical gestures which would reveal something of the Pope's personal character and aspirations from a world perspective. The Pope summarized his experience at the Angelus on the Sunday following his return from Turkey. It is worth quoting that address in full.

I n the first place I wish to express again my joy at the visit that was granted to me to pay to the sister Church of Constantinople and to Patriarch Dimitrios I on the solemnity of Saint Andrew the Apostle, who is the patron saint of that Church.

The tradition of Andrew, who was Peter's brother, brings back to my mind the image of the Church, which is constructed and grows on the cornerstone, Jesus Christ, and at the same time on the foundation of the Apostles and the Prophets [Eph 2:20], with the strength of her original unity, and at the same time with the desire of that perfect unity which will have to be reached in a time known only to God, by means of the Holy Spirit, because he is the Spirit of truth and love. The Church, in her bimillenary history, has developed from her primordial cradle along the way of great and distinct traditions: the Eastern and the Western. For many centuries these two traditions manifested the common riches of the Body of Christ, completing one another in the heart of the People of God and also in hierarchical institutions, in liturgical rites, and in the doctrines of the Fathers and theologians.

The Second Vatican Council pointed out to us that these riches and this tradition do not cease to be a common good of the whole of Christianity and that—on the basis of this good and under the action of the Holy Spirit—we must overcome the division that has weighed upon us since the eleventh century and seek rapprochement and union again. In this connection I am happy to recall here what the Council Fathers recognized, pointing out that "from their very origins the Churches of the East have had a treasury from which the Church of the West has drawn largely for its liturgy, spiritual tradition, and jurisprudence" (Decree *Unitatis Redintegratio,* 14) and, especially, in the field of devotion to the Blessed Virgin, to whom "the Eastern Christians pay high tribute, in beautiful hymns of praise" [ibid., 15] and in that of monastic spirituality, "a source from which Latin monastic life took its rise and has often drawn fresh vigor ever since" [ibid.].

The Eastern Churches, therefore, the Council Fathers concluded authoritatively, "although separated from us, yet possess true sacraments, above all—by apostolic succession—the priesthood and the Eucharist, whereby they are still joined to us in closest intimacy" [ibid.].

It is a pleasure for me to recall here the special merits that the Church of Constantinople had in the evangelization of the Slavs. It was the Church of Constantinople which, responding to the invitation of Prince Rastislav, sent the brothers Cyril and Methodius to Great Moravia, where they started a work of thorough evangelization, continued by their disciples.

It was precisely in this spirit of communion that I undertook and carried out, with the help of God, the recent pilgrimage. I hope that it will yield abundant fruit for the ecumenical cause. I call upon you all to pray for this intention. ✠

ZAIRE 1980

In 1980 during Pope John Paul's first apostolic journey to the continent of Africa, he visited six different countries: Zaire, Congo, Kenya, Ghana, Upper Volta, and the Ivory Coast. One of the Pope's themes throughout his journey is the encouragement of the inculturation of Christianity with the rich heritage and traditions of the African people.

Though he spent time addressing many, visiting with university students, and ordaining eight new bishops, his remarks to the Zairean bishops on 3 May vividly reflect his thoughts on inculturation:

The Gospel, certainly, is not identified with cultures, and transcends them all. But the Kingdom that the Gospel proclaims is lived by men deeply tied to a culture; the construction of the Kingdom cannot dispense with borrowing elements of human cultures [*Evangelii Nuntiandi,* n. 20]. Indeed, evangelization must help the latter to bring forth out of their own living tradition original expressions of Christian life, celebration, and thought [Exhortation *Catechesi Tradendae,* n. 53]. You wish to be at once fully Christians and fully Africans. The Holy Spirit asks us to believe, in fact, that the leaven of the Gospel, in its authenticity, has the power to bring forth Christians in the different cultures, with all the riches of their heritage, purified and transfigured. ✠

CONGO 1980

During a homily in Brazzaville, Congo, the Pontiff continued his thoughts on inculturation by painting a metaphor of the Church's expansion to the Congo and its meaning to the rest of the world's Catholics. The address was delivered on 5 May.

I am thinking of your integration in the universal Church. It is a great and beautiful mystery. The tree of the Church, planted by Jesus in the Holy Land, has not ceased to develop. All the countries of the old Roman Empire have been grafted onto it. My own country, Poland, had its hour of evangelization, and the Church of Poland has been grafted onto the tree of the Church, to make it produce new fruit. Now your community of Congolese believers has been grafted, in its turn, onto the tree of the Church. The graft lives on the sap that circulates in the tree; it cannot survive unless closely united with the tree. But as soon as it is grafted, it brings to the tree its heritage and produces its own fruit. It is only a metaphor. The Church causes the new peoples that have come to her to live by her life. No new community grafted onto the tree of the Church can live its life independently. It lives only by participating in the great vital current that makes the whole tree live. Then the Church receives new treasures of vitality and can thus manifest a greater variety of fruits in the world. ✠

KENYA 1980

IN A SPEECH OF 6 MAY delivered to the Diplomatic Corps in Nairobi, Kenya, the Pontiff pointed out Africa's contribution to a moral ethos and also to its particular place at this moment in history.

A frican society has also—built into its life—a set of moral values, and these values shed further light on the true identity of the African. History testifies how the African continent has always known a strong sense of community in the different groups that make up its social structure: this is especially true in the family, where there is strong coherence and solidarity. And what better insight can be found into the necessity for the peaceful solution of conflicts and difficulties—a way that is in keeping with human dignity—than that innate propensity for dialogue, that desire to explain differing views in conversation, to which the African turns so easily and which he accomplishes with such natural grace? A sense of celebration expressed in spontaneous joy, a reverence for life and the generous acceptance of new life—these are some more of the elements that are part of the heritage of the African and help define his identity.

It is against this background that the Catholic Church, in the light of her own convictions drawn from the message of Christ, views the realities of Africa today, and proclaims her trust in this continent.

A few days before leaving on this pastoral visit, I expressed my joy in being able to visit the peoples of Africa, in their own countries, in their own sovereign states, where they are "the true masters of their own land and the helmsmen of their own destiny" [Angelus, 27 April 1980]. In Africa, most of the nations have known colonial administration in the past. While not denying the various achievements of this administration, the world rejoices in the fact that this period is now drawing to a final close. The peoples of Africa, with a few painful exceptions, are assuming full political responsibility for their own destiny—and I greet here, particularly, the recently achieved independence of Zimbabwe—but one cannot ignore the fact that other forms of dependence are still a reality or at least a threat.

Political independence and national sovereignty demand as a necessary corollary that there be also economic independence and freedom from ideological domination. The situation of some countries can be profoundly conditioned by the decisions of other powers, among which are the major world powers. There can also be the subtle threat of interference of an ideological nature that may produce, in the area of human dignity, effects that are even more deleterious than any other form of subjugation. There are still situations and systems, within individual countries and in the relationships between states, that are "marked by injustice and social injury" [Address to the United Nations Organization, 2 October 1979, no. 17] and that still condemn many people to hunger, disease, unemployment, lack of education, and stagnation in their process of achieving development.

The state, the justification of which is the sovereignty of society and to which is entrusted the safeguarding of independence, must never lose sight of its first objective, which is the common good of all its citizens—all its citizens without distinction—and not just the welfare of one particular group or category. Another problem on which the truth about man, and about the African in particular, impels me to speak out, is the persistent problem of racial discrimination. The aspiration to equal dignity on the part of individuals and peoples, together with its concrete implementation in every aspect of social life, has always been strongly supported and defended by the Church. ✠

GHANA 1980

SINCE THE CLOSE OF THE SECOND VATICAN COUNCIL, while he was yet Cardinal Archbishop of Kraków, the Pontiff was a permanent member of the Pontifical Council for the Laity. The formation of a lay spirituality has always personally been close to his heart since the time of his ordination. Some ten years before, a Pan-African conference on lay formation was held under the auspices of the Vatican's Council for the Laity in Accra, Ghana. Recalling that event, Pope John Paul spoke directly to this aspect of the Church's life on 9 May.

The laity of the Church in Africa have a crucial role to play in meeting the urgent problems and challenges which face this vast continent. As Christian laity, the Church expects you to help shape the future of your individual countries, to contribute to their development in some particular sphere. The Church asks you to bring the influence of the Gospel and the presence of Christ into every human activity, and to seek to build a society where the dignity of each person is respected and where equality, justice, and freedom are protected and promoted.

Today, I also wish to emphasize the need for the continuing instruction and catechesis of the laity. For only a serious spiritual and doctrinal formation in your Christian identity, together with an adequate civic and human preparation in secular activities, can make possible that contribution of the laity to the future of Africa which is so greatly desired. In this regard, we are reminded of the exhortation of Saint Paul: "We urge you and appeal to you in the Lord Jesus to make more and more progress in the kind of life you are meant to live: the life that God wants" [1 Thes 4:1]. In order to accomplish this goal, greater knowledge is needed of the mystery of Christ. It is necessary for the laity to enter into this mystery of Christ and to be trained especially in the word of God which leads to salvation. The Holy Spirit is calling upon the Church to pursue this path with loving tenacity and perseverance. Hence I wish to encourage the worthy initiatives on all levels which have already been undertaken in this field. May these efforts continue and increasingly equip the laity for their mission so that with holiness of life they may meet the many needs that lie ahead, so that the whole Church in Africa will ever more effectively communicate Christ. ✠

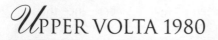UPPER VOLTA 1980

WHEN POPE JOHN PAUL II ARRIVED at Ouagadougou Airport in Upper Volta (now Burkina Faso) on 10 May, he was greeted by the Cardinal Archbishop, Paul Zaungrana, and the president of the republic, Sangoule Lamizuna. The nation was experiencing a drought in the Sahel region. The disease and death caused by the drought moved the Pope deeply. With all the moral force that he could derive from his office, the Pope made a world appeal:

That is why from this place, from this capital of Upper Volta, I launch a solemn appeal to the whole world. I, John Paul II, Bishop of Rome, and successor of Peter, raise my suppliant voice because I cannot be silent when my brothers and sisters are threatened. I become here the voice of those who have no voice, the voice of the innocent, who died because they lacked water or bread;

the voice of fathers and mothers who saw their children die without understanding, or who will always see in their children the after-affects of the hunger they suffered; the voice of the generations to come, who must no longer live with this terrible threat weighing upon their lives. I launch an appeal to everyone!

Let us not wait until the drought returns, terrible and devastating! Let us not wait for the sand to bring death again! Let us not allow the future of these peoples to remain jeopardized forever! The solidarity shown in the past has proved, through its extent and efficacy, that it is possible to listen only to the voice of justice and charity, and not that of selfishness, individual and collective.

Listen to my appeal! ✠

VORY COAST 1980

FROM THE REPUBLIC OF THE IVORY COAST, the Pope took his leave of Africa on 12 May.

F arewell now, Africa, this continent which I love so much already and which I have been longing since my election to Peter's See to discover and traverse. Farewell to the peoples that have received me, and to all the others to whom I should like so much, one day, if providence permits, to bring my affection personally. I have learned a great many things during this journey. You cannot know how instructive it has been. In my turn I would like to leave to Africans a message which has sprung from my heart, which has been meditated upon before God, and which is demanding because it comes from a friend for friends.

Africa struck me as being a vast work yard, from all points of view, with its promises and also, perhaps, its risks. Wherever you go, you admire a considerable undertaking in favor of development and of raising the standard of living, in favor of the progress of man and society. There is a long way to go. Method can be different and turn out to be more or less suitable. But the desire to advance is undeniable. Already, considerable results have been obtained. Education is spreading, diseases that used to be fatal are overcome, new techniques are started, success is beginning to be achieved in the struggle against certain natural obstacles. The value of the riches peculiar to the African soul is also being felt more, and that arouses pride. Parallel, accession to national sovereignty and respect for it seems to be the object of everyone's aspirations.

There is here an important heritage, which must absolutely be safeguarded and promoted harmoniously. It is not easy to control this seething life, to make sure that its living forces are used for true development. There is a great temptation in fact to demolish instead of constructing, to acquire at a high price arms for populations that need bread, to want to seize power—were it by setting some ethnic groups against others in bloody and fratricidal struggles, whereas the poor are longing for peace, or else to succumb to the intoxication of profit for the benefit of a privileged class.

Do not get caught up, dear African brothers and sisters, in this disastrous mechanism, which has really nothing to do with your dignity as creatures of God, or with what you are capable of. You have not to imitate certain foreign models, based on contempt of man or on interest. You have not to run after artificial needs which will give you an illusory freedom or which will lead you to individualism, whereas the community aspiration is so strong in you. Nor have you to delude yourselves about the virtues of ideologies which hold upright prospects of complete happiness but always postpone to tomorrow.

Be yourselves! I assure you: You can. You who are so proud of your possibilities, give the world the proof that you are capable of solving your own problems yourselves, with the humanitarian, economic, and cultural assistance which is still useful for you and which is only justice, but taking care to turn all that in the right direction.

Farewell, Africa! I take with me all that you have so generously given me and all that you have revealed to me in the course of this journey. May God bless you and each of your children, and may he let you enjoy peace and prosperity. ✠

RANCE 1980

WHEN HE DEPARTED FOR FRANCE on 30 May 1980, Pope John Paul announced the scope of his visit from the tarmac of Fiumicino Airport. It was to strengthen the faith of the children of France. Invited to address the 109th session of the Executive Council of UNESCO, the Pope addressed the importance of culture in human formation. He also addressed assemblies of seminarians, religious, and clergy. He called for a renewed spirit of self-sacrifice. He also exhorted the workers of Paris, as well as leaders of lay apostolic movements, to deeper piety. His strongest words were for the bishops and, in a way, were intended for the entire Church of France. When the French hierarchy met at Issy-les-Moulineaux on 1 June, he addressed the question of modern man before God.

The fundamental question that we must ask ourselves, we bishops on whom there weighs a special responsibility as regards the truth of the Gospel and the mission of the Church, is that of the credibility of this mission and of our service. In this field, we are sometimes questioned and judged severely; did not one of you write: "Our age will have been harsh with regard to the bishops"? Then, too, we are ready to judge ourselves severely, and to judge severely the religious situation of the country and the results of our apostolate. The Church in France has not been free from such judgments; it is enough to recall the famous book of Abbé Godin: *France, Pays de Mission?* [a.k.a. *France Pagan?*] or else the well-known statement: "The Church has lost the working class."

These judgments sometimes call for a perspicacious moderation to be observed. It is also necessary to think for the long term, for that is essential for our mission. But it cannot be denied that the Church in France has undertaken, and is undertaking, great efforts in order "to reach those who are far away," especially in the de-Christianized working class and rural environments.

These efforts must preserve fully an evangelical, apostolic, and pastoral character. It is not possible to succumb to "the challenges of politics." Nor can we accept many resolutions which claim to be only "just." We cannot let ourselves be shut up in overall views which are in reality one-sided. It is true that social mechanisms, and also their political and economic characteristic, seem to confirm these overall views and certain painful facts: "mission country," "loss of the working class." It seems, however, that we must be ready not only for "self-criticism," but also for criticism of the mechanisms themselves. The Church must be ready to defend the rights of the workers, in every economic and political system.

Above all, the very great contribution of the Church and of French Catholicism in the missionary field of the Church, for example, or the field of Christian culture, cannot be forgotten. It cannot be accepted that these chapters should be closed! What is more, it cannot be accepted that, in these fields, the Church in France should change the quality of its contribution and the orientation it had taken, which merits complete credibility.

Your responsibility extends in fact—as among other episcopates, but in a different way—beyond "your" Church, beyond France. This is something you must accept and you cannot shake it off. ✠

ℬRAZIL 1980

THE APOSTOLIC VISIT OF POPE JOHN PAUL II to Brazil from 30 June to 12 July 1980 was his second to Latin America. The text of his addresses closely follows the lines of his earlier exhortation at Puebla de los Angeles, Mexico. Everywhere, he was moved by the plight of the poor. In one slum section, the Pope removed the ring given him by Pope Paul VI when he was created Cardinal. He asked the pastor to sell the ring for the sake of the poor of the parish. Again, he reminded the bishops of their special ministry to the disfranchised. Skirting the ideologies of Marxism and capitalism, he said, "The achievement of justice on this continent is confronted by clear choice.

Either it is to be carried out by means of peaceful and courageous reform, or it is to be carried out by the forces of violence." The central occasion of his visit was the opening of a Eucharistic Congress at Fortaleza on 9 July, when he was hosted by Cardinal Aloysius Lorscheider, O.F.M. In his many discourses in Brazil, he follows a pattern of reiterating the theme of "communion," which is central to his homily at the Inaugural Mass of the Congress. It is that of communion, human and divine.

T he sacred banquet in which the bread is Christ, in which his passion is relived by us, our soul is filled with grace, and there is offered to us a pledge of future glory."

From this moment and for several days Fortaleza becomes in quite a special way the upper room where this banquet is celebrated, singing and affirming the Church's faith in the Blessed Sacrament.

This celebration reminds us again that the God of our faith is not a distant being, who contemplates with indifference the condition of men, their difficulties, their struggles, and their anxieties. He is a Father who loves his sons, to such an extent as to send his Son, his Word "that they may have life, and have it abundantly" [Jn 10:10].

It is this loving Father who now gently draws us with the action of the Holy Spirit who dwells in our hearts [see Rom 5:5].

How often in our lives have we seen separated two persons who love each other. During the severe and ugly war in my youth, I saw fathers torn away from their homes, without hope of return, without knowing whether they would meet their dear ones again someday. At the moment of departure, a gesture, a photo, an object, which passes from one hand to the other to prolong, somehow, presence in absence. And nothing more. Only human love is capable of these symbols.

As a testimony and as a lesson of love, at the moment of separation, "when Jesus knew that his hour had come to depart out of this world to the Father, having loved his own who were in the world, he loved them to the end" [Jn 13:1]. And thus, on the eve of that last Passover spent in this world with his friends, Jesus "took bread, and when he had given thanks, he broke it, and said, 'This is my body which is for you. Do this in remembrance of me.' In the same way also the cup after supper, saying: 'This cup is the new covenant in my blood. Do this, as often as you drink it, in remembrance'" [1 Cor 11:23–25].

In this way, the Lord Jesus Christ, perfect God and perfect man, departing from his friends, leaves them not a symbol but the reality of himself. He returns to the Father, but he remains among us. He does not leave a mere object to conjure up his memory. Under the species of bread and wine it is he, really present with his Body, his Blood, his Soul, and his Divinity. As one of your classical authors said [Fr. Antonio das Shagas, *Sermoni,* 1764]: "From the union of infinite power with infinite love what was there to follow if not the greatest miracle and the greatest marvel?"

Eucharistic communion is therefore the sign of the meeting of all the faithful. A truly inspiring sign, because at the holy table all differences of race or social class disappear, leaving only the participation of all in the same holy food. This participation, identical in all, signifies and realizes the suppression of all that divides men, and brings about the meeting of all at a higher level, where all opposition is eliminated. Thus the Eucharist becomes the great instrument of bringing men closer to one another. Whenever the faithful take part in it with a sincere heart they receive a new impetus to establish a better relationship among themselves, leading to recognition of one another's rights and corresponding duties as well. In this way a satisfaction of the requirements of justice is facilitated, precisely because of the particular climate of interpersonal relations that brotherly charity creates within the same community.

Using the theme of communion and solidarity to reinforce that of evangelization, which he first spoke of in Mexico, the Pope applied it in a brief pastoral visit to prisoners at Papuda Jail near Brasília on 1 July.

The visit I am paying to you today, though a short one, means a great deal for me. It is the visit of a Pastor who would like to imitate the Good Shepherd [Jn 1:10ff.], in his act of seeking with greater concern the sheep that for some reason had got lost [Lk 15:4], and is then happy to find it. It is the visit of a friend. As a friend

I would like to bring you at least a little serenity and hope, in order to find the will and the courage to be better.

It is the visit of the Vicar of Christ. You know, from reading the Gospel, that he, Christ, being without sin, detested sin but loved sinners, and visited them to offer them forgiveness. I would like to bring you the call and the consolation of the Redeemer of Man.

In you I find human persons, and I know that every human person corresponds to a "thought" of God. In this sense, every human being is fundamentally good and made for happiness. There was in the life of nearly all of you a moment in which you departed from God's plan. You should regret the wrong done, but not consider it an evil destiny. You can return to reflecting God's thought. You can be happy again.

I find in you men redeemed by the precious blood of Jesus Christ. This blood speaks to you of the infinite love of the Father and of his Son Jesus for you as for all men. He offers you the greatest joy in the world, which is that of loving and of feeling one's self-love. From above he gives you the strength to change your life.

I find in you real brothers and I want to tell you that, in moments of loneliness and sadness, you can be certain, you can have the certainty that this common father is close to you and that in him you can find all your brothers who are the Christians and Catholics of the whole world.

May this prison, like all the others in Brazil and in the world, say in its mute language: no to hatred, to violence, to evil; yes to love, because only love saves and constructs! ✠

WEST GERMANY 1980

WHEN POPE JOHN PAUL FIRST VISITED GERMANY from 15 to 19 November 1980, it was still a divided nation. The invitation, which came from the hierarchy for a pastoral visit, included ecumenical

and academic goals. The Pope likewise addressed life in the ex-
panding economy of the Federal Republic of Germany. His host
was Joseph Cardinal Hoffner, president of the German Episcopal
Conference. Among the cities visited were Cologne, Fulda, Mainz,
and Munich. In this last city, the Pope gave an address to the elderly that is both creative and comforting. It is presented here in its
entirety.

M y dear brothers and sisters who are advanced in age!
It fills me with special joy that during my visit to Germany I am allowed to meet with you in a special hour of
prayer. I come as to familiar friends: for I know that in my service I
am supported in a special way by your concern, prayer, and sacrifice.
So I greet you here in the Cathedral of Our Lady in Munich with
heartfelt gratitude. Especially I thank you for the profound words of
welcome and for your prayer, by which you accompanied me during
these days. Together with you I greet all the people of your age group
in your country, especially those who through radio and television are
united with us in this moment. *Gruss Gott* to all of you who longer
than I have "endured the work and heat of the day" [Mt 20:12], who
longer than I have exerted yourselves to meet the Lord and to serve
him in all fidelity, in the great things and in the small ones, in joy and
suffering!

The Pope bows with devotion before old age, and he invites all
people to do the same with him. Old age is the crown of the steps of
life. It gathers in the harvest, the harvest from what you have learned
and experienced, the harvest from what you have done and achieved,
the harvest from what you have suffered and undergone. As in the fi-
nale of a great symphony, all the great themes of life combine to a
mighty harmony. And this harmony bestows wisdom—the wisdom
which young King Solomon is praying for [see 1 Kgs 3:9–11] and which
means more to him than power and riches, more than beauty and
health [see Wis 7:7, 8, 10]—the wisdom about which we read in the
rules of life of the Old Testament: "How attractive is wisdom in the
aged, and understanding and counsel in honorable men! Rich experience is the crown of the aged, and their boast is the fear of the Lord"
[Sir 25:5–6].

To today's older generation, that is to you, my dear brothers and sisters, this crown of wisdom is due in a very special way: Some of you had in two world wars to see and to endure immense pain; many of you have thereby lost your relatives, your health, your profession, your house, and your home country; you have come to know the abyss of the human heart, but also its ability for heroic willingness to help, and for loyalty to the faith, as well as its power to dare a new beginning.

Wisdom confers distance, but not a distance that stands aloof from the world; it allows people to be above things, without despising them; it allows us to see the world with the eyes—and with the heart!—of God. It allows us with God to say "yes," even to our limitations, even to our past—with its disappointments, omissions, and sins. For "we know that in everything God works for good with those who love him" [Rom 8:28]. From the conciliative power of this wisdom spring up kindness, patience, understanding, and—that precious ornament of age—the sense of humor.

You yourselves know best, my dear brothers and sisters, that this precious harvest of life which the Creator has apportioned to you is not an uncontested possession. It requires vigilance, carefulness, self-control, and sometimes even a resolute battle. Otherwise it is endangered, easily to be eaten away or to be corroded by idleness, by moods, by superficiality, by arrogance, or even by bitterness. Do not lose heart; with the grace of our Lord start over and over again, and use the sources of power which he offers you: in the Sacraments of the Bread and of Forgiveness; in the word which comes to you in sermons and in reading and in spiritual conversation! In this place I am sure that I am allowed also in your name most cordially to thank the priests who reserve a decisive place in their work and in their hearts for their pastoral work among the aged. In this way they at the same time render their best service to the whole community; for thereby they win for it, in a sense, a legion of faithful intercessors.

Next to the priests who serve you with their pastoral work I should like to address myself to the priests of your age group. My dear confreres! The Church thanks you for your lifelong work in the vineyard of the Lord. To the younger priests Jesus says in the Gospel of John [4:38]: "Others have labored, and you have entered into their

labor." Most venerable priests, keep on bringing the needs of the
Church before God through your priestly service of prayer—"*ad
Deum, qui laetificat iuventutem vestram*" [Ps 43:4]!

Brothers and sisters of the older generation, you are a treasure for
the Church, you are a blessing for the world! How often you have to
relieve the young parents, how well you know how to introduce the
youngsters to the history of your family and of your home country, to
the tales of your people and to the world of faith! The young adults
with their problems often find an easier way to you than to their parents' generation. To your sons and daughters you are the most precious support in their hours of difficulty. With your advice and your
engagement you cooperate in many committees, associations, and
initiatives of ecclesiastical and public life.

You are a necessary complement in a world that shows enthusiasm for the vitality of youth and for the power of the so-called "best
years," in a world where what can be counted counts so much. You
remind it that it continues building upon the diligence of those who
have been young and strong earlier, and that one day it, too, will place
its work in younger hands. In you it becomes apparent that the meaning of life cannot consist in earning and spending money, that in all
our external activities there has to mature something internal, and
something eternal in all the temporal—according to the words of
Saint Paul: "Though our outer nature is wasting away, our inner nature is being renewed every day" [2 Cor 4:16].

Indeed, old age deserves our devotion, a devotion which also
shines forth from Holy Scripture when it places before our eyes Abraham and Sarah, when it calls Simeon and Anna to the Holy Family in
the temple, when it calls the priests "elders" [Acts 14:23; 15:2; 1 Tm
4:14; 5:17, 19; Ti 1:5; 1 Pt 5:1], when it sums up the worship of the
whole of creation in the adoration of the twenty-four elders, and
when finally God calls himself: "the Ancient of Days" [Dan 7:9, 22].

Is it possible to intone a higher song in honor of the dignity of
old age? But, my dear elder listeners, I am sure you would be disappointed if the Pope would not also mention another aspect of
becoming old; if he would have brought you only—maybe unexpected—the honors, but would have failed to bring you consolation.
Just as to the beautiful season in which we are not only belong the

harvest and the solemn splendor of color, but also the branches' being stripped of their leaves, the leaves falling and decaying; not only the soft and full light, but also the wet and dreary fog—in the same way old age is not only the strong final accord or the conciliative sum of life, but also the time of fading, a time where the world becomes strange and life can turn into a burden, and the body into pain. And so I add to my call "Be aware of your dignity," the other one, "Accept your burden."

For most people the burden of old age means in the first place a certain frailty of the body; the senses are no longer as acute, the limbs no longer as pliable as they used to be, the organs become more sensitive [cf. Sir 12:3f]. The things one may experience in younger years in days of sickness often become one's daily—and nightly!—companions in old age. One is forced to give up many activities that used to be familiar and dear.

Also the memory may refuse its service: new facts are no longer received easily, and old ones fade away. And so the world ceases to be familiar: the world of one's own family, with the living and working conditions of the adults utterly changed, with the interests and forms of expression of young people so completely different, with the new learning goals and methods of the children. The home country becomes strange with its growing cities, the increasing density of population, and the landscape many times remodeled. The world of politics and economics turns strange, the world of social and medical care becomes anonymous and unintelligible. And even that domain where we should feel at home most of all—the Church in her life and doctrine—has become strange to many of you through her effort to meet the demands of the time and the expectations and needs of the younger generation.

By this world which is hard to understand, you feel misunderstood and often enough rejected. Your opinion, your cooperation, your presence is not asked for—that is how you feel and how, unfortunately, sometimes it actually is.

What can the Pope say to this? How shall I console you? I do not want to take it too easy. I do not want to belittle the anxieties of old age, your weaknesses and illnesses, your helplessness and loneliness. But I would like to see them in a conciliatory light—in the light of our Savior "who for us did sweat blood, who for us was scourged at the pillar, who for us was crowned with thorns." In the trials of old age he is the companion of your pain and you are his companions on the way of the cross. There is no tear you have to shed alone, and none you shed in vain [see Ps 5:9]. By this suffering he has redeemed suffering, and through your suffering you cooperate in his salvation [see Col 1:24]. Accept your suffering as his embrace and turn it into a blessing by accepting it from the hand of the Father, who in his inscrutable yet unquestionable wisdom and love is using just this to bring about your perfection. It is in the furnace that metal turns into gold [1 Pt 1:7]; it is in the press that the grape becomes wine.

In this spirit—which God alone can give us—it becomes also easier to be understanding with those who through negligence, carelessness, heedlessness contribute to cause our need, and it becomes possible for us to forgive also those who knowingly and even intentionally make us suffer without, however, completely conceiving how much pain they cause us. "Father, forgive them; for they do not know what they are doing!" [Lk 23:34]. Also with regard to us has this word been spoken which alone brings salvation.

In this Spirit—whom we want to implore together and for each other in this hour—we are also going to be awake and grateful for all loving thoughts, words, and deeds that we receive each day, which we so easily get used to and which therefore we easily take for granted and which we overlook. We are celebrating today the feast of St. Elizabeth, a saint your nation has given to the whole world as a symbol of self-sacrificing charity. She is the sublime example and great patroness for all who serve their fellow creatures in need—be it through their profession or on a volunteer basis, be it in the circle of their friends and relatives—and who meet Christ in them, whether they know it or not. That, my dear elder people, is the reward which you give to those for whom you dislike being a burden. You are the occasion for them to meet the Lord, the opportunity to outgrow themselves, and by your turning to them you let them share in the already mentioned fruits of life which God allowed to mature in you! Therefore do not bury your requests in a timid, disappointed, or reproachful heart, but express them in all naturalness—being convinced of your own dignity and of the good in the hearts of the others. And be happy over each opportunity to practice that royal word of "Thank you" which rises from all altars and which is going to fill our eternal beatitude.

And so I am sure that I will be allowed together with you to thank all those people who work for the well-being of the older generation, for their well-being in body and mind, in order to help them find a fulfilled life and a permanent home in society, all those who work in the many ecclesiastical, civil, and public organizations, associations, and initiatives, on a communal or on a higher level, in legislature and administration, or just on a private basis. I commend especially the fact that working for the elder people is becoming more and more working with the elder people.

With this I turn again to you, my elder brothers and sisters, and to the consolation you expect from me. There is a saying: "When you are lonely, go and visit somebody who is still lonelier than you!" This wisdom I would like to recommend to you. Open your mind for those companions on your road who in whatever respect are in a still poorer condition than you, whom you can help in one way or the other—through a conversation, through giving a hand, some favor, or at least your expressed sympathy! I promise to you in the name of Jesus: in this you are going to find strength and consolation [see Acts 20:35].

In this way you simultaneously practice in small matters what we all are as a whole. We are one body in many members: those who bring help and those who receive help; those who are more healthy and those who are more sick; those who are younger and those who are older; those who have stood the test of life, those who are still standing it, and those who just are growing into it; those who are young and those who once have been young; those who are old and those who are going to be old tomorrow. We all together represent the fullness of the body of Christ, and we all together mature into this fullness—"into the perfect Man, fully mature with the fullness of Christ" [Eph 4:13].

The last consolation we are seeking together, my dear fellow pilgrims "in this vale of tears" [*Salve Regina*], is the consolation in the face of death. Since our birth we are going to meet it, but in our old age we become more conscious of its approaching from year to year—if only we do not forcefully suppress it from our thoughts and feelings. The Creator has arranged it so that in old age accepting and standing the test of death is being prepared, made easier and learned, in an almost natural manner. Because becoming old, as we have seen, means a slow taking leave of the unbroken fullness of life, of the unimpeded contact with the world.

The great school of living and dying then brings us to many an open grave; it makes us stand at many a deathbed before it will be us around whom other people will be standing in prayer—so may God grant it. An old person has experienced such lessons of life in a greater number than young ones do, and he is seeing them with increasing frequency. That is his great advantage on the way to that great threshold which we often in a biased way conceive of as being an abyss and night.

The view across the threshold is dark from our side; but to those who have gone before us God will allow in his love to accompany our lives and to surround us with care more often than we possibly think. It has been the conviction of deep and living faith that gave to a church in this city the name of "All Souls Church." And the two German churches in Rome are called: Santa Maria in Campo Santo and Santa Maria dell'Anima. The more the fellow beings of our visible world reach the limits of their ability to help, the more we should see the messengers of the love of God in those who already have passed the test of death and who are now waiting for us over there: the saints, especially our personal patrons, and our deceased relatives and friends who we hope are at home in God's mercy.

Many of you, my dear sisters and brothers, have lost the visible presence of your partner. To you I direct my pastoral admonition. Allow God ever more to be the partner of your lives; then you will also be united to the one whom he gave you as a companion once upon a time and who himself now has found in God his center.

Without familiarity with God there is in the last end no consolation in death. For that is exactly what God intends with death, that at least in this one sublime hour of our life we allow ourselves to fall into his love without any other security than just this love of his. How could we show him our faith, our hope, our love in a more lucid manner!

One last consideration in this context. I am sure it echoes the conviction of many a heart. Death itself is a consolation! Life on this earth, even if it were no "vale of tears," could not offer a home to us forever. It would turn more and more into a prison, an "exile" [*Salve Regina*]. "For all that passes is just a parable" [Goethe, *Faust,* II, final chorus]! And so the words of Saint Augustine which never lose their color come to our lips: "You have created us for yourself, Lord; and our heart is restless until it finds its rest in you!" [*Confessiones* I. 1. 1].

And so there are not those who are destined to die and those who stand in the so-called life. What is awaiting all of us is a birth, a transformation whose pains we fear with Jesus on the Mount of Olives, but whose radiant exit we already carry within ourselves, since at our baptism we have been submerged into the death and victory of Jesus [see Rom 6:3–6; Col 2:12]. ✠

PART II

SOLIDARITY
AND
UNITY

ℛKISTAN 1981

ON 16 FEBRUARY 1981, Pope John Paul made a brief visit to Karachi, Pakistan. He was greeted by the president of the Islamic Republic of Pakistan, General Muhammad Zia Ul-Haq, and the Cardinal Archbishop of Karachi, Joseph Cordeiro. During his greetings, the Pope spoke of a mutual spirit of collaboration found among all the children of Abraham:

The Church, without forgetting that her primary mission is a spiritual one, always seeks to collaborate with individual nations and people of goodwill in promoting the dignity and advancement of the human person. She carries out these endeavors by various means, such as schools and programs of education, and through charitable and social institutions. In this regard, it is gratifying to see how the Catholic Church and the government of Pakistan have worked together here in harmony for the benefit of so many. I pray for the continued success of these endeavors. One of the special concerns of the Church at the present time is the plight of refugees, a problem faced by your nation and by many other countries as well. May I take this occasion to express my admiration for the efforts that Pakistan has made, and is still making, on behalf of these displaced persons. And I would assure you that just as the Church has already assisted in these efforts, so she wishes to continue to do so, within the limited means available to her.

One of the salient characteristics of Abraham—to whose faith Christians, Muslims, and Jews alike eagerly link their own—was his good spirit of hospitality, as displayed in a particular way when he welcomed three guests by the Oak of Mamre [Gen 18:1 ff]. The warm welcome which you and the beloved people of Pakistan extend to me on this happy occasion gives expression to the same spirit of hospitality. For this I am deeply grateful and I would like to reciprocate your kindness with the assurance of my prayers. ✠

PHILIPPINES 1981

POPE JOHN PAUL LANDED AT THE MANILA INTERNATIONAL AIRPORT on
17 February 1981, to be greeted by President Ferdinand Marcos and
by Cardinal Jaime Sin. In his opening remarks, the Holy Father stated
that the purpose of his visit was to celebrate the first beatification of
Servants of God outside of Rome. He further indicated that this was
at the specific request of Cardinal Sin during the first week of Pope
John Paul's pontificate. Therefore, on 18 February the Pope beatified
sixteen martyrs who had shed their blood in persecutions conducted
in Japan in the seventeenth century. Many of the martyrs were Spanish or Japanese, but one of them, Lorenzo Ruiz, was a native Filipino,
the son of a Chinese father and a Tagalog mother. Although associated with the Dominican Order, Blessed Lorenzo was a married man
and the father of children. The Pontiff explained that he had come
to Manila to praise the history of faith exercised in that country and
to encourage the evangelical activity of the Catholic Church within
the Philippine nation as well as among the other nations. Using
Blessed Lorenzo as an example, the Pope spoke of the significance
of martyrdom:

This is what Lorenzo Ruiz did. Guided by the Holy Spirit to an
unexpected goal after an adventurous journey, he told the
court at Nagasaki that he was a Christian, and must die for God
and would give his life for him a thousand times [*Positio*, p. 417].

"Even if this body would have a thousand lives / I would let all of
them be killed / if you force me to turn my back to Christ." Here we
have him summed up. Here we have a description of his faith and the
reason for his death. It was at this moment that this young father of
the family professed and brought to completion the Christian catechesis that he had received in the Dominican Friars' school in Binondo:
a catechesis that cannot be other than Christ-centered, by reason
both of the mystery it contains and the fact that it is Christ who
teaches through the lips of his messenger [*Catechesi Tradendae*, 5–6].

This is the Christian essence of the first beatus of the Philippine nation, today exalted as a fitting climax to the fourth centenary of the Archdiocese of Manila. Just as the young Church in Jerusalem brought forth its first martyr for Christ in the person of the deacon Stephen, so the young Church in Manila founded in 1579 brought forth its first martyr in the person of Lorenzo Ruiz, who had served in the parish Church of St. Gabriel in Binondo. The local parish and the family, the domestic church, are indeed the center of faith that is lived, taught, and witnessed to.

The example of Lorenzo Ruiz reminds us that everyone's life and the whole of one's life must be at Christ's disposal. Christianity means daily giving in response to the gift of Christ, who came into the world so that all might have life and have it to the full [Jn 10:10]. Or, as so aptly expressed in the theme of my visit to this country: "To die for the faith is a gift to some, to live the faith is a call for all." I, too, have come from the city of the martyrs Peter and Paul to this capital city to speak to you about the meaning of our existence, about the value of living and dying for Christ. And that is what I wish to affirm by this act of beatification, desired by myself and by my predecessor Paul VI, and requested by the various local churches and by the Dominican Order.

ON 18 FEBRUARY, the Holy Father addressed the entire student body of the Pontifical University of St. Thomas in Manila. Here, he defined "youth":

First and foremost, be genuine young people. What is it to be young? To be young means possessing within oneself an increasing newness of spirit, nourishing a continual quest for good, and persevering in reaching a goal. Being genuinely young in this sense is the way to prepare for your future, which is to fulfill your vocation as fully mature adults. Never try to ignore then the irresistible force that is driving you toward the future.

The Church is not frightened at the intensity of your feeling. It is a sign of vitality. It indicates pent-up energy, which of itself is neither good nor bad, but can be used for good causes or for bad. It is like rainwater that accumulates on the mountains after days and days of raining. When whatever holds it bursts, it unleashes forces capable of wiping whole towns off the map, overwhelming their inhabitants in a sea of tears and blood. But, if properly channeled, dry fields are irrigated, producing the necessary food and much needed energy. In your case it is not only food or material things that are involved; it is the destiny of your country, the future of your generation, and the security of children yet unborn.

ON **21 FEBRUARY,** the Pontiff made an important radio address to all the peoples of Asia from the studios of Radio Veritas Asia in Manila. The address was unprecedented and was intended to penetrate such nations as China, North Korea, and Vietnam, as well as those nations which had not ever received a pontifical visit.

The Pope foresaw an emerging alliance toward economic progress among the entire family of Asian nations. His prayer was for peace in the quest for prosperity:

To you the people of Asia.

To you the hundreds of millions of men, women, and children living on the immense mainland of this continent and in its archipelagos.

To you especially who are suffering or who are in need.

To all of you I address my heartfelt greetings. May almighty God bless you all with lasting peace and harmony. It is with great joy that I have come to Asia for my first visit as Bishop of Rome and successor of the apostle Peter. I have come to visit the Catholic communities and to bring a message of fraternal love to all the people of the Philippines and Japan, two countries among the many that make up Asia. My journey is meant to be a journey of brotherhood, in fulfillment of a mission that is entirely religious. But I have also come with the desire of being able in the future to travel to other Asian countries, in order to convey personally to them, too, my sentiments of deep respect and esteem.

In order to succeed, the development of nations must take place in an atmosphere of peace. I cannot address myself to you, peoples of Asia, without touching upon this most important issue, for peace is the necessary condition for every nation and people if they are to live and develop. My heart is heavy when I think of the many parts of your continent where the sound of war has not yet died down, where the people involved might have changed, but not the reality of war, where weapons alone are thought to provide security, or where brother fights against brother in order to redress real or alleged injustices. Asia has not been spared the lot of many other parts of the world where peace—true peace and freedom, mutual trust and fraternal collaboration—still remains but a dream. Too many men, women, and children on Asian soil suffer and die; too many families are disrupted, are forced to flee their homes and villages; too much hate still creates sorrow and destruction. I shall not cease to raise my voice to plead for peace. As I have constantly done in public appeals and in private conversations with the leaders of the world, so now again I beseech each and every one to respect the values and rights of peoples and nations.

My final word is a prayer for Asia. Upon the heads of state and the governments of Asia, I invoke wisdom and strength, that they may lead their nations toward full humanity and progress. Upon the leaders of the religions in Asia, I invoke assistance from on high, that they may always encourage believers in their quest for the Absolute. I pray that the parents and children of Asia will grow in love for each other and in service to their fellow citizens. And I commend to the almighty and merciful God the dignity and destiny of every man, woman, and child on this continent—the dignity and destiny of all Asia. ✠

$\mathcal{G}$UAM 1981

ON 22 FEBRUARY, Pope John Paul briefly visited the American island of Guam, the largest of the Marianas, discovered by Magellan in 1521. The following day, the Pontiff addressed the religious and clergy of that region, reminding them of the richness of the missionary tradition which they represent. He spoke of the biblical foundation of their vocation as derived from the New Testament:

For the Church in every age and in every place is called by Christ to make of many individuals a single people, united in "one Lord, one faith, one baptism" [Eph 4:5]. As one body, the Church must radiate the presence of her Lord in the world. Jesus Christ, therefore, is the reason for everything the Church says and does! Jesus Christ is the focal point for that living communion which constitutes the Church!

It is good for us to return often to those sacred accounts of the Church's early life and to reflect on those elements which made up her ecclesial communion. In the Acts of the Apostles we read: "And they devoted themselves to the apostles' teaching and fellowship, to the breaking of bread and the prayers" [Acts 2:42].

From the beginning, the Church recognized her duty to hand on what she had received from the Lord. The apostolic teachings enabled the disciples to be of "one heart and one mind" [Acts 4:32]. Thus the early Christians confessed a common faith before the world, and no authentic communion was possible where fidelity to the apostolic tradition was lacking. Today no less than before the Church is called to preserve the integrity of Christ's message. For his word is not entrusted to her to do with as she pleases. Rather, the Church is an instrument of evangelization imparting Christ's message in its entirety, with the rich fullness of its content. At the same time this Gospel message is not intended to be displayed as in a museum showcase, where it can only be studied and admired. No, it must be shared, passed on, so that others may hear it, accept it, and be initiated into the community of the faithful.

But where does the community receive the impulse for being a true communion? The Church finds this source in "the breaking of the bread." In the Eucharist, ecclesial communion is not only manifested but it is, in fact, brought about. "Because there is one bread, we who are many are one body, for we partake of the one bread" [1 Cor 10:17].

Lastly, the call of faith implies for each believer a continual call to holiness nurtured by prayer. Left to his own devices, man does not possess the necessary strength to overcome the sin of the world. It is only the Holy Spirit who can ensure a true and lasting unity, since by his presence each member of the community is impelled toward more generous expressions of charity and mercy. With all my heart I encourage this interest, and I pray that the Holy Spirit will instill into every sector of the Church a fervor of holiness that will prefer the love of God and the love of neighbor to every other consideration. ✠

JAPAN 1981

On 23 February 1981, Pope John Paul commenced a four-day visit to Japan, where he spoke often of the sixteen martyrs of Nagasaki whom he had beatified in Manila. Nine of those martyrs were Japanese. The others were Spaniards, French, Italian, and Filipino. As if to reiterate and exemplify the text of his message to all Asia in the radio address of 21 February, the Pope spoke emphatically of the closing days of the Second World War. He recalled Hiroshima.

To remember the past is to commit one's self to the future. To remember Hiroshima is to abhor nuclear war. To remember Hiroshima is to commit one's self to peace. To remember what the people of this city suffered is to renew our faith in man, in his capacity to do what is good, in his freedom to choose what is right, in his determination to turn disaster into a new beginning. In the face of the man-made calamity that every war is, one must affirm and reaffirm again and again that the waging of war is not inevitable or unchangeable. Humanity is not destined to self-destruction. Clashes of ideologies, aspirations, and needs can and must be settled and resolved by means other than war and violence. Humanity owes it to itself to settle differences and conflicts by peaceful means. The great spectrum of problems facing the many peoples in varying stages of cultural, social, economic, and political development gives rise to international tension and conflict. It is vital for humanity that these problems should be solved in accordance with ethical principles of equity and justice enshrined in meaningful agreements and institutions. The international community should thus give itself a system of law that will regulate international relations and maintain peace, just as the rule of law protects national order. And to the Creator of nature and man of truth and beauty I pray:

Hear my voice, for it is the voice of the victims of all wars and violence among individuals and nations;

Hear my voice, for it is the voice of all children who suffer and will suffer when people put their faith in weapons and war;

Hear my voice when I beg you to instill into the hearts of all human beings the wisdom of peace, the strength of justice, and the joy of fellowship;

Hear my voice, for I speak for the multitudes in every country and in every period of history who do not want war and are ready to walk the road of peace;

Hear my voice and grant insight and strength so that we may always respond to hatred with love, to injustice with total dedication to justice, to need with the sharing of self, to war with peace.

O God, hear my voice and grant unto the world your everlasting peace. ✠

UNITED STATES—ALASKA 1981

ON THE 26 FEBRUARY 1981, Pope John Paul II made his second visit to the United States with a short stopover in Anchorage, Alaska, where he was greeted by the Most Reverend Francis Hurley, Archbishop of Anchorage. Here, the Pontiff spoke of the unique beauty of the land and the many ethnic groups who constitute its population:

Being here in Alaska, so richly endowed with the beauties of nature, at once so rugged and yet so splendid, we sense the presence of God's Spirit in the manifold handiwork of creation. And not only do we feel this presence in inanimate nature and in the order of plants and animals, but all the more so in the precious gift of life which God has breathed into each one of his sons and daughters. Having fashioned man and woman in his own image, God remains with each individual on the pilgrimage of this earthly life, inviting, calling, prompting through his Spirit an acceptance of the salvation offered in Christ.

As I look over this gathering here, I see the evidence of the Holy Spirit's call of faith in Alaska. Here many peoples of diverse backgrounds and cultures are drawn into one community of faith. Here native Alaskans—Eskimos, Aleuts, and Indians—join together with people from all parts of the United States to form one ecclesial community. Here in recent years Hispanics have come in increasing numbers to join in the united fellowship of the Church. In acknowledging this activity of the Spirit, are we not impelled to make a joyful song to the Lord? Do not our hearts overflow in speaking of all the wonderful blessings that the Spirit has infused into the Church? ✠

NIGERIA 1982

ON 13 MAY 1981, Pope John Paul II was wounded in an assassination attempt in St. Peter's Square. He did not undertake, therefore, any further apostolic visits in 1981. Early in 1982, he undertook his second journey to Africa, arriving in Lagos, Nigeria, on 12 February. The occasion for this visit was to encourage seminarians as well as novices and junior religious in the rapidly growing Catholic Church of Nigeria. His remarks are oriented toward the character of future leaders of the faith. Other nations visited during this time were Benin, Gabon, and Equatorial Guinea. The following is from a talk delivered to aspirants of the ministry in Enugu on 13 February:

God has blessed Nigeria with many junior and senior seminarians. Indeed your Bigard Memorial Seminary in Enugu and Ikoh Ekpene is one of the largest in the world. The high number of your seminarians must never be used as a reason for accepting a lower quality of performance. Of first importance in the seminary must be friendship with Christ centered on the Eucharist and nurtured especially by prayer and meditation on the word of God. This friendship with Christ is authentically expressed in sacrifice, love of neighbor, chastity, and apostolic zeal. It likewise demands fidelity to studies and a certain detachment from the things of this world.

No priest can carry out his ministry well unless he lives in union with Christ. His life, like Christ's, must be marked by self-sacrifice, zeal for the spreading of the Kingdom of God, unblemished chastity, unstinted charity. All this is possible only when the priest is a man of prayer and Eucharistic devotion. By praying the liturgy of the hours in union with the Church he will find strength and joy for the apostolate. In silent prayer before the Blessed Sacrament, he will be constantly renewed in his consecration to Jesus Christ and confirmed in his permanent commitment to priestly celibacy. By invoking Mary, the Mother of Jesus, the priest will be sustained in his generous service to all Christ's brothers and sisters in the world. Yes, the priest must not allow the passing needs of the active apostolate to elbow out or eat into his prayer life. He must not be so engrossed with working for God that he is in danger of forgetting God himself. He will remember that our Savior warned us that without Him we can do nothing. Without Him, we can fish all night and still catch nothing.

No priest can work all by himself. He works with his brother priests and under the leadership of the bishop, who is their father, brother, coworker and friend. The authentic priest will maintain the love and unity of the presbyterium; he will reverence and obey his bishop as he solemnly promised on ordination day. The presbyterium of the bishop with all of his priests, diocesan and religious, should function as a family, as an apostolic team marked with joy, mutual understanding, and fraternal love. The presbyterium exists so that, through the renewal of Christ's sacrifice, the mystery of Christ's saving love may enter the lives of God's people. Priests must not forget to help their brother priests who are in difficulty: moral, spiritual, financial, or otherwise. And the sick and the old priests find in your warmth of brotherly charity both solace and support.

No state of life escapes temptations, and you will try to identify your own. By God's grace and with persevering effort you must strive to resist whatever temptation may come your way: whether, for example, to laxity in discipline or to laziness, instability, unavailability, too much traveling, or dissipation of apostolic energy. Relying on grace, you will reject temptations against celibacy by watchfulness, prayer, and mortification. You will refuse to be captured by the attraction of material things and will not put your joy in money, big cars, and a high position in society. Party politics are not for you. It is the proper area of the lay apostolate. Rather you are the chaplains of the laity, who in political matters should assume their own distinctive role [*Gaudium et Spes*, 43]. In strengthening you against temptation the sacrament of Penance has great importance for every priest. Here, for our own lives, we ministers of reconciliation find Christ's healing and sustaining action, his forgiving and merciful love.

Nigerians love to study. This is good. Learned priests are required in order to answer the needs of Church and society. Every priest should continue to improve himself by the private study of theology, catechetics, and other such sacred sciences. Strive to make time for some such study frequently.

The priest must be a leaven in the Nigerian community of today. In a country in which many are overconcerned with making money, the priest by word and example must call attention to higher values. Man does not live by bread alone. The priest must identify with the poor, so as to be able to bring them the uplifting Gospel of Christ. Remember that Jesus applied these words to himself: "The spirit of the Lord is upon me, because he has anointed me to preach good news to the poor" [Lk 4:18].

ON THE FOLLOWING DAY, the Pope deepened his message to the future leaders of the Church in Nigeria when he ordained ninety-two priests in the city of Kaduna. The following is an excerpt from his homily. To the newly ordained, he spoke of the realism that must accompany their ministries:

The Letter to the Hebrews also instructs us that our Lord and Master, during his life on earth, "learned to obey through suffering" [Heb 5:8]. Suffering is an inevitable part of discipleship. That is why Jesus told his followers: "anyone who does not carry his cross and come after me cannot be my disciple" [Lk 14:27]. This is not to forget or overlook the fact that faith in Christ is the source of deep joy [Jn 15:11], and that Jesus promised his disciples a peace which the world cannot give [Jn 14:27]. But it remains true that suffering will be part of serving Christ. And suffering is closely related to obedience, for when we accept the suffering which divine providence allows we are conforming ourselves more closely to the will of the Heavenly Father.

FOLLOWING THE PUBLICATION of the apostolic letter *Evangelii Nuntiandi* in 1975, the Joint Working Group of the World Council of Churches and the Secretariat for Promoting Christian Unity developed a document on "Common Witness" in the field of ecumenism. In his address to representatives of the various Christian denominations in Lagos, Pope John Paul used the term "common witness" as an ecumenical incentive for the first time in a papal discourse and explained its significance.

My pastoral visit from its very planning was meant to have an important ecumenical dimension, for I see work for the unity of all Christians as an essential element in my own ministry as Bishop of Rome and Pastor of the Catholic Church. This encounter therefore fills one of my deepest desires. I am very pleased to greet you in the love of our common Lord: "the grace of our Lord Jesus Christ be with you all" [2 Thes 3:17].

The Catholic Church has much in common with your various ecclesial communities. We are all baptized in Christ, whom we confess as our Lord and Savior and whom we acknowledge as the "one Mediator between God and men" [1 Ti 2:5]. The Bible and especially the Gospels are dear to us all, because they are the word of God and the revelation of his saving love. Our fundamental religious orientation is directed by our faith in Christ, our love for him, and our desire to help in the spreading of his Kingdom into the hearts of all, among all peoples and at all times.

We also share common views on fundamental human rights, on justice and peace, on development, and on the need to live according to one's faith. We believe that there must be no dichotomy between the Gospel message and Christian living . . . all of this constitutes a common witness to the charity of Christ.

Moreover, your common efforts with the Catholic Church in the Bible Society of Nigeria have yielded dividends especially in joint projects of Bible translation into your many languages, and in the subsidizing of Bibles so that the poor can buy them, too. These efforts are the expression of true zeal "that the word of the Lord may speed on and triumph" [2 Thes 3:1].

You also issue joint statements when the occasion demands it. You show concern for the place of the Church and religion in Nigerian schools and you promote national unity and understanding in other ways too. May God bless all these efforts. ✠

ℬENIN 1982

ON 17 FEBRUARY 1982, Pope John Paul II made a one-day visit to the People's Republic of Benin. The previous decades had seen tension between the government and religion. In his address to the president, Mathieu Kérékou, the Pontiff spoke of the participation of Catholics in society and their usefulness in human development.

Through you, who have with the government the exalted responsibility of the temporal affairs of the country, I greet and thank the people of Benin, without distinction of race or religion, for their welcome. This country hopes to develop—with the help given in the spirit of brotherhood and with respect for its own genius—all its resources, material and human, so that its people may lead their lives in increasing dignity and take their place freely in the family of nations. I understand and share this hope because it is the will of God. It will involve the whole nation, and I express to all its citizens my solidarity, my good wishes, and my encouragement in this work on behalf of their motherland.

Catholics have their part in this and, as you know, Mr. President, they can make an important contribution to it in the economic, social, and cultural fields, both because of their numbers and by reason of their vision of things, which is at once profound and open to all aspects of life. During 120 years of evangelization, the ancestral qualities, which are notable, have not been overlooked or hindered by the Church. Rather they have been strengthened, purified when necessary, improved and developed by the Christian faith. The faith was able to deliver the children of this country from a certain fear by putting their souls at peace with the Creator. The faith calls on them always to be loyal, to have respect for love and life, to work in solidarity, to share, to give disinterested service, to pardon, to be courageous in time of trial, to hope. Christians spontaneously attach great importance to works of education and healing, as being exalted forms of service. The fruits of this work are authentically African and Christian. ✠

ℰQUATORIAL GUINEA 1982

ON 18 FEBRUARY 1982, the day after his visit to Gabon, Pope John Paul celebrated the Eucharist in the city of Bata in Equitorial Guinea, where he identified the vitality of the local Church in each nation. Again his theme was evangelization in order to promote the faith.

The Pope has come to you to promote the work of evangelization also in your lands. That kind of evangelization that means a deeper growth in faith and generous dedication to whatever promotes the personal dignity of every man, and loyalty to Christ and to his Church. I come to you as a brother and as a friend, as a representative of Christ in whom you already believe, as a herald of his message of salvation, as a sower of encouragement for your Christian community. Urged by my duty as evangelizer, I come to this Church that is part of the flock of Christ entrusted to me as Peter's Successor. Therefore I wish to imitate Paul the Apostle and rejoice in your perseverance in the Gospel "which you received, in which you stand, by which you are saved, if you hold it fast as I have announced it to you" [1 Cor 15:1ff].

Today we thank God because of the seed that the first missionaries sowed in 1645, which only many years later was spread in a more continuous and vast manner, and has yielded abundant fruits. These are reflected in the major Catholic population found in Bata and Malabo. Our mind can imagine how many sufferings the successive missionaries—Capuchins, diocesan priests, Jesuits, and above all Claretians—had to face, faithful to the Master's commandment to teach all nations [Mt 28:19f] with every effort to show to the brethren the way to salvation. It is just, then, that we pay a tribute of gratitude and appreciation to that long-lasting evangelizing effort that little by little rooted the Church among you.

This work of evangelization tends by its nature to enable each Church to govern itself sufficiently with its own powers. Not to close in upon itself, but to become an evangelizer of other Churches. In this way, each shows its full maturity in faith, returning what it received in the phase of its growth.

But while we await a major consolidation with regard to evangelizing workers, your Church has already given some consoling proofs of maturity and faithfulness to the Lord. There are indeed not few among your brethren who have given courageous witness, even in the midst of persecution, of their Christian faith. And if some have been weak, many more have given wonderful examples of constancy in their intimate religious convictions.

These examples must encourage and stimulate you to follow

with renewed fervor the teachings of the Gospel: "Who shall separate us from the love of Christ? Shall tribulation, or distress, or persecution, or famine, or nakedness, or peril, or sword? . . . In all these things we are more than conquerors through him who loved us" [Rom 8:35–37]. ✠

$\mathscr{P}$ORTUGAL 1982

ON 13 MAY 1982, Pope John Paul paid a special visit to the Shrine of Our Lady of Fatima in Portugal to render thanks for the preservation of his life against an assassination attempt in Rome one year before.

In 1917, three children reported experiencing visions of the Blessed Mother at Fatima. The piety of Catholicism of the twentieth century has often been identified with this place of pilgrimage. Now it has a definite place in the pontificate of Pope John Paul.

And so I come here today because on this very day last year in St. Peter's Square in Rome, the attempt on the Pope's life was made in mysterious coincidence with the anniversary of the first apparition at Fatima, which occurred on 13 May 1917.

I seem to recognize in the coincidence of the dates a special call to come to this place. And so today I am here. I have come in order to thank divine providence in this place which the Mother of God seems to have chosen.

Mary's motherhood in our regard is manifested in a particular way in the places where she meets us: her dwelling places, places in which a special presence of the mother is felt.

There are many such dwelling places. They are of all kinds: from a special corner in the home or little wayside shrines adorned with an image of the Mother of God, to chapels and churches built in her honor; however, in certain places the mother's presence is felt in a particularly vivid way. These places sometimes radiate their light over a great distance and draw people from afar. These places are the Marian sanctuaries or shrines.

In all these places that unique testament of the crucified Lord is wonderfully actualized: in them man feels that he is entrusted and confided to Mary; he goes there in order to be with her as with his Mother; he opens his heart to her and speaks to her about everything; he "takes her to his own home," that is to say, he brings her into all his problems which at times are difficult.

Mary's spiritual motherhood is therefore a sharing in the power of the Holy Spirit of "the giver of life"; it is the humble service of her who says of herself, "Behold, I am the handmaid of the Lord" [Lk 1:38]. ✠

RGENTINA 1982

At the time of his visit to Great Britain, that nation was at war with Argentina over possession of the Falkland Islands (the Malvinas). Unwilling to take sides in the conflict, Pope John Paul flew to Argentina for a two-day visit immediately following his pastoral activities in Britain. In his discourse to the bishops of Argentina, Pope John Paul outlined the role of bishop as peacemaker, but applied it to all Christians. His visit lasted over 11 to 12 June 1982.

A s successor of the Apostle Peter, your elder brother and servant in unity, why not proclaim before you that in the face of the sad events in the South Atlantic, I also wanted to be with you as the herald and minister of reconciliation?

I well knew that in directing my steps toward Great Britain—in carrying out a strictly pastoral mission which was not only the Pope's but the entire Church's—that someone could perhaps have interpreted such a mission in political terms, deflecting it from its purely evangelical significance. In any case, I maintained that fidelity to my own ministry required that I not halt in the face of possible inexact interpretations but carry out the mandate to proclaim with gentleness and firmness the *verbum reconciliationis*.

It is true that I first wished to meet repeatedly with authoritative representatives of the Episcopate of Argentina and of Great Britain in order to ask their opinion and advice on a problem of such importance for the concerned nations and for the Churches which are located in them. Therefore, I wished to celebrate a solemn Eucharist in the Basilica of St. Peter with some pastors of the countries involved in the conflict. The moving witness of communion which, even in the midst of the battle between their countries of origin, those pastors gave "in one cup and in one bread," was enriched even more by the joint statement.

And I do not need to comment here upon the already mentioned letter signed by my own hand which, as Saint Paul often did, I wrote (to the beloved sons and daughters of the Argentine nation). It was a message which came from my heart in an hour of suffering for your people, whose scope was to announce my burning desire to come visit you.

But not only in the Argentine society. At this moment when all Latin America gives proof of greater cohesion, when it is anxiously looking for its deepest identity and its own character, the peacemaking presence of the Church is important, so that a continent which possesses a "true Catholic foundation" [Puebla, 412], may preserve the ideal inspirations which have distinguished it.

In the midst of the hopes and the dangers which can be glimpsed on the horizon, and in view of the latent tensions which arise from time to time, it is necessary to offer a service of pacification in the name of faith and of mutual understanding, so that the religious and spiritual riches, true foundations of unity, may be much stronger than any seed of disunity. ✠

 WITZERLAND 1982

IN 1959 POPE JOHN XXIII ISSUED AN ENCYCLICAL, *Ad Petri Cathedram,*
in which he spoke of the need for unity in the world. Among the
groupings in need of that human unity identified was the relationship between workers and employers. On 15 June 1982 Pope John
Paul accepted an invitation to address the International Labor Organization (ILO) in Geneva, Switzerland. Here, he spoke to the assembled representatives, basing his talk on a word which he was to
help make popular in the Eastern European situation: "solidarity." At
this very time, labor issues were making headlines in news about
Poland and the other countries of the Soviet bloc.

The problems of work—problems that have repercussions in so
many spheres of life and at all levels, whether individual, family, national, or international—share one characteristic, which
is at one and the same time a condition and a program and which I
would like to stress before you today: solidarity. I feel impelled to
place these considerations before you partly because solidarity is inherent, in one way or another, in the very nature of human work and
also because of the objectives of your organization and above all the
spirit which imbues it.

Confronted with the blatant injustices arising out of the systems
of the last century, workmen, especially in industry, reacted and
thereby discovered not only their common poverty, but the strength
that comes from concerted action. As victims of the same injustices,
they combined in a joint effort. In my encyclical *On Human Work,* I
called this reaction a "just social reaction"; this situation "caused the
impetus for emergence of a great burst of solidarity between workers, first and foremost industrial workers. The call to solidarity and
common action addressed to the workers—especially to those engaged in narrowly specialized, monotonous, and depersonalized
work in industrial plants where the machine tends to dominate
man—was important and eloquent from the point of view of social
ethics. It was the reaction against the degradation of man as the sub-

ject of work. . . . This reaction united the working world in a community marked by great solidarity" [*Laborem Exercens,* n. 8].

Despite subsequent improvements, despite the greater and more effective respect for workers' fundamental rights in many countries, various systems based on ideology and on power have allowed flagrant injustices to persist or have created new ones. Moreover, the enhanced awareness of social justice which, because of their geographical extent or contempt for the inalienable dignity of the human person, are nothing less than challenges to mankind. *The need today is to forge a new solidarity based on the true significance of human work.* For it is only through a just concept of work that it will be possible to define the objectives of this *solidarity* and the various forms it should take. ✠

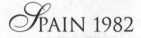

✐PAIN 1982

FROM 31 OCTOBER TO 9 NOVEMBER 1982, Pope John Paul made a pastoral visit to Spain. Welcomed in Madrid by King Juan Carlos and Queen Sofia, he had come to celebrate the closure of the fourth centenary of Saint Teresa of Avila. From his youth he had been influenced by Carmelite spirituality. For him, this visit was at once personal and pastoral. On 1 November he celebrated a Mass in honor of Saint Teresa at the Cathedral of Avila. His entire visit lasted ten days, and included visits to Salamanca and Alba de Tormes.

B y means of prayer, Teresa has searched and found Christ. She found him in the words of the Gospel which from her youth "took hold of her heart" [*Life,* 3,5]: she found him "having carried him in her being" [ibid., 4,7]: she learned to gaze on him with love in the images of the Lord to which she was so devoted [ibid., 7, 2; 22:4]: with the "Bible of the poor"—images, and this "Bible of the heart"—meditation on the word, she was able to relive interiorly the scenes of the Gospel and draw near to the Lord with great confidence.

How often did Saint Teresa meditate on those Gospel scenes of Jesus speaking to some women! What joyful interior liberty did the caring attitude of the Master bring to her in times of a marked antifeminism—Jesus with Magdalene, with Martha and Mary in Bethany, with the Canaanite and Samaritan women, those feminine personages which the Saint recalls so many times in her writings! There is no doubt that from this evangelical perspective Teresa has been able to defend the dignity of women and their potential for an appropriate service in the Church: "You did not disdain women, Lord of my soul, when you walked the Earth: you favored them always with much mercy" [*Way of Perfection,* Autograph of El Escorial, 3, 7].

The scene of Jesus with the Samaritan woman near the well of Sicar, which we have recalled in the Gospel, is very significant. "Every one who drinks of this water will thirst again, but whoever drinks of the water that I shall give him will never thirst; the water that I shall give him will become in him a spring of water welling up to eternal life" [Jn 4:13–14].

Among the holy women in the history of the Church, Teresa of Jesus is without a doubt the one who has responded to Christ with the greatest fervor of heart: Give me this water! She herself confirms this when she recalls her first encounters with the Christ of the Gospel: "How often I remember the living water of which the Lord spoke to the Samaritan woman! And so I am much attracted to that episode of the Gospel" [*Life,* 30, 19]. Today Teresa of Jesus, like a new Samaritan woman, invites all to come close to Jesus, who is the fountain of living water.

Christ Jesus, our Redeemer, was the model for Teresa. In him she encountered the majesty of his divinity and the humility of his humanity: "It is a wonderful thing that while we are living and human we have him as human" [ibid., 22, 9]: she saw that even though he was God, he was human, that he was not frightened of human weakness. What horizons of familiarity with God does Teresa reveal to us in the humanity of Christ! With what precision does she affirm the faith of the Church in Christ who is truly God and truly human! How she feels him near, "our companion in the most Blessed Sacrament" [ibid., 22, 6].

From the mystery of the most sacred humanity which is the door, way, and light she has arrived at the mystery of the Most Holy Trinity [ibid., 7, 1, 6], the source and goal of human life, "which is a mirror reflecting the image according to which we are sculpted" [ibid., 2, 8]. From the height of the mystery of God she has understood the human worth of a person's dignity whose vocation is to the infinite.

ON 9 NOVEMBER Pope John Paul assumed the role of medieval pilgrim and traveled to the tomb of Saint James the Apostle at Santiago de Compostela. Here in the presence of the king of Spain and the presidents of all the Episcopal Conferences of Europe he spoke of the possibilities of the future of a Europe united in faith. His words were personal.

Therefore, I, John Paul, son of the Polish nation which has always considered itself European by its origins, traditions, culture, and vital relationships, Slavic among the Latins and Latin among the Slavs; I, Successor of Peter in the See of Rome, a See which Christ wished to establish in Europe and which he loves because of its efforts for the spread of Christianity throughout the whole world; I, Bishop of Rome and Shepherd of the universal Church, from Santiago, utter to you, Europe of the ages, a cry full of love: *Find yourself again. Be yourself.* Discover your origins, revive your roots. Return to those authentic values which made your history a glorious one and your presence so beneficent in the other continents. Rebuild your spiritual unity in a climate of complete respect for other religions and other genuine liberties. Give to Caesar what belongs to Caesar, and to God what belongs to God. Do not become so proud of your achievements that you forget their possible negative effects. Do not become discouraged for the quantitative loss of some of your greatness in the world or for the social and cultural crises which affect you today. You can still be the guiding light of civilization and the stimulus of progress for the world. The other continents look to you and also hope to receive from you the same reply which James gave to Christ: "I can do it." ✠

ℬORTUGAL 1983

From 2 to 10 March 1983 the Pontiff made a pastoral journey to Central America, where he visited Costa Rica, Nicaragua, Panama, El Salvador, Guatemala, Belize, Honduras, and Haiti. While on the way to this part of Latin America, the Pope's aircraft paused for a technical stopover in Lisbon on 2 March. The Pontiff shared a few thoughts with the small crowd at the airport. He reflected again on his devotion to Our Lady of Fatima. He also mentioned the special jubilee year then being celebrated in Rome. His passage through Lisbon was in the middle of the night of the Redemption.

A s the person most responsible for the message of Christ, which is above all a message of peace, I came to you in an attitude of dialogue, with respect to all that is human. But, the indelible memory of my story in Fatima (in May of last year), a stay that is at once essentially pastoral, religious, and Marian in nature, is very much alive. During this brief stopover in the "Land of Holy Mary," I wish to renew my appeal so that the "message" that comes to us from Fatima may be heard, a message which coincides with the call of the imminent Jubilee Year of the Redemption echoing "Our Lady of the Message." I repeated in my appeal that Redemption is always more powerful than man's sin and the "sin of the world," and that the Redemption infinitely surpasses every kind of evil which may exist in man and in the world. "A pilgrim among pilgrims," I had occasion to say then that I came with the name of Our Lady on my lips and with the canticle of God's mercy in my heart.

Once more in the role of a pilgrim, the thoughts which guide me are the same, and my lips speak of the fullness I carry in my heart: the love of God, rich in mercy; the power of Christ's Redemption; Our Lady, mother of our confidence; and love and peace among men. ✠

COSTA RICA 1983

ON 2 MARCH 1983 the Pontiff began a history-making tour of Central America by touching down in Costa Rica. The times were indeed troubled, and he focused his attention on the resolution of many civil wars which were at that time being waged in the nations throughout the region. He was to receive mixed reactions from the several countries of his visit. Still, he identified himself with the terrible suffering that was caused in an area where the poor not only were made to suffer but where they "disappeared." Immediately upon his arrival at the airport in San José he noted the specific reasons for his pastoral presence:

There echoes in my mind with urgent emphasis the rending cry which arises from these lands and which invokes peace, an end to war and violent death; which implores reconciliation, with the end of divisions and hatred; which yearns for ample justice, until now futilely awaited; which wants to be called to a greater dignity without renouncing its Christian religious essence.

I would like to give voice to this pained outcry with my visit; the voice which fades away with the already customary images of tears or of the death of an infant, of the discomfort of the elderly, of the mother who loses her children, of the long line of orphans, of so many thousands of refugees, exiled and forced to flee in search of a home, of the poor person without hope or work.

I come to share the pain of the peoples to try to understand them firsthand, to leave a word of encouragement and hope, based on a necessary change of positions.

This change is possible if we welcome the voice of Christ, which urges us to love and respect each man as our brother; if we know how to renounce the practices of blind selfishness; if we learn to be more united; if we rigorously apply the rules of social justice proclaimed by the Church; if a growing sense of the distributive justice of tasks and duties among the various sectors of society makes its way among the leaders of the peoples; and if each people could face its problems in an atmosphere of sincere dialogue, without foreign interferences.

Mine is the word of peace, of concord, and of hope. I have come to speak to you with love for all and to exhort you, as children of the same Father, to brotherhood and understanding. It is precisely this reality which moves me to knock at consciences, so that from an adequate response the hope, that they so much need, can be born in these lands. ✠

NICARAGUA 1983

WHEN POPE JOHN PAUL II LANDED IN MANAGUA, Nicaragua, on 4 March 1983, he was greeted by the head of the Junta, Daniel Ortega Saavedra, and the members of the government. He found a country politically divided in the wake of the regime of Anastasio Somoza. The nation was in the midst of a hidden civil war between factions, such as the Sandinistas and the Contras. The division likewise affected the Catholic Church. Here the titles varied, with names such as "Loyalists" and the "Popular Church." The Pope's open-air Mass marks the only time he received publicly hostile reactions, and he had to shout for silence above the crowd. His calls for unity are among the most memorable of all his visitation discourses.

The Church is the family of God (Puebla, 238–49), and just as in a family, unity in order must reign; so likewise in the Church. In it no one has a greater right to citizenship than anyone else; neither Jews, nor Greeks, nor slaves, nor freedmen, nor men, nor women, nor the poor, nor the rich, since all "are one in Jesus Christ" [Gal 3:28].

This unity is based on "one Lord, one faith, one baptism, one God and Father of all, who is over all, and works through all, and is in all," as is stated in the text of the Letter to the Ephesians, which we have just heard [Eph 4:5], and as you often sing during your celebrations.

We must appreciate the profundity and the solidity of the foundations of this unity which we enjoy in the universal Church, in that of all Central America, and to which the local Church in Nicaragua must steadfastly aspire. Precisely for this reason we must give due value also to the dangers which threaten it and to the need to maintain and deepen this unity, a gift of God in Christ Jesus.

As I wrote in my letter to the bishops of Nicaragua last August, this "gift" is perhaps more precious precisely because it is "fragile" and "threatened" [*L'Osser-vatore Romano,* Spanish language edition of 8 August 1982, p. 9].

In effect the unity of the Church is called into question when the powerful factors which constitute and maintain it—faith itself, the revealed Word, the sacraments, obedience to the bishops and to the Pope, the sense of vocation, and mutual responsibility in Christ's mission in the world—are relegated to a position inferior to earthly considerations, unacceptable ideological commitments, temporal options, even concepts of the Church which supplant the true one.

Yes, dear Central American and Nicaraguan brothers, when the Christian, whatever his condition may be, prefers any other doctrine or ideology to the teaching of the Apostles and of the Church, when these doctrines are made the criterion of our vocation, when an attempt is made to reinterpret according to their categories the catechesis, religious teaching, and preaching, when "parallel magisteria" are established, as I said in my inaugural address at the Puebla Conference [28 January 1979], then the unity of the Church is weakened, the exercise of its mission of being the "sacrament of unity" for all men is made more difficult.

The unity of the Church means and demands from us the radical overcoming of all these tendencies towards separation; it means and demands the reexamination of our scale of values; it means and requires the submission of our doctrinal concepts and of our pastoral projects to the *Magisterium of the Church,* represented by the Pope and the bishops. This also applies to the field of the social teaching of the Church set out by my predecessors and by myself. ✠

ANAMA 1983

WHILE IN CENTRAL AMERICA, the Pontiff took the occasion to address the subject of marriage and the family as a means of protecting stability in an otherwise chaotic society. On 5 March at Albrook Fields Airport in Panama, he spoke about family as a fundamental human value. He also spoke of the need to sustain and promote harmony among the generations.

In the will of Christ, reflected in his words, we must discover something more than an external law; in those words is God's mysterious design for spouses. Marriage is the story of mutual love, a path to human and Christian maturity. Only in the persons' progressive self-manifestation can a relationship of love be consolidated which involves the totality of the spouses' life.

The path is arduous, but not impossible. And the grace of marriage also includes the necessary help in overcoming these inevitable difficulties. On the contrary, breaking the marriage covenant not only strikes out against the law of God, but it blocks the maturing process, the individuals' full realization. Therefore, a certain mentality which filters into society and foments marital instability and egoism in favor of unconditioned sexual freedom is not acceptable.

The spouses' Christian love has its example in Christ, who gives himself completely to the Church and is inscribed in the Paschal Mystery of death and resurrection, of loving sacrifice, of joy and hope.

Even when difficulties increase, the solution is not flight, nor the breaking of the marriage, but rather the perseverance of the spouses. You know it by experience, beloved husbands and wives: conjugal fidelity shapes and matures; it reveals the energies of Christian love; it creates a new family, with the newness of a love which has passed through death and resurrection; it is the proof of a fully Christian relationship between spouses, who learn to love each other with the love of Christ; it is the guarantee of a stable environment for the children's formation and balance.

The relationship between parents and children is an important aspect of family life. In fact, the authority and obedience which are lived in the Christian family must be imbued with the love of Christ and directed to the fulfillment of the persons. Saint Paul summarizes this in a phrase full of meaning: *Acting in the Lord* [Eph 6:1–4], that is, according to his will, in his presence, since he presides over the domestic Church, which is the family [*Lumen Gentium,* 11]. The conflicts which arise between the generations are overcome only through the proof of true love. The complementary values which are borne by every generation can be integrated in patience, in the search for truth.

For this reason, may families not neglect prayer in common, according to the best traditions of your people, in order to be constantly renewed in good and in the sense of God. In this atmosphere, the necessary vocations to the priesthood and the religious life, which are the sign of God's blessing and special love, can flourish. ✠

El SALVADOR 1983

THROUGHOUT HIS VISIT TO CENTRAL AMERICA the Pontiff maintained his theme of unity. On 6 March 1983, he paid tribute to the memory of Archbishop Oscar Romero, the champion of the poor in San Salvador, who was cut down by the bullets of a sniper as he concluded the celebration of Mass in 1980. During a private visit to the cathedral, Pope John Paul recalled Romero's memory.

Within these walls rest the mortal remains of Monsignor Oscar Arnulfo Romero, a zealous pastor whom love for God and service to his brothers brought as far as the very sacrifice of his life in a violent way, as he was celebrating the Sacrifice of pardon and reconciliation.

For him, as for all the other venerable pastors who in their time have guided the flock of El Salvadoran faithful, we address our prayer to the just and merciful God, that his light might shine perpetually on them who sacrificed themselves for all and invited all to be inspired by Jesus, who had compassion for the multitudes at the very moment in which he committed himself to forging a more just, human, and fraternal world in which we all want to live. ✠

GUATEMALA 1983

POPE JOHN PAUL II ARRIVED IN GUATEMALA on 6 March 1983 and was welcomed by President Rios Montt. The following day he celebrated Mass in the esplanade Campo di Marte in the City of Guatemala. In a nation torn by class distinction and civil war, the Pope pleaded for peace and reconciliation.

Faith teaches us that man is the image and likeness of God [Gen 1:27]. This means that he is endowed with immense dignity and that when man is abused, when his rights are violated, when flagrant injustices are committed against him, when he is subjected to torture, when violence is done to him by unlawful restraint or his right to life is violated, a criminal and most grave offense is committed against God. At that moment, Christ retraces the steps of his Passion and suffers the horrors of the crucifixion in the victimized and the oppressed.

Men of all positions and ideologies who are listening to me: Pay heed to the appeal I address to you; listen to it because it comes from the depths of my faith, of my trust, and of my love for the man who suffers; listen to it because it comes in the name of Christ. Remember that every man is your brother and be converted into respectful defenders of his dignity. And may the life of your brother, of every man, always be assured in the first place beyond any social, political, ideological, racial, and religious difference.

Dear brothers and sisters, may faith in Jesus Christ shine in your lives like the sun on the waters of your seas, on the craters of your magnificent volcanoes, on the wings of your swift *quetzales*.

May this Christian faith, the glory of your nation, the soul of your people and of Central Americans, be manifested in practical, well-defined attitudes, above all toward the poorest, weakest, and simplest of your brothers and sisters. This faith must lead to justice and peace. No more divorce between faith and life. If we accept Christ, we do Christ's work, we treat each other as brothers and sisters, we walk the ways of the Gospel. ✠

ONDURAS 1983

THE POPE WAS IN HONDURAS FOR ONE DAY, 8 March 1983. He was welcomed at the Toncontin-Tegucigalpa Airport by the president, Roberto Suazo Cordova. Like the other states he visited, the nation was afflicted by poverty and internal civil strife. The population was not unfamiliar with the presence of guerrillas from other nations. Honduras also was experiencing a clergy shortage. A society known as the "Delegates of the Word," a group of laypeople who catechize and teach in the course of a service of the Word, assembled for an instruction by the Pontiff.

Every preacher must always remember that the Word we preach is not ours: We do not preach "ourselves" but "Jesus Christ" and him "crucified" [1 Cor 1:23]. Christ himself, the first sower, and the Church entrust us with the Word we must proclaim. We find it in the Sacred Scriptures, read in the light of the Church's constant tradition.

Therefore let the Bible, the Word of God, be your continuous reading, your study and your prayer: in the Liturgy and outside of it, as the last Council has taught us. But always read it according to

the correct interpretation made by the Church's legitimate authorities.

By virtue of the mission you have received, you must help the
members of your communities to accept and to deepen their knowledge of the faith, their love and their allegiance to the Church; and at
the same time you must teach them to practice their traditional devotions with the true sense of what they signify in the context of
Christian Life. Thus be aware of your responsibility and of your high
mission.

Your preaching is very valuable, without a doubt. It is the witness
you give to the truth with your lips. However, to be credible witnesses, your life must faithfully reflect what you preach. Otherwise
you would destroy with one hand what you build with the other. This
means that your life as a family, parents, spouses, children, citizens,
your fidelity to the duty of solidarity with the poor and the oppressed,
your exemplary charity, your honesty, are the unavoidable demands
of your vocation as Delegates of the Word. ✠

ELIZE 1983

On 9 March Pope John Paul briefly visited the nation of Belize, formerly known as British Honduras. Addressing the very new nation
with a large English-speaking population, the Pontiff reiterated the
theme of unity that predominated throughout his Central American
visit. In this situation he located the theme in ecumenism.

You have perhaps heard that in different places in Central America, during my mission, I have insisted on the theme of unity,
the unity of the local church, united with its bishop, and with
the other local churches, in the unity of the universal Church. Today,
I would like to consider with you and for you another aspect of the

major theme of unity. Namely, the unity to which the various Churches and ecclesial communities are called, in the supreme, organic unity of the one Church of Christ.

The Lord then as he approached his own sacrificial death, which he suffered "to gather into one the children of God who are scattered abroad" [Jn 11:52], foresaw the tragedy and scandal of division among Christians. And by the same token he taught us that unity is not to be dismissed as impossible or unnecessary, and that division is not to be accepted as a necessary evil. No, it is his will and the content of his prayer that we "be one" as he and the Father are one [Jn 17:22; 10:30].

This, however, is not all. The decree on ecumenism speaks also about holiness of life [*Unitatis Redintegratio*] and, indeed if we pay careful attention to what our Lord, in his priestly prayer, presents as the ultimate model of Christian unity, we cannot but be convinced that unity depends on holiness. Because he prays "that they may all be one, even as thou, Father, art in me, and I in thee, that they also may be one in us" [Jn 17:21]. And again: "that they may be one even as we are one" [V. 22]. The reading from the Letter to the Ephesians also puts Christian unity at the same lofty level when it says "I . . . , a prisoner for the Lord, beg you to lead a life worthy of the calling to which you have been called, . . . eager to maintain the unity of the Spirit in the bond of peace" [Eph 4:1, 3].

Yes, dear brethren, nothing short of the unity of the Holy Trinity in itself and our unity with the Holy Trinity can bring about full unity among Christians. When we strive for this perfect communion among all Churches and ecclesial communities, this is what we mean: unity shaped, modeled on, and given to us by the Holy Trinity. Let us remember that unity and holiness in the Church go together. When we strive, then, to be good Christians, and true Christians, unity among us should be one of our main goals. ✠

HAITI 1983

On 9 March 1983 the Pope arrived at Port au Prince, Haiti. Here he presided at the nineteenth ordinary Plenary Assembly of the Latin American Episcopal Council (CELAM), where he instructed the bishops to be faithful to their ideals of a "preferential option to the poor." Prior to this meeting he celebrated the closing Mass for Haiti's Eucharistic Congress. In his homily, he encouraged devotion to the Eucharist, but at the same time he spoke to the needs of the nation.

You have chosen as the theme of your Congress: "Something must change here." Very well, you may find in the Eucharist the inspiration, the strength, and the perseverance for your commitment in this process of change.

Things must indeed change. In preparing the Congress, the Church has had the courage to face up to the hard realities of the present, and I am sure that the same goes for all men of goodwill, for all who are profoundly attached to their fatherland. Certainly, you have a beautiful country, one with numerous human resources. In your case, one can speak of an innate and generous religious sentiment, of a vitality, and of the popular character of the Church. But the Christians have also experienced division, injustice, excessive inequality, a degradation of standards of living, misery, hunger—a fear experienced by many. Their mind has turned to their fellow countrymen who are incapable of living off their land, to the people who are packed together without work in the cities, to displaced families, to victims of various forms of frustration. And nevertheless they are convinced that there are solutions, in solidarity. The poor of every kind must regain hope. The Church maintains in this domain a prophetic mission, inseparable from her religious mission, and she demands the freedom to fulfill this: not in order to accuse and not merely to take cognizance of the evil, but to contribute in a positive manner to its relief by engaging the consciences of all, and more particularly of those who bear responsibility in the villages, in the cities, and at the national level, so that they can act in conformity to the Gospel and to the social doctrine of the Church.

ON THE EVENING OF 10 MARCH 1983 Pope John Paul addressed the opening of the nineteenth ordinary Plenary Assembly of the Latin American Episcopal Council (CELAM). This speech is considered to be a watershed in his pontificate. For the first time he used the term "new evangelization." His administration until this point had been very much influenced by Pope Paul VI's Apostolic Letter *Evangelii Nuntiandi* (1975). In addressing the forthcoming fifth centenary of the discovery of America, he challenged the bishops to place a new emphasis on their ministry of preaching and proclamation. Thus he concluded his speech:

With this aim in mind, allow me to present briefly what strikes me as fundamental conditions for this new evangelization. The first one refers to ordained ministers. As she comes to the end of her first half millennium of existence and approaches the door to the third Christian millennium, the Church in Latin America will need much vitality, impossible without numerous, well-trained priests. The fostering of new vocations and their adequate training in spiritual, doctrinal, and pastoral dimensions is, for a bishop, a prophetic action, in which he advances the future of the Church. Hence, I entrust to you this task which will require watchfulness and suffering, but will also bring joy and hope.

The second condition refers to the laity. Both the shortage of priests and the self-understanding of the Church in Latin America, in the light of Vatican II and of Puebla, speak forcibly of the place of the laity in the Church and in society.

As the five hundredth anniversary of your evangelization draws near, bishops, together with their Churches, must commit themselves to forming an increasing number of laypeople willing to collaborate effectively in the work of evangelization. A light which can guide this new evangelization—and this is our third condition—should be the Puebla document dedicated precisely to this theme, impregnated with the teachings of Vatican II and in consonance with the Gospel. In this sense it is necessary to spread and eventually regather with integrity the Puebla message, without distorted interpretations, deforming reductionism, or incorrect application of some parts to the exclusion of others.

As we prepare for such significant events over the next few years, dear brothers, may you be full of confidence in this new evangelizing enterprise. May the three characteristics that distinguish the piety of your peoples—love for the Eucharist, devotion to the mother of God, affectionate union with the Pope as Saint Peter's successor—be a pledge and guarantee of success in this mission. ✠

ℬOLAND 1983

FROM 16 TO 23 JUNE 1983, Pope John Paul II visited his homeland. It was a time of great international unrest in East Europe. In particular, the world watched the labor and economic problems of Poland. Under the title of the "Holy Cross," Pope John Paul affiliated himself with the history and destiny of his own Polish people. In particular, he pointed to the leadership of the late Stefan Cardinal Wyszyński. The Pope was recovering from his wounds when Cardinal Wyszyński died and could not return to Poland to be with the Cardinal in his last hours. In this visit he paid tribute to the late Archbishop of Warsaw.

C hrist was obedient unto death for us so that we might have life and have it abundantly [Jn 10:10]. I wish my pastoral service in my native land to contribute to this "abundance of life," which everyone receives from the Father in Jesus Christ, crucified and risen. I wish it to contribute to that abundance of life which everyone has in Christ through the work of the Holy Spirit. In fact, in his invisible working—the work of sanctification—Christ's salvific "going away" through his death and Resurrection has continued even to the end of the world.

Today's Gospel bears witness to that "going away." We hear Jesus cry out in a loud voice: "My God, my God, why hast thou forsaken me?" [Mk 15:34], expressing the unfathomable depth of his salvific suffering. We are witnesses of how he "breathed his last" [v., 37] on the Cross. We hear finally, after the Sabbath, what the women who came to the tomb heard: "You seek Jesus of Nazareth, who was crucified. He has risen, he is not here; see the place where they laid him" [Mk, 16:6].

Through the words of the Gospel we are in close contact with the very center of the events through which the redemption of the world was accomplished. These events have passed into history; we are separated from them by nineteen hundred and fifty years. But the Redemption of the world continues inexhaustibly and is always available anew to each person, to every man and woman. In a special way it is available to those who suffer (and perhaps suffer more intensely because they cannot fully perceive the meaning of their own suffering and, even more, the meaning of their own existence).

Let us allow ourselves to be caught up in the mystery of the Redemption! Like that centurion beneath the Cross who at the moment of Christ's death confesses, "Truly this man was the Son of God!" [Mk 15:39]. Let us allow ourselves to be caught up in the mystery of the Redemption! We all stand beneath the Cross. All humanity stands continually beneath the Cross. Let us allow ourselves to be caught up in the mystery of the Redemption: the mystery of the Son of God! In it there is also fully revealed what is at times so difficult to solve: the mystery of man. And there is manifested through all his sufferings and humiliations, the supreme vocation of him—of man.

Together with all my compatriots, especially with those who are most acutely tasting the bitterness of disappointment, humiliation, suffering, of being deprived of their freedom, of being wronged, of having their dignity trampled upon, I stand beneath the Cross of Christ, to celebrate on Polish soil the extraordinary jubilee of the Year of the Redemption. I stand here and I know that, as once on Calvary at the foot of this Cross, there stands the Mother of Christ.

The first stage of my pilgrimage is to Jasna Góra on the occasion of the six hundredth anniversary of the Image of the Mother of Christ, and leads to the Cathedral of Warsaw, to the tomb of the great primate of the millennium, Cardinal Stefan Wyszyński.

I was not able to come to Warsaw for his funeral, on 31 May 1981, because of the attempt on my life on 13 May that resulted in some months in the hospital. Today, however, as I have been able to come to my homeland, I direct my first steps to his tomb and I come to the altar of the Cathedral of St. John to celebrate my first Mass on Polish soil for him. I celebrate it for the soul of the late Cardinal Stefan, but I celebrate this holy Sacrifice with a deep sense of thanksgiving. I give thanks to Divine Providence that in the difficult period of our history, after the Second World War, in the transition from the first to the second millennium, we were given this primate, this man of God, this man so in love with the Mother of God of Jasna Góra, this intrepid Servant of the Church and of the homeland.

On 18 June, Pope John Paul visited the site of Niepokalanow, "the City of the Immaculate," the large convent of the Conventual Franciscans. This together with the basilica was founded by Saint Maximilian Kolbe, whom the Pope had canonized during the previous October. Maximilian Kolbe had offered his life in place of another while a prisoner in Auschwitz Concentration Camp. The references to the heroism of Saint Maximilian provided clear comfort to the Polish faithful in a year of political uncertainty.

Maximilian Kolbe was a minister: he was, in fact, a priest, a son of Saint Francis. Every day he celebrated sacramentally the mystery of the redeeming death of Christ on the Cross. He often repeated these words of the psalm, recalled in today's liturgy:
    "What shall I give back to the Lord
        for everything that he has given to me?
    I will lift up the cup of salvation
        and call on the name of the Lord" [Ps 116:12–13].
So it was. Every day, he lifted up the cup of the new and eternal covenant, in which, under the appearance of wine, the Blood of the Redeemer is sacramentally shed for the remission of sins. Besides the sharing in the mystery of the Eucharistic Chalice, there matured in him that hour of decision at Auschwitz: "Shall I not drink the cup which the Father has given me?" [Jn 18:11]. And he drank, he drank the chalice to the last drop, in order to bear witness before the world

that love is stronger than death. The world needs this witness in order to shake off the bonds of that civilization of death which, especially at certain moments of the present day, shows its menacing face.

Today at Niepokalanow, at the center of our celebration in the land of our birth—after his canonization—is Saint Maximilian Maria Kolbe: the first saint of Polish stock at the beginning of our second millennium. The first and second millennium of Poland and of Christianity in Poland meet in an eloquent symbol. The patron of the Poland of that time—is he the patron . . . only of Poland? Is he not rather the patron of our whole difficult century? Yes, but since he is the son of this land—one who shared in its trials, its sufferings, and its hopes—therefore, in a certain special way he is the patron of Poland.

Precisely of this Poland which from the end of the eighteenth century people began to condemn to death: to partition, to deportations, to concentration camps, to starvation bunkers. And when after one hundred twenty years it had returned to a state of independence, they waited till 1939 in order to repeat yet again this sentence of death. Indeed, Saint Maximilian's gesture at Auschwitz was born from the very heart of these struggles between the life and the death of the homeland. *Mores et vita duello conflixere mirando* (death and life opposed each other in a terrible duel), as we read in the sequence of Easter. The son of Polish soil, who fell on his Calvary, "giving his life for a brother" in the bunker of death through starvation, comes back to us in the glory of holiness. Love is stronger than death.

IN THE CITY OF POZNAŃ, Pope John Paul beatified Sister Ursula Ledochowska, foundress of the Ursuline Sisters of the Sacred Heart of Jesus, who died in 1939. Mother Ursula was the second member of her family to be raised to the altar. Her blood sister, Blessed Maria Teresa Ledochowska, foundress of the Sodality of Saint Peter Claver, was beatified by Pope Paul VI. Her brother, Father Vladimir Ledochowski, was General of the Society of Jesus in the early part of this century, while her uncle, Mieszyslaw Cardinal Ledochowski, was both primate of Poland and later prefect of the Congregation for the Propagation of the Faith.

On 22 June, he beatified two further Servants of God from

Poland, Blessed Raphael Kalinowski and Blessed Brother Albert Chmielowski, founder of the Albertine Brothers and Sisters. Both individuals suffered as a result of the Polish Insurrection of 1863. Not yet a priest, Kalinowski was sentenced to deportation to Siberia. Upon his return, he entered the Discalced Carmelite Friars, where he remained for the rest of his life. Once ordained he was noted for his skills in the confessional. Brother Albert was mutilated by the Russian Army and dedicated himself to living and working among the outcasts as a kind of hermit. In beatifying both these individuals, the Pontiff again holds up the heroism of two Polish citizens who were faithful in the practice of virtue, even in a time of suppression from the East.

B oth one and the other could repeat with Saint Paul: "I count everything as loss because of the surpassing worth of knowing Christ Jesus my Lord, for whom I have suffered the loss of all things" [Phil 3:8]. Father Raphael and Brother Albert are examples of the admirable evangelical mystery of *"kenosis,"* of detachment, of renunciation, which opens the door to the fullness of love. Father Raphael wrote to his sister: "God gave himself completely for us and we must sacrifice ourselves to God" [Letter of 1 July 1866 to his family].

And Brother Albert confessed: "I look at Jesus in his Eucharist. Could his love have provided anything more beautiful? If he is bread . . . let us give ourselves" [W. Kluz, *Adam Chmielowski,* p. 199].

In this way, each one of them is "won by Jesus Christ" [ibid., 12].

In this way, each one of them has gained Christ and has found in him the righteousness that comes from God . . . "Becoming like him in his death that if possible I may attain the resurrection from the dead" [ibid., 8, 9, 10–11].

In this hope, Father Raphael ended his life within the walls of the Carmelite monastery at Wadowice, my native town, in 1907; Brother Albert died in his "beggars' refuge" in Kraków in 1916.

These two great sons of the Polish land, who showed the paths of holiness to their contemporaries and to the successive generations, ended their lives at the dawn of this century, on the eve of the regained independence of Poland. ✠

 FRANCE 1983

POPE JOHN PAUL II VISITED LOURDES, France, from 14 to 15 August 1983 for the occasion of the Feast of the Assumption of Mary. While he was there, news reached him of the shooting down of a Korean airliner which had strayed into Russian territory. The tragedy moved the Pontiff deeply. He expressed his sentiments in a telegram to Steven Cardinal Kim, Archbishop of Seoul. The event dramatized further the Pontiff's remarks which were oriented to the meaning of Our Lady of Lourdes. Throughout his travels during the Jubilee Year of the Redemption, he explains the relation of Mary to the act of Christ's Passion:

The Virgin, Our Lady of Lourdes! Tomorrow we shall celebrate her in her risen glory, sharing with body and soul in the heavenly life of her Son. The woman clothed with divine life as with the Son, and with a crown of stars, to use the language of the book of Revelation. In the apparitions of Bernadette Soubirous, she certainly radiated this happiness; but she rather recalled the young woman of the Annunciation, young, always young, younger than sin, as was well explained by one of your writers, Georges Bernanos. She recalled the preliminaries to the Incarnation of Christ, the preparation for his coming by baptism and penance, Advent. And, especially, she recalled the grace of her own Immaculate Conception which made her the forerunner of redeemed humanity by preserving her from original sin, that separation from God which is the common lot of all men at their birth and which leaves in their hearts an inclination to suspicion, mistrust, disobedience, revolt, and even breaking with that God who has never stopped loving them. The Virgin was from the very first in loving relationship to God.

Why then did she choose this aspect and this name to reveal herself here? Quite frankly, our world needs to be converted. It has been this way in every age. In the middle of the nineteenth century, this need manifested itself in a particular way with the unbelief of certain scientific circles, of certain philosophies, and even in daily life. Today, even the sense of sin has partly disappeared, because the meaning of God is being lost. Some have thought of evolving a humanism without God, and the faith might easily be seen as something peculiar to a few, without its necessary role for the salvation of all. Consciences have become dulled, as on the occasion of the first sin, no longer able to distinguish between good and evil. Many no longer know what sin is, or do not want to know, as if this knowledge would destroy their freedom. And yet, what marvelous efforts our contemporaries are doing to improve the natural talents God has given them and to create better living conditions for themselves and for others! But it remains difficult to convince this world of the misery of its own sin and of the salvation which God offers unceasingly through the reconciliation stemming from the Redemption. This is especially what the Church is trying to do during this Jubilee Year of the Redemption.

The Virgin without sin reminds us here of this basic need. She tells us, as she told Bernadette: Pray for sinners, come wash yourselves, purify yourselves, draw forth new life. "Reform your lives and believe in the Gospel" [Mk 1:15]. She gives a new meaning to these first words of Jesus in the Gospel.

Yes, awareness of sin is possible at the same time as awareness of the merciful love of God, or rather thanks to him, for it is he who transforms the heart of the sinner, making him pure and repentant. This is not humiliating, this is not shocking, this is liberating! Only pride is an obstacle to it. And Bernadette reminds us by her whole life what Mary proclaimed in her Magnificat: "He has looked upon his servant in her lowliness . . . and raised the lowly to high places" [Lk 1:48–52]. Apparently, the interior and exterior obstacles to conversion might today seem insurmountable. But everything is possible to God. What it takes is a gift of God, and this we will ask for. It is like the spring which suddenly gushed forth between Bernadette's fingers and which will never cease to flow. We must wash ourselves in it. "Though your sins be like scarlet, they shall be as white as snow" [Is 1:18]. And we must prepare ourselves for this with humility, acts of penance, prayer, request for pardon; there is no other way. This is what was said by the prophets who came before Christ, especially John the Baptist; this is what Christ himself stated; and this is what the Church and Mary repeat in bringing us his message, and Bernadette who transmitted it to us so simply and faithfully.

EVERY YEAR THOUSANDS OF SICK PEOPLE make a pilgrimage to the Shrine of Our Lady of Lourdes to seek a cure or to search for comfort in their suffering. During the procession of the Blessed Sacrament at the grotto of Massabielle, the Pope spoke directly to them:

I n the face of any kind of suffering, the healthy have a primary duty: that of respect, sometimes even of silence. Was it not Cardinal Pierre Veuillot, Archbishop of Paris, so quickly carried off by an implacable illness fifteen years ago already, who asked the priests who visited him to speak of suffering only with much circumspection? Neither fair nor unfair, suffering remains, even with partial explanations, difficult to understand and accept even by those who have faith. Faith does not remove pain, but binds it invisibly to that of Christ the Redeemer, the Lamb without blemish, who immersed himself, as it were, in the sin and misery of the world in order to be in full fellowship with humanity, to give the world new meaning, to sanctify in advance all the trials and even death that cling to the flesh and the heart of his human brothers. "Through Christ and in Christ, the riddles of sorrow and death grow meaningful. Apart from his Gospel, they overwhelm us." This affirmation is taken from the admirable Constitution on the Church in the Modern World [*Gaudium et Spes,* 22]. The prophet Isaiah, from whom we read a short while ago, was right when he said to the people of his time: "Be strong, fear not! Here is your God . . . he comes to save you" [Is 35:4]. And Jesus spoke truly when he said: "Come to me, all you who are weary and find life burdensome, and I will refresh you" [Mt 11:28].

You who are ill, I would like you to keep in your hearts and minds three small lights that seem to me very precious.

First of all, whatever may be your suffering, physical or moral, personal or familial, apostolic or even ecclesial, it is important that you be fully aware of it without minimizing it or exaggerating it, and that you be aware of the effects it has on your human sensibility: failure, uselessness of your life, and so on.

Then, it is indispensable to go on ahead to acceptance. Yes, to accept that things are what they are, not through more or less blind resignation, but because faith assures us that the Lord can and will draw good from evil. How many there are here present who could testify that trial, accepted in faith, gave rise to new serenity and hope. . . . In seeking to draw good from evil, the Lord invites you yourselves to be as active as you can despite sickness, and, if you are handicapped, to assume responsibility for yourselves using all the strength and talent that you have despite your infirmity. Those who give you their love and help, as well as the associations for the sick to which you belong, rightly seek to have you love life and to make it grow in you as much as possible, as a gift of God.

Finally, the finest gesture is yet to be made: that of oblation. The offering of suffering, made through love of the Lord and of our fellows, leads to the attainment of a sometimes very high degree of the theological virtue of charity, that is, becoming absorbed into the love of Christ and of the Holy Trinity for humanity. These three stages, lived by each suffering person according to his or her rhythm or grace, give rise to an astonishing interior liberation. Is not this the paradoxical teaching reported by the Evangelists: "Whoever loses his life for my sake will find it" [Mt 16:25]? Is not this the evangelical impulse of abandonment so deeply felt by Bernadette of Lourdes and Thérèse of Lisieux, who were sick almost all of their lives? Dear suffering brothers and sisters, return home strengthened and renewed for your "special mission"! You are the precious cooperators of Christ in the application throughout time and space of the Redemption that he acquired once for all for the benefit of all humanity through the historical mysteries of his Incarnation, Passion, and Resurrection. And Mary, his Mother and your Mother, will always be close to you! ✠

$\mathscr{A}$ustria 1983

On 11 September 1983 Pope John Paul made a four-day visit to Austria. The occasion was the close of the Great *Katholikentag,* an assembly of bishops, clergy, religious, and laity to promote enthusiasm for the apostolate. The assembly chose the theme of "hope," and the Pope addressed his remarks in terms of the parable of the Prodigal Son. The parable contains the joint themes of family and of reconciliation:

Y ou chose the motto of "hope" for your *Katholikentag.* You know from experience that many people, young and old, have lost all hope. But in the long run you cannot live without hope. How, then, can we find new hope? How can we show others the road to hope?

The parable of the Gospel we have just heard tells of a young man who proudly and self-confidently left his father's house for a distant country where he expected more freedom and happiness. But when he had squandered his fortune and suffered the indignities of bondage such as he had never experienced before, his hope sank. Finally admitting his guilt to himself, he remembered his father and set off for his father's house, hoping against hope.

It is at this very point in the Gospel that we read, "I will set off and go to my father." This profound parable, in fact, epitomizes the eternal drama of man: the drama of freedom, the drama of ill-used freedom.

Christ's parable, however, does not leave us in utter darkness in the misery of the sinner in all his abasement. The words "I will set off and go to my father" make us aware of the longing for the good that still persists in the heart of the prodigal son and of the light of unfailing hope. In these words the perspectives of hope open before him. And such a perspective will always be open to us, since each individual, and, indeed, all mankind, may set off to go to the Father. This is the essential truth, the essential message of the Gospel.

The words "I will set off and go to my father" are evidence of the change of heart. For the Prodigal Son continues, "I will say to him, 'Father, I have sinned against God and against you'" [Lk 15:18]. At the very center of the Good News, we find the truth of *metanoia,* of penance, of a change of heart.

Starting from this spiritual program I should like to consider with you some of the elements of the change of heart in the sphere of the family and society.

Marriage and the family are in grave danger today. This means great suffering for many people: for husbands and wives, and even more for their children, but ultimately for all of society. Basing myself on the experience of bishops throughout the world, two years ago I characterized today's crisis of the family in the following words: "There are signs of an alarming degeneration of fundamental values: an erroneous . . . conception of the mutual independence of the partners in marriage; grave misconceptions with regard to the relations of authority between children and their parents; the concrete difficulties frequently experienced by families when they try to pass on lasting values to their children; the increasing number of divorces; the widespread evil of abortion" [Apostolic letter *Familiaris Consortio,* n. 6]—an evil which we have not yet found the right way to curb, and the horrible nature of which far too few people have yet come to understand.

This crisis seems to be rooted above all in the wrong conception of freedom. Freedom seen, not as the "capacity to realize the divine plan for marriage and the family, but rather as an autonomous force of self-realization, selfishly aiming at one's personal well-being and frequently directed against one's fellow human beings" [ibid.]. These negative tendencies are yet fostered by public opinion, which calls into question the very institution of marriage and the family and seeks to justify other forms of living together. Though many profess that the family is of crucial importance to society, far too little is still being done to protect it actively. Marriage and the family are in danger because in many people faith and a sense of religion have faded and because husbands and wives themselves, and thus also their children, have become indifferent to God.

Dear mothers and fathers, dear families! Set off to return to the Father! You can understand and experience the full depth and wealth of married life and the family only as you recognize your responsibility before God. ✠

United States—Alaska 1984

On 2 May 1984, Pope John Paul II arrived in Fairbanks, Alaska, on his way to South Korea. Here he was greeted by President Ronald Reagan and his wife, Nancy. The Pope would also visit Papua New Guinea, the Solomon Islands, and Thailand.

When I arrived on my first visit to your beautiful state, dear people of Alaska, I remember being welcomed by a lovely little child, Mollie Marie, who reached out and handed me a bouquet of forget-me-nots, your state flower. Shortly afterwards, that little girl was called home to her heavenly Father, but her loving gesture is not forgotten and her memory is held in blessing.

In some ways, Alaska can be considered today as a crossroads of the world. President Reagan is returning from visiting the beloved people of China, even as I am making my way to a neighboring area in the Far East. The city of Fairbanks reminds us also of another direction, for it is called "The Heart of the Golden North." Here in this vast state, sixty-five languages are spoken and peoples of many diverse backgrounds find a common home with the Aleuts, Eskimos, and Indians.

This wonderful diversity provides the context in which each person, each family, each ethnic group is challenged to live in harmony and concord, one with the other. ✠

$\mathscr{S}$OUTH KOREA 1984

ON 3 MAY, the Pope arrived in South Korea with the principal intention of beatifying 103 Korean martyrs. The following day, he
spoke about an "elusive peace" which pervades the contemporary
world. In a speech to the Diplomatic Corps at the Apostolic Nunciature in Seoul in the presence of the Archbishop of that city, Steven
Cardinal Kim, he invoked the symbolism of a divided Korea.

I n your diplomatic service in Korea you can see how contrasting
ideologies and the passions they unleash give rise to intense suffering. The anguish and pain of a divided Korea are emblematic
of a divided world that lacks trust and fails to achieve reconciliation
in brotherly love. They are a symbol of a world situation that cries out
for a response: a new attitude, a new heart. Your mission here, therefore, assumes a particular meaning and weight. I pray that your experience will convince you that only a committed affirmation of
fundamental human rights and values, together with an effective respect for the dignity of every human person, will bring an abiding answer to the heartfelt aspirations of all the peoples of the world to live
in peace and brotherhood.

ON SUNDAY 6 MAY the Pope canonized 103 martyrs in the Diocesan
Cathedral at Seoul. Since French missionaries were among their
number, representatives of the French hierarchy were present. In his
homily, the Pope likened their deaths to the death of Jesus on the
Cross. He likewise traced the history of the primitive Church of Korea,
which has burgeoned into a Christian nation where the Gospel today
is still the Good News. The first group of Koreans to be beatified were
killed in persecutions of 1839 and 1846. The first Korean martyrs
were beatified by Pope Pius XI in 1925. At the end of his homily,
Pope John Paul singled out Saint Laurent Imbert, the first Vicar Apostolic of Korea.

Yearning for an ever-greater share in the Christian faith, your ancestors sent one of their own in 1784 to Peking where he was baptized. From this good seed was born the first Christian community in Korea, a community unique in the history of the Church by reason of the fact that it was founded entirely by laypeople. This fledgling church, so young and yet so strong in faith, withstood wave after wave of fierce persecution. Thus in less than a century it could already boast of some ten thousand martyrs. The years 1791, 1801, 1827, 1839, 1846, and 1866 are forever signed with the holy blood of your martyrs and engraved in your hearts.

Even though the Christians in the first half-century had only two priests from China to assist them, and these only for a time, they deepened their unity in Christ through prayer and fraternal love; they disregarded social classes and encouraged religious vocations. And they sought an ever-closer union with their bishop in Peking and the Pope in faraway Rome. After years of pleading for more priests to be sent, your Christian ancestors welcomed the first French missionaries in 1836. Some of these, too, are numbered among the martyrs who gave their lives for the sake of the Gospel and who are being canonized today in this historic celebration.

The splendid flowering of the Church in Korea today is indeed the fruit of the heroic witness of the martyrs. Even today, their undying spirit sustains the Christians in the Church of silence in the North of this tragically divided land.

From the thirteen-year-old Peter Yu to the seventy-two-year-old Mark Chong, men and women, clergy and laity, rich and poor, ordinary people and nobles, many of them descendants of early or unsung martyrs—they all gladly died for the sake of Christ.

Listen to the last words of Teresa Kwon, one of the early martyrs: "Since the Lord of heaven is the Father of all mankind and the Lord of all creation, how can you ask me to betray him? Even in this world anyone who betrays his own father or mother will not be forgiven. All the more may I never betray him who is the Father of us all."

A generation later Peter Yu's father Augustine firmly declares: "Once having known God, I cannot possibly betray him." Peter Cho goes even further and says, "Even supposing that one's own father committed a crime, still one cannot disown him as no longer being one's father. How then can I say that I do not know the heavenly Lord Father who is so good?"

And what did the seventeen-year-old Agatha Yi say when she and her younger brother were falsely told that their parents had betrayed the faith? "Whether my parents betrayed or not is their affair. As for us, we cannot betray the Lord of heaven whom we have always served." Hearing this, six other adult Christians freely delivered themselves to the magistrate to be martyred. Agatha, her parents, and those other six are all being canonized today. In addition, there are countless other unknown, humble martyrs who no less faithfully and bravely served the Lord.

The Korean martyrs have borne witness to the crucified and risen Christ. Through the sacrifice of their own lives they have become like Christ in a very special way. ✠

$\mathscr{P}$APUA NEW GUINEA 1984

FROM 7 TO 9 MAY, Pope John Paul visited the Church of Papua New Guinea. In his introductory homily, he outlined the heroism of early missionary activity in that land, which commenced in 1847. He singled out Blessed Giovanni Mazzucconi of the Pontifical Institute for Foreign Missions (known as the PIME Missionaries), who died in 1855 and whom the Pontiff had recently beatified in Rome. He mentioned, too, the work of the Marists, the Missionaries of the Sacred Heart, and the Society of the Divine Word. In a later speech, on 8 May, he praised the genius of the missionary activity in Papua New Guinea as flowing from the care for the sick. In a homily connected with the anointing of the sick on 8 May, he united the two concepts of evangelization and personal compassion.

It is not surprising, then, that the missionaries who came to Papua New Guinea not only brought the good news of salvation but also cared for the sick. Indeed their loving compassion for those who were suffering made a very deep impression on your ancestors. Seeing this example of charity and faith, they made the missionaries welcome among them and opened the doors of their hearts to the Gospel of our Lord Jesus Christ.

With similar sentiments I come to you today. I come to tell you of my love for you in Christ, and to assure you of the pastoral concern of the whole Church. The Church, like Jesus her Redeemer, desires always to be close to those who suffer. She lifts them up to the Lord in prayer. She offers them conciliation and hope. She helps them to find meaning in their fear and pain by teaching them that suffering is not a punishment from God, nor something caused by witchcraft or evil spirits. Rather, the Church points to Christ who, by his Cross and Resurrection, has redeemed all human suffering and has thus given meaning to this mystery of human existence. ✠

Solomon Islands 1984

ON 9 MAY, Pope John Paul II paid a brief visit to the Solomon Islands at Honiara. Upon landing, he expressed why this visit brought him personal joy:

From the beginning of my pontificate, I have had a special interest in the Solomon Islands. Only a month after I was elected Bishop of Rome and Successor of Saint Peter, I had the joy of establishing the first ecclesiastical province of the Catholic Church in this land, with Honiara being designated as the Metropolitan See and the Diocese of Gizo as its Suffragan See. Then less than a year and a half ago, I had the further pleasure of establishing the new Diocese of Auki, making it too a Suffragan of the Archdiocese of Honiara. These historic moments are signs of the vigorous life and growing maturity of the Christian faith in your country. And it is because of this vitality of your faith that I have greatly looked forward to being in your midst.

In the tradition of the Bishops of Rome, I come among you as "the servant of the servants of God," on a pastoral visit to the Catholic faithful of this young nation. ✠

HAILAND 1984

FROM 10 TO 12 MAY, Pope John Paul visited the nation of Thailand. On the second day he paid a visit to a refugee camp at Phanat Nikhon. Here he addressed the problem of displaced persons and international migration of peoples. In the context of the aftermath of the Southeast Asian wars, his words were poignant.

I want you to know that my words transcend all barriers of speech: they are spoken in the language of the heart. My heart goes out to you. It is the heart of a brother who comes to you in the name of Jesus Christ to bring a message of compassion, consolation, and hope; it is a heart that embraces each and every one of you as friends and fellow human beings; a heart that reaches out to all those around the world who share your condition and experience life as refugees.

Listen to these words that come from my heart: I want you to know of my love. We are truly brothers and sisters, members of the same human family, sons and daughters of the same loving Father. I wish to share with you your sufferings, your hardships, your pain, so that you may know that someone cares for you, sympathizes with your plight, and works to help you find relief, comfort, and a reason for hope.

Have faith in yourselves. Never forget your identity as free peo-

ple who have a rightful place in this world. Never lose your personality as a people! Remain firmly rooted in your respective cultures,
from which the world can learn much and come to appreciate you in
your uniqueness.

Have hope in the future. Our world is in full development. It
needs you and your contributions. Take every opportunity offered
you to study a language and perfect a skill in order to be able to adapt
socially to the country that will open its doors to you and be enriched
by your presence.

To the Catholics among you I wish to say a special word: God
never said that suffering is a good thing in itself; but he taught us
through his Son, our Lord Jesus Christ who suffered and died for our
sins, that our sufferings, when joined to those of Christ, have value for
the salvation for the world. Jesus Christ, the Son of God, who rose on
the third day, is the foundation of our hope, now and in the future. ✠

*S*WITZERLAND 1984

By his own words, Pope John Paul undertook a second visit to
Switzerland, from 12 to 17 June 1984, especially to make a pilgrimage to the memory of Saint Nicholas of Flue (1417–87). Known
as *Bruder Klaus,* this husband and father of ten ultimately became
known as the Hermit of Ranft. Despite his contemplative vocation,
he became a "promoter of reconciliation and peace" among his fellow countrymen. Largely due to his efforts, the multilingual cantons
of Switzerland came together in an alliance of neutrality which has
come to characterize that nation over the last five hundred years.
Says the Pope himself, "With the neutrality of Switzerland, as a country, there is certainly also explained the fact that at present numerous international organizations have sought, and still seek, a
headquarters there." Among the significant sites of the papal visit
were the hermitage of Saint Nicholas himself, the World Council of
Churches headquarters in Geneva, and the monastery at Einsiedeln,

where he praised Swiss monastic life. This first citation is taken from the June 14 Mass at the birthplace of Saint Nicholas in Flueli (Flue):

My dear brothers and sisters:
"Let the name of Jesus be your greeting!"
With these, your patron's words of greeting, I wish to come among you here in Flueli. Here is where Saint Bruder Klaus lived and worked. Here he lived a happy family life for twenty-three years with his wife, Dorothy, and brought up his ten children. Here, after a difficult interior struggle, he came to the decision to leave brothers, sisters, wife and children, lands and home for love of Christ's name [Mt 19:29], in order to serve God alone. Here in Ranft, on his own land, he led the life of a hermit for twenty years, detached from the world though open to the needs of the world and of his homeland.

"The kingdom of God is not a matter of eating and drinking, but of justice, peace, and the joy that is given by the Holy Spirit" [Rom 14:17]. We have just heard these words from the Letter to the Romans. The Apostle Paul wrote these words to the community of Rome in the context of what was then a concrete situation. We want to interpret them today in the light of this land and this saint who is a symbol for the country and the people, Nicholas of Flue and Switzerland.

In the life and works of Brother Nicholas of Switzerland the Kingdom of God was shown as "justice, peace, and the joy that is given by the Holy Spirit." Over five centuries ago, there went out from this place, from the silence of prayer and union with God in Ranft, his message of peace which brought together into unity at the Diet of Stans the citizens of the divided and torn confederation, opening a new chapter in your history. Here in Flueli, where the figure of Brother Nicholas is still vivid in our eyes, we seem still today to hear his voice, calling us to peace, peace in your own land, to responsibility to peace in the world.

Your patron still exhorts you today to peace in your own land. "My counsel is also that in these matters you will be friendly, for one good thing leads to others. But if the matter cannot be reconciled in friendship, then let justice be the best thing." So wrote Bruder Klaus in 1482 to the mayor and council of Constance.

Goodness and kindness are the first and fundamental condition for peace in the life of a community, as in the life of the individual. "Clothe yourselves with heartfelt mercy, with kindness, humility, meekness, and patience. Bear with one another: forgive whatever grievances you have against one another," Saint Paul urges the baptized [Col 3:12–13]. If this exhortation is not to remain merely a pious ideal in the hard political and social reality of a nation, we must see how it can be transferred into public life. The history of what happened at Stans can show us how: it is necessary to accept one another with all the differences and therefore to be able to refrain from claiming many rights, even though justified.

IN 1969, Pope Paul VI visited the World Council of Churches headquarters in Geneva as an expression of the ecumenical ministry defined by Roman Catholicism during the Second Vatican Council. Some fifteen years later, Pope John Paul II visited the World Council for the only time during his pontificate. Greeted by Dr. Philip Potter, president of the World Council of Churches, he addressed the ecumenical representatives, expressing the themes of "baptism as the source of unity" and "common witness." At the same time, Dr. Potter and Cardinal Johannes Willebrands, president of the Secretariat for Promoting Christian Unity in Rome, expressed a joint statement regarding common witness and a document on consensus beliefs regarding Baptism, Eucharist, and Ministry.

The simple fact of my presence here among you, as Bishop of Rome paying a fraternal visit to the World Council of Churches, is a sign of the will for unity. From the beginning of my ministry as Bishop of Rome, I have insisted that the engagement of the Catholic Church in the ecumenical movement is irreversible and that the search for unity was one of its pastoral priorities [see Invitation to Prayer for the Sixth Assembly of the WCC, 24 July 1983, *L'Osservatore Romano* of 25 July 1983]. The New Code of Canon Law as well expresses very clearly the obligation of the Catholic bishops to promote the ecumenical movement in conformity with Christ's will [Can. 755, 1].

To begin with, we have become aware of our common baptism and its significance. Hear the affirmations of the New Delhi or Evanston assemblies express the same conviction as the Second Vatican Council's Decree on Ecumenism: "By the sacrament of baptism, whenever it is properly conferred in the way the Lord determined and received with proper dispositions of soul, man becomes truly incorporated into the crucified and glorified Christ." . . . "Baptism therefore constitutes the sacramental bond of unity existing among all who are reborn through it" [*Unitatis Redintegratio,* n. 22]. Sure enough, baptism of itself is only a beginning, a point of departure, for it is wholly directed toward the acquiring of fullness of life in Christ" [ibid.]. But baptized with the true baptism we are all enveloped with the same indivisible love of the Father, given life by the same indivisible Spirit of God incorporated into the only Son. If we are divided among ourselves, we are all held in the same clasp, by what Saint Irenaeus called "the two hands of the Father" [The Son and the Spirit]. That is what impels us to knit again the communion between us. It is a matter of accepting to be what we are for God in virtue of "one baptism" because of "one God and Father of us all, who is above all and through all and in all" [Eph 4:6]. Although we are still divided, we are nevertheless all in the mystery of Pentecost, reversing Babel. In this way our divisions stand out against the existing unity and because of it are only more scandalous.

. . . The Catholic Church hopes that other Christian Churches and communities will raise their voices along with hers so that the citizens' authentic freedom of conscience and of worship be guaranteed, as well as the liberty of the Churches to train their ministers and to provide them with the means they need to develop the faith of their peoples. Many persons of goodwill and many international organizations understand today the importance of this fundamental right. But faced with the gravity of the facts, it seems to me necessary that together, all Christians and Christian communities—when they have the possibility of expressing themselves—*should give their common witness on what is vital to them.*

We also find ourselves together in apprehension about the future of humanity. Our faith in Christ lets us share in the same hope for facing the forces of destruction which assail the human family, erode its spiritual foundations, and lead it to the brink of the abyss. The creative and redemptive work of God cannot be swallowed up by all that sin kindles in the human heart nor be definitively blocked. But that leads us to a key perception of our own responsibility as Christians facing the future of humanity and also to awareness of the gravity of our divisions. To the extent that they obscure our witness in a world tempted by suicide, they are an obstacle to the proclamation of the good news of salvation in Jesus Christ.

IN AND NEAR THE ABBEY OF EINSIEDELN, the Holy Father addressed various groups of the Swiss Church, including the Episcopal Conference, the clergy, and the lay leadership. He did so in terms of the monastic spirituality which dominates the environment. On 15 June he blessed a new altar in the Abbey Basilica and celebrated the Eucharist for all those with whom he met.

N ear the cross of Jesus there stood his mother" [Jn 19:25]. As pilgrims in the presence of our beloved Lady of Einsiedeln, we have gathered today in your sanctuary to celebrate the Eucharistic sacrifice of Christ in common prayer with you in this venerable place. Your Chapel of Grace stands on the historic site where the Benedictine hermit Meinrad [A.D. 861], over a thousand years ago, by his saintly life and death, lit the torch of faith and divine worship in the so-called "dark forest." The sons of Saint Benedict, by their faithful prayer and the witness of their lives, have kept that torch burning down through the centuries and have handed it on to succeeding generations right to our own times. In this place of prayer, dedicated to the Divine Redeemer, his mother too, under the title of Our Blessed Lady of Einsiedeln, have found among the people of Switzerland a lasting place and a center of special veneration.

Our whole life must be a purifying preparation for our encounter with God: tomorrow in eternity, but also today in the Eucharist. The Gospel in today's liturgy reminds us explicitly: "If you are bringing your offering to the altar and there remember your brother has something against you, leave your offering there before the altar; go and be reconciled with your brother first, and then come back and present your offering" [Mt 5:23–24]. Our preparation for the Eucharist, which is the source of our reconciliation with God, must also be our source of reconciliation with man.

Our everyday life unremittingly sets before us conflicts and tensions, hate and enmity: in our heart, in the family, in the parish community, at work, among nations. The more men yearn for mutual understanding and harmony, the more unattainable they seem for them. All the more strongly then is the Church today where God has entrusted to her the message of reconciliation [2 Cor 5:19]. God, who requires of us that we be reconciled with others before we bring our gift to the altar, is at the same time ready to make us disposed to this reconciliation through Christ and before the Church. For God "in Christ" was reconciling the world to himself [2 Cor 5:19] and has given us in the Church the precious sacrament of Reconciliation. True reconciliation between divided and hostile men is possible only when they allow themselves to be reconciled also with God. Authentic brotherly love is founded on love for God, who is the common father of all.

The solemn lighting of the candles on the altar during the consecration reminds us of Christ "a revealing light to the Gentiles" [Lk 2:32]. Christ, present in the fraternal love of a community, is a light that shines on the whole Church. He is a light with a missionary power. So it is said of the first Christian community "day by day the Lord added to their number those who were being saved" [Acts 2:47]. Dear brothers and sisters, celebrate the Holy Eucharist always in such a way that the light of Christ may shine forth from it into your daily lives and into the world. Celebrate the "Mass" so that it leads to "mission"—*Missa–Missio*—to the Christian mission among men. ✠

CANADA 1984

THE VISIT OF POPE JOHN PAUL to Canada lasted from 9 to 20 September 1984, during which he again addressed several contemporary pastoral questions such as evangelization, personal suffering, education, and catechesis. He also spoke to several ethnic groups, including: Native Americans, immigrant Slovaks and Ukrainians, and the Anglophone and Francophone communities. In the beginning of his visit, he acknowledged the special richness of the Catholic culture with its element of mysticism and apostolic outreach that found its home in colonial Canada. Among those whom he cited were Saint Marguerite Bourgeoys, Blessed Marie of the Incarnation, Mother Marguerite d'Youville, Father André Grasset, Mother Marie-Rose Durocher, Blessed François de Laval, first Bishop of Canada, Blessed André Bessette, Blessed Katarie Tekawitha, Saint Jean de Brébeuf, and the other Jesuit martyrs of the seventeenth century. To their number he added Mother Marie-Leone Paradis (1840–1912), foundress of the Little Sisters of the Holy Family. This beatification, which took place on 11 September 1984, was the first to take place in North America. Blessed Marie-Leone established a congregation dedicated to practical work in the service of the clergy. Referring to her experience of God as the Burning Bush, he also spoke of her pragmatism.

N ever doubting her call, she often asked: "Lord show me your ways," so that she would know the concrete form of her service in the Church. She found and proposed to her spiritual daughters a special kind of commitment: the service of educational institutions, seminaries, and priest's homes. She never shied away from the various forms of manual work which is the lot of so many people today and which held a special place in the Holy Family and in the life of Jesus of Nazareth himself. It is there that she saw the will of God for her life. It was in carrying out these tasks that she found God. In the sacrifices which were required and which she offered in love, she experienced a profound joy and peace. She knew that she was one with Christ's fundamental attitude: he had "come not to be served, but to serve." She was filled with the greatness of the Eucharist and with the greatness of the priesthood at the service of the Eucharist. That was one of the secrets of her spiritual motivation.

The saints and the blessed, and all those guided by the spirit of God, can make their own the words of the Letter to the Ephesians which we have heard: "Blessed be God the Father of our Lord Jesus Christ, who has blessed us with all the spiritual blessings of heaven in Christ" [Eph. 1:3]. Yes, the names of the saints confirm in a special way the truth of our existence in Jesus Christ. The truth and the call to holiness, that is, union with God through Christ. Let us again listen to this Letter to the Ephesians: God "before the world was made, chose us, he chose us in Christ"; out of love he determined that we should become his adopted sons through Jesus Christ"; in him, "through his blood we gain our freedom, the forgiveness of our sins," and this, through the "richness of his grace"; he has united everything under Christ, as head, everything in the heavens and everything on earth"; in him, we too have been made heirs; in him, we have been stamped "with the seal of the Holy Spirit . . . the pledge of our inheritance which brings freedom for those whom God has taken for his own, to make his glory praised" [Eph 1:4–14].

THROUGHOUT HIS VISIT TO CANADA, Pope John Paul was clearly taken with the country's rich tradition of saints and beati, with their unique expressions of spirituality. In fact, he concluded the homily for the beatification of Blessed Marie-Leone in terms of the book of Exodus and the image of the burning bush, by referring to Canada as "holy ground." He reiterated this point when he departed the nation from Uplands Military Airport in Ottawa on 20 September. He invited the nation to be faithful to the inspiration of their saints. He likewise referred to the beauty and the diversity of the nation, and the generosity of Canada in the community of nations. Yet in Canada, too, he made a profound statement about the relationship between the nations of the Northern and Southern Hemispheres. This was the first time on a pontifical journey that he made such a statement about global balance.

S o it is that Christ the Judge speaks of "one of the least of the brethren," and at the same time he is speaking of each and of all.

Yes. He is speaking of the whole universal dimension of injustice and evil. He is speaking of what today we are accustomed to call the North-South contrast. Hence not only East-West but also North-South: the increasingly wealthier North and the increasingly poorer South. Yes, the South—becoming always poorer, and the North—becoming always richer. Richer, too, in the resources of weapons with which the superpowers and blocs can mutually threaten each other. And they threaten each other—such an argument also exists—in order not to destroy each other.

This is a separate dimension—and according to the opinion of many it is the dimension in the forefront—of the deadly threat which hangs over the modern world, and which deserves separate attention. Nevertheless, in the light of Christ's words, this poor South will judge the rich North. And the poor people and poor nations—poor in different ways, not only lacking food, but also deprived of freedom and other human rights—will judge those people who take these goods away from them, amassing to themselves the imperialistic monopoly of economic and political supremacy at the expense of others. ✠

$\mathcal{D}$OMINICAN REPUBLIC 1984

ON 12 OCTOBER 1984, in the presence of the Latin American Episcopal Conference in the Dominican Republic, Pope John Paul II began a novena of years to prepare for the fifth centenary of the discovery of America by Christopher Columbus in 1492. Here he delivered an address which would characterize his future pontificate. Using language that he had coined for his visit to Haiti one year before, the Pope spoke about the *new evangelization*. In this address he explains the concept. He based his ideas on the history of missionary activity and Church life in Latin America as well as on the ideas inherent in the 1975 apostolic letter of Pope Paul VI, *Evangelii Nuntiandi:*

I said that you must celebrate this centenary with "an attitude of thanksgiving to God for the Christian and Catholic vocation of Latin America, and to all who were living and active instruments of evangelization. With an attitude of fidelity to your past history of faith. With a look at the challenges of the present and the efforts that are being made. With a glance to the future to see how to consolidate the work already begun," a work that was to be "a new evangelization: new in its zeal, its methods, and its expression" [Allocution on March 1983, III].

The Pope, to whose ecclesial ministry in the first place falls Christ's mandate to preach the faith, could not neglect to make his personal contribution to this mission, when there is a plan for such a large portion of the Church—all of Latin America—the objective of a new evangelization, an evangelization which will continue to complete the work of the first evangelizers.

To face the problems and challenges that the Church has before her with regard to evangelization at the present moment, she needs a clear vision of her origins and development.

This is not for mere academic interest or a nostalgia for the past, but to find her own firm identity, to draw from the living current of mission and holiness that inspired her history, and to understand better the problems of the present and to project herself more realistically toward the future. In its evangelizing aspect, it marked an unprecedented missionary unfolding which, starting from the Iberian Peninsula, would soon give a new configuration to the ecclesial map. And it would do so at a time when the religious upheavals in Europe were provoking struggles and partial visions which needed new lands into which to pour the creativity of faith.

In the heart of a society inclined to see the material benefits that it could gain by slavery and by the exploitation of the Indians, there arose the clear protest of the critical conscience of the Gospel, which denounced the nonobservance of the demands of human dignity and brotherhood, which have their foundation in creation and the divine filiation of all persons. How many missionaries and bishops struggled for justice against the abuses of the Conquistadores and *"En Comenderos"*?

Evangelizing activity in its social aspect is not limited to the denunciation of the sin of mankind.

Under this cultural aspect the evangelizers had to invent methods of catechesis which did not exist; they had to create "schools of doctrine," instruct children and catechists and overcome language barriers.

A fact consigned to history is that the first evangelization essentially marked the historicocultural identity of Latin America [Puebla,

412]. Proof of this is that the Catholic faith was not uprooted from the hearts of its peoples, despite the pastoral vacuum created in the period of independence or the subsequent hostilities and persecutions.

That Catholic cultural substratum is manifested in the full living of the faith, in the vital wisdom in regard to the great questions of life, in its baroque forms of religiousness, with a profound Trinitarian content and with the devotion to the passion of Christ and to Mary. These are aspects to keep well in mind also in a renewed evangelization.

It is a substratum with its undeniable vitality and present-day youth, which seeks effective ways of insertion in today's society, which is awaiting an evangelization that is renewed and full of hope in order to revitalize its own richness of faith and to stir up vigorous energies of deeply Christian roots in order to be able to create a new Latin America confirmed in its Christian vocation, free and brotherly, just and peaceful, faithful to Christ and to Latin American man.

The restrictions sometimes placed on free profession of the faith are, unfortunately, verifiable facts in various places. The counter-witness of some inconsistent Christians or ecclesial divisions create evident scandal in the Christian community.

The impelling cry for a justice that is too long awaited is raised by a society that seeks its due dignity.

Corruption in public life, armed conflicts, huge expenditures to procure death and not progress, the lack of ethical sentiment in so many fields, all cause weariness and destroy dreams of a better future. To all of this are added the rivalries among nations, and incorrect behavior in international relations and in commercial interchanges, which create new imbalances. And now there is the serious problem of the foreign debt of third world countries, especially of Latin America.

Resist the temptation of those who want to forget your undeniable Christian vocation and the values that shape it, in order to seek social models that prescind from it or contradict it.

Resist the anti-Christian temptation of those who do not believe in dialogue and reconciliation and resort to violence, and who substitute the power of arms or ideological oppression for political solutions.

The coming fifth centenary of the discovery of the first evangelization calls us then to a new evangelization of Latin America, which will develop more vigorously, as it did in its beginnings, a potential for sanctity, a great missionary thrust, a vast creativity in catechesis, a fruitful manifestation of collegiality and communion, and an evangelical battle for the dignity of man, in order to generate a great future of hope in the bosom of Latin America.

All this has a name: "the civilization of love." This name, which Paul VI already indicated, a name to which I myself have repeatedly alluded and which the message of the Latin American bishops in Puebla picked up, is an enormous task of responsibility. ✠

$\mathcal{P}$UERTO RICO 1984

HAVING OUTLINED THE CONTENT OF HIS PHRASE "the new evangelization," Pope John Paul II flew to San Juan, Puerto Rico, on 12 October 1984. His talks there referred again to the meaning of the "new evangelization." In San Juan, he spoke in terms of the Blessed Mother and the new evangelization, applying his language to the meaning of the family:

B eloved sons and daughters of Puerto Rico, the Mother of Divine Providence is present in a special way in the midst of your community. Pointing to Christ the Lord, she repeats the words spoken at Cana of Galilee: "Do whatever he tells you."

What does she have to say to you today?

Without any doubt, one of the areas to which her maternal concern is directed is that of the family. A profound esteem for the family is one of the elements which make up your religious and cultural patrimony. This institution transmits those cultural, ethical, civic, spiritual, and religious values which contribute to the development of its members and of society. Within the bosom of the family, the different generations help each other to grow, and to harmonize their own rights with the needs of the others. For this reason, the home environment ought to be the field of a vigorous evangelization, so that it may be impregnated with Christian values and reflect the exemplary life of the Holy Family. ✠

VENEZUELA 1985

Pope John Paul visited Venezuela from 26 January until 29 January 1985. In the course of this visit to Latin America and the Caribbean, Pope John Paul reconfirmed his message of the "new evangelization" and unity in the faith. He especially emphasized the importance of education and catechesis. To illustrate the importance of the education of youth, he publicly entered into dialogue with young adults in the Olympic Stadium of Caracas. In a question-and-answer forum, he showed himself to be a shepherd. This innovation was to be repeated on other visits.

THE FIRST QUESTION WAS: *What are your fears and hopes for the future?*

ANSWER: Your fears and your hopes in the presence of the future are concentrated in this question which you often ask: What meaning has my life?

The answer to such a question, beloved young people, is to be found in your very being, created in the image and likeness of God [Gen 1:26–27]. It is to be found in the Christian faith which teaches you with certainty: you are called to an eternal destiny, to be sons of God and brothers of Christ [1 Jn 3:1], to be creators of brotherhood out of love for Christ. He—Christ—is your answer. He teaches you always to help man, to give yourselves for man. This is the word revealed in the Bible. If I were to talk to you differently, I should betray my service to God and I should betray you yourselves, who have the right to the full truth.

Remember always that, since you are made in the image of God, you are able to understand him. It is for this that God calls you to participate in his life, in which you will find your own fullness and your crown [*Populorum Progressio,* 16]. The opening to God and the relationship with him are inscribed, so to speak, in the lost intimate depth of your being. It follows that religiousness is not something added on to the structure of your humanity, but is the first dimension of your identity.

THERE WERE MANY QUESTIONS POSED. The next two are examples.

Q UESTION: *What do you believe the Church must do in the face of the situation in the country?*
ANSWER: What better place than the Church could you find, beloved young people, for the development of your personality! In her, you receive orientation from the word of God, which gives meaning to your lives: the action of Christ that makes all men brothers, making them sons of the common Father; the force that will propel your energies to create a new world that is just and fraternal.

I am convinced that one of the best things that the Church can do in order to revive the faith of the Venezuelans, and to contribute to creating a better society, is to dedicate herself to a serious Christian formation of youth, and to the unification of this same youth. For this, there must be a revitalizing action in the parishes and in the Christian families, in the primary and secondary school and in the university. It is a challenge for the Church in your country.

QUESTION: *What do you think about the Pope?*
ANSWER: I must thank you here for your answer since most of you replied that he is your friend. I want to tell you that this is true. I want to tell you that the Pope considers himself to be a friend who is very close to young people and to their hopes. Therefore he has confidence in them, in you. Therefore esteeming you and having confidence in you he says to you:

Compared with the past, youth is modernity: compared with the future, it is hope and the promise of discovery and innovation: compared with the present, it must be a dynamic and creative force. ✠

*E*CUADOR 1985

THE POPE LANDED IN QUITO, ECUADOR, on the evening of 29 January. The purpose of his visit was to sustain the rich tradition of education, Spanish culture, and religious piety for which Ecuador is noted. The smallness of the nation provides a sense of community and interchange of which the citizens are proud. In the presence of the president of the republic, León Febres Cordero, the Pope also applauded the fact that the nation had consecrated itself one hundred years before to the Sacred Heart of Jesus.

A consecrated nation. This nation has been consecrated as a people to the Sacred Heart of Jesus for more than a century. There still resounds in many hearts the echo of their act of consecration: "This is your people, Lord. It will also acknowledge you as its God. It will not turn its eyes to lights other than that one of love and mercy which shines in the midst of your breast, the sanctuary of divinity, the ark of your heart."

This solemn profession of popular faith honors this nation which numbers among its children illustrious examples of holiness such as the saints Mariana De Jesus and Brother Miguel, and Mother Mercedes De Jesus Molina, whom I will have the joy to proclaim blessed the day after tomorrow at Guayaquil. They are the choice fruit of the evangelization of Ecuador. They encourage and serve as examples for many sons and daughters of the Church who wish to follow Christ faithfully every day of their lives and to consecrate themselves to him and to others through him.

ON 1 FEBRUARY Pope John Paul celebrated Mass at the "Los Samanes" esplanade in Guayaquil. In the course of the ceremony he beatified Mother Mercedes De Jesus Molina. In the nineteenth century she established a congregation of religious women dedicated to the memory of another Ecuadorian saint, Mariana De Jesus. This institute, known as the Marianites, dedicated itself to abandoned children and orphans. The Pope noted this new *beata* as an example of wisdom.

T he Spirit of Wisdom had purified in love and in sorrow the charism of a spiritual fruitfulness transmitted to her daughters by the example of her life, along with her direct care for the religious sisters, personally tending the "rosebush" of Christ Crucified and of the Virgin Mary, seat of wisdom.

This was in reality the sanctity of this woman of the coast of Ecuador: living the love of Jesus in the love of her neighbor. The contemplative gaze of Mother Mary Mercedes was captivated by the poverty of the Child of Bethlehem, by the suffering on the pained face of the Crucified. She wanted to be simply and clearly loved for suffering, according to the motto recounted in early biographical notes: "As much love for as many sufferings as there are in the world"; to practice charity toward all those who, in poverty, suffering, and abandonment, reflected the mystery of the poor Child of Bethlehem or of Christ's suffering on Calvary.

She was mother and educator of orphans, a poor missionary and peacemaker among the Indians, foundress of a religious family. To her daughters she transmitted her same spirit, which identifies sanctity with apostolic love for the most poor, the most disdained, the most abandoned. It was her mission "to announce salvation to the poor without shelter and support," to dry the tears of contrite hearts, to call for the liberation of those suffering imprisonment or condemnation, to comfort all the afflicted. This was love without limits, able to bring aid and comfort, as Mother summarized in her constitutions, "to as many afflicted hearts as there are in the world." ✠

$\mathscr{P}$ERU 1985

ON THE EVENING OF 1 FEBRUARY Pope John Paul landed in Lima, Peru. Upon arrival, he directly addressed the political atmosphere of the nation.

I know of the repulsion that disturbs hearts on seeing the world exalt the excessive and cruel greed for possessions, power, and pleasure. But Christ is with you as a friend; he knows what you mean for the Church and the sacrifices of your mission as witnesses of the faith and servants of your brothers and sisters. For this reason the Pope says to you: Renew your optimism. Your hope will not be frustrated. Christ accompanies you and has conquered the world.

ON 2 FEBRUARY, presiding at a double ceremony at San Augustine in Arequipa, the Pontiff crowned an image of the Madonna and beatified Sister Ana de los Angeles Monteagudo. This seventeenth-century contemplative nun was noted for her mysticism and personal suffering. Misunderstood by both family and the Dominican community to which she belonged, she showed patience, gentleness, and a prayerful watchfulness. Known as the Peruvian "Angel of the Andes," she joins the company of other holy heroes from the colonial period in Peru: Turibius de Mogrovejo, Rose of Lima, Martin de Porres, and Juan Marcias.

I n Sister Ana we admire above all the exemplary Christian, the contemplative Dominican nun of the famous monastery of Saint Catharine—a monument of art and devotion of which the people of Arequipa rightfully felt proud. She carried out in her life the Dominican program of light, of truth, of love, and of life, summed up in the well-known phrase "contemplate and transmit what is contemplated." Sister Ana de los Angeles carried out this program with an intense, austere, radical surrender to the monastic life, according to the manner of the Order of Saint Dominic, in the contemplation of the mystery of Christ, the Truth and Wisdom of God.

But at the same time, her life held a singular apostolic irradiation. She was a spiritual teacher and faithful implementer of the norms of the Church that urgently sought the reform of the monasteries. She knew how to accept everyone who turned to her, teaching them the paths of pardon and the life of grace. Her hidden presence became noticed, beyond the walls of her convent, by the fame of her sanctity. With her prayer and her advice she helped bishops and priests; with her prayer she accompanied travelers and pilgrims who came to her.

Sister Ana de los Angeles confirmed with her life the apostolic fruitfulness of the contemplative life in the mystical Body of Christ which is the Church. A contemplative life which took root very quickly here as well from the very beginning of evangelization and continues to be a mysterious wealth of the Church in Peru and in all of Christ's Church. ✠

*T*RINIDAD TOBAGO 1985

ON 5 FEBRUARY THE POPE passed a few hours in Port of Spain, Trinidad and Tobago. While celebrating Mass in the presence of President Ellis Clarke and Archbishop Gordon Anthony Pantan, the Pontiff outlined the history of mission activity in these Caribbean islands. Citing, among others, Saint Louis Bertrand, he also mentioned the apostolic activity of the Anglican communion. In departing the nation, he spoke directly to its national image.

Historians tell us that, when the explorer Christopher Columbus first saw this island's three mountain peaks, he was reminded of the Most Holy Trinity. The mystery of the three persons in one God. And thus he named the island Trinidad. Nearly five hundred years later, I too have had the joy of coming to these shores. While I readily acknowledge the beauty of your country, what most reminds me of the mystery of the Holy Trinity is not your majestic mountains, but your cheerful faces, which reflect the glory of God.

The high moral standards, the discipline, the self-sacrifice, and the genuine concern for the common good which mark your public service are ways of witnessing to the authenticity of your belief in the Paschal Ministry, of the Redeeming Death and Resurrection of our Lord and Savior Jesus Christ. Yours is a work of service and of brotherhood. As such, it needs the support of a profound sense of the unique dignity of every human being. The special value of each person can only be fully understood where each one is accepted as an image of God himself and a brother or sister of Christ. ✠

∕ETHERLANDS 1985

POPE JOHN PAUL II's VISIT TO THE NETHERLANDS beginning on 11 May 1985 coincided with the fortieth anniversary of the liberation from Nazi forces. But the Pope also recalled the more distant history at his first Mass there, in Utrecht, citing Saint Willibrord, its first bishop, and Pope Adrian VI, elected in 1522. In his homily, he spoke of the unity of the Dutch Church, focusing on the Eucharist and love.

We have gathered together to participate in the Eucharist. It is the sacrifice of expiation for the sins of the world, for our sins, and precisely for this reason it is the sacrifice of salvation. In it love overcomes sin, overcomes hate, overcomes death. This was accomplished once and for all on Calvary through the cross and resurrection of Christ—and it is effected sacramentally, by virtue of Christ's institution, in the Eucharist, in every Holy Mass.

We are gathered together, therefore, to participate in the sacrament of love, the sacrament of salvation. We unite ourselves with those who first participated in this sacrament. Christ said to them, to the Apostles: "As the Father has loved me, so I have loved you. Remain in my love" [Jn 15:9]. These words are laden with a grandiose content: a salvific content! Christ transfers to us this love with which he himself is eternally loved by the Father, and in which he eternally loves the Father. He transfers to men this love which saves. He implants it in men: in their hearts, consciences, wills, and works.

Love is a gift: it "has been poured into our hearts by the Holy Spirit which has been given us" [Rom 5:5] through the work of Christ. In the same way it was poured into the hearts of the Apostles in the Cenacle; and into the hearts of the centurion Cornelius and his servants, who were visited by the Apostle Peter at Caesarea, through a clear disposition of the Holy Spirit, as we see from today's first reading, from the Acts of the Apostles. ✠

✐UXEMBOURG 1985

LUXEMBOURG RECEIVED THE HOLY FATHER ON 15 MAY 1985 for only a day and a half. At an outside Mass near the Arbed steel mill of Esch-sur-Alzette, the Pope spoke on labor to the workers gathered there, using the "Our Father" as his theme. The theme of labor was often to appear in his homilies and exhortations. Pope John Paul published his encyclical *Laborem Exercens* in 1981, early in his pontificate. It was his third encyclical. His themes are found here.

Creating man, God willed to clothe him with unequaled dignity, he made him in his image and likeness, capable of doing a work for which he is responsible. In this way human work itself pertains to the work of creation, as we see already in the first chapter of Genesis.

God, in fact, creating man and woman, says to them: "Be fertile and multiply; fill the earth and subdue it" [Gen 1:28]. This is, in a manner of speaking, the first commandment of God, inherent in the very order of creation.

Thus human work corresponds to the will of God. When we say "Thy will be done," we also apply these words to the work which fills all the days of our lives! We see that we conform to this will of the Creator when our work and the human relations which it implies are imbued with the values of initiative, courage, trust, and solidarity, which are so many reflections of the divine likeness in us. But we also know that many workers find themselves in situations which are difficult or contrary to the will of the Creator.

The Creator has invested man with the power to dominate the earth; he also asks him to dominate with his work, the sphere which he entrusts to him, to employ all his capacities to reach the happy development of his own personality and the entire community. With his work man obeys God and responds to his trust. That is not extraneous to the request of the "Our Father"—"thy kingdom come"; man acts to carry out the plan of God, conscious of having been made in God's likeness and thus having received from him his strength, his intelligence, and his aptitudes for bringing about a community of life through the unselfish love that each man brings to his brethren. All that is positive and good in man's life develops and reaches its true goal in the Kingdom of God. You have fittingly chosen the motto: "Kingdom of God—Life of Man." Since God's cause and man's cause are tied to one another the world advances toward the Kingdom of God thanks to the gifts of God which permit the dynamism of man. In other words, to pray that the Kingdom of God might come is to incline one's whole being toward the reality which is the ultimate end of human work. ✠

ℬELGIUM 1985

POPE JOHN PAUL II FINISHED HIS TOUR OF THE BENELUX countries in a five-day visit to predominantly Catholic Belgium, 19 to 23 May. Developing the theme of the relationship of faith and culture, the Pope addressed the communities gathered at the Flemish University of Louvain, east of Brussels. Welcomed by King Baudouin, with whom he enjoyed a personal friendship, the Pope's concern was for materialism and spiritual inertia, which affected the times.

D ear friends, it is a beautiful and noble adventure that the Church, through my voice, calls you to live: Be men and women of culture and of faith for our time! More than ever our modern society, faced with the threats of disintegration which it carries within itself, has need of men and women well prepared to meet all of today's challenges; to overcome its own doubts, its temptations, its weaknesses.

Increasing your knowledge, broadening your culture, deepening your faith, affirming your convictions, you prepare yourselves to be those vigorous witnesses to truth and to love that our age calls for, our age in which man, isolated in the lonely crowd, no longer knows what it is to live, to love, to suffer, and to die. What is man? This question must be answered: the challenge of practical materialism, religious indifference, caustic skepticism must be met. Yes, what is man, lacerated between the infinitude of his desires and the finiteness of his pleasures, between his persistent search for the truth and the bit-by-bit knowledge which comes to him? Today even those who have doubts about God, and from this arrive pretty quickly at having doubts about man, feel with a more or less vivid awareness the need to establish and to guarantee respect for man, respect for his life in all of its phases of development, respect for the love he has for others, respect for the liberty of his convictions and of his conscience. Must not the Catholic university contribute in responding to these fundamental questions regarding man with all the seriousness that their gravity demands? ✠

$\mathscr{T}$OGO 1985

From 8 to 19 August 1985, the Holy Father visited the continent of Africa for the third time. It was his first visit, however, to the countries of Togo, Cameroon, the Republic of Central Africa, and Morocco. He addressed often the Church's missionary zeal during his visit, as well as Christian renewal and the common good, as he did in his homily during Mass in Lomé, Togo, on 8 August 1985. All of these are components of his central theme for Africa: inculturation of the Gospel.

T he spirit of Christian renewal should, moreover, be exercised with regard to that which the modern civilizations of developed countries bring to your country. It is often a matter of wonderful successes in technique which can be used for economic, health, or cultural welfare of the community. But you also discern the limits of the mentality that often accompanies them—for example, the temptation to lower man to matter, human love to egoistic pleasure, liberty to caprice, autonomy of the mind to forgetfulness or rejection of God. The reception of all these possibilities, at times ambiguous, demands from you much discernment and courage. I think that the texts of Vatican Council II bring you a light to trace your path in the midst of these new realities, joining timely "updating" with essential fidelity.

In considering these different spheres, on which precise points can the moral renewal, for which our faith calls, bear? I can only mention them, leaving to you the responsibility to reflect on this with your bishops, your priests, your catechists.

Taken as a whole, this will always be in the way of fraternal love. Christ gave us "a new commandment," his commandment, to love one another as he has loved us [see Jn 13:34; 15:12]. To love, in your circles, is to regard the other person with respect; it is to support him despite his defects; it is to suppress animosity or hatred toward him; it is to pardon him; to share with him when he is in need, hungry, homeless, in prison, ill, a stranger. To love is to open oneself to others in a spirit of peace and cooperation, beyond the frontiers of one's group, one's tribe, one's nation.

You are likewise called to a "social love," that is, to work for the common good of the nation, to take your share of responsibility in the social life so as always to promote there an increase of justice and concord, in order to create the conditions which respect each man's dignity and his fundamental rights. Your profession, especially if you are civil servants, already contributes to that when you exercise it with integrity, with professional conscience, as a service. If you are students, you seek to acquire a true competence so that one may count on you tomorrow. It is thus that, step by step, one can renew the texture of society. The Christian, in social life, is concerned to protect the most deprived, to help; he feels that he has a joint responsibility for the most disadvantaged regions of his country and also of the world.

Finally, conjugal family love has ceaseless need for renewal. The sacrament of Matrimony enables the union and the whole life of the spouses to be sanctified, and it is important that Christians prepare themselves for it with care. It does not dispense from the daily efforts to strengthen, with Christ's help, the unity of the home, the permanent fidelity of the spouses, the delicacy of mutual love, the concern to educate the children in the faith. Family pastoral care, in the sense explained by the exhortation *Familiaris Consortio,* should have a select place in this Church. ✠

IVORY COAST 1985

ON 11 MAY 1980, the Holy Father had been invited to bless the foundation stone of the new Cathedral of Abidjan, Ivory Coast. Five years later, on 10 August 1985, he consecrated the new cathedral, and delivered his homily on the symbols used in the liturgy as well as the symbol of the cathedral itself. The building of this church is a symbol of the growth of believers on the continent of Africa.

You have completed the building, but you are well aware that the construction of the Church goes on. It is a task for all times and all generations. In order to accomplish this task, men must be purified and constantly renewed, converted by the grace of God and turned from sin which is the work of death. That is why at the same time that we sprinkled baptismal water on the walls of this building, we also sprinkled it over all of us; it is in this water that we have been purified and united in new life in Christ. This is the water which Jesus promised to the Samaritan woman in the Gospel, saying to her, "The water that I shall give will become a spring of water welling up to eternal life" [see Jn 4:14].

Before consecrating the cathedral we will chant the Litany of the Saints. We will thus recall that the living Church has its foundation in the Apostles and the saints of all ages. This church is dedicated to Saint Paul. What a joy it is to invoke the patronage of the Apostle of the gentiles on this land of Africa! What a pleasure it is for the Bishop of Rome to entrust this church in Abidjan to him who ended his missionary journey making the land of Rome fertile with the gift of his blood! The people called to holiness today are the people from which God raised up numerous saints who are examples for us; they live in the kingdom of heaven and intercede for us. May the patronage of Saint Paul and the communion of all the saints be a ferment of unity and love for the Church that gathers here! I would also like to recall that you are particularly honoring the Queen of Apostles under the title of Our Lady of Africa by building another sanctuary, the foundation stone of which I blessed. May she guide you and be helpful to you; may she accompany you along your paths of service to God and men! ✠

$\mathcal{C}$AMEROON 1985

IN YAOUNDÉ, CAMEROON, on 12 August 1985, the Holy Father addressed civil and diplomatic officials, with President Biya in attendance, on their duties to promote the unity and well-being of their country. Pope John Paul was especially concerned that the civil authorities foster peace and eliminate violence from their midst. In the postcolonial period, continuous unrest threatened the stability of the entire continent. The message was meant to carry beyond the frontiers of Cameroon.

A ll countries, but most especially those of the third world, have to take up the economic and social challenge with limited means and they must mobilize all their energies. It is important to devise a manner of doing this which in itself develops the best qualities of the human being without resorting to a constraining system which makes man lose his liberty; without, too, letting the influences of money blindly and egotistically increase their control to the profit of a few. It falls on all to avoid the paralyzing effects of excess bureaucracy and the evils of corruption, fraud, and waste. One must rejoice to see the degree to which you have put into practice the call of the officials of this country for a moralization of behavior; for a strictness of management; for professional integrity, competence, and conscience; for work done well; for perseverance in effort; for a sense of responsibility; for a concern for the common good; for self-sacrifice; and for the search for social justice for all.

Africa needs peace. She cannot tolerate wars, not even the ruinous guerrilla wars which take their toll in human life and destruction, which necessitate a buildup in military expenses and inflame passions, changing brothers into enemies. Who could take part in these fratricidal, and in some cases even genocidal, wars?

In the face of continuing or reawakening conflicts, everyone must honestly question their causes. The injustices committed by certain regimes against the rights of man in general or the legitimate claims of a part of the population which is denied participation in common responsibilities, unleash upheavals of a regrettable violence; it cannot be appeased, however, except by the reestablishment of justice. It is also true that certain external interferences inflame the guerrillas with the sole goal of destabilizing the area [see Address to Diplomatic Corps, 14 January 1984, n. 4]. Lastly, it is certain that the sale of arms for profit alone encourages the belligerents.

Whoever loves Africa will at least avoid fanning the embers of violence, or even more will do everything to lead the parties to the wisdom of peace which corresponds to the profound desire of a number of Africans, sufficiently experienced too.

In reality whoever loves Africa discerns, besides these miseries which are inherently attached to human weakness, a certain number of human, moral, and spiritual values which need only to be extended, and Christianity for its part would like to encourage and ennoble them by the grace of the peace and love which comes from Christ. Among other things, Africa can offer the world the example of generous and untiring hospitality, of the solidarity which exists so strongly among the members of a family or tribe to the point that no one is ever left uncared for, the example of a spontaneous religious sense which renders the invisible familiar. These are the values of which the modern world would have great need in order to counteract the contradictions and snares of a humanism deprived of its fundamental religious dimensions and to achieve a happy coexistence at all the levels of society. ✠

CENTRAL AFRICA 1985

ON HIS FIRST VISIT TO THE REPUBLIC OF CENTRAL AFRICA on 14 August 1985, Pope John Paul II celebrated Mass in Bangui and preached to those gathered on the fruits of their faith as well as the challenge that still faces them. With the overall theme of the "new evangelization" for his journey on the continent of Africa, the Pope reinforced the need to adhere to Christ and his Gospel in all things.

Dear brothers and sisters, Jesus still has a word to confide to you, a beautiful and serious word: "I am the vine, you are the branches. He who abides in me, and I in him, he it is that bears much fruit, for apart from me you can do nothing" [Jn 15:5].

All the fruits of which we have spoken, in your personal, family, social, and national life, will not be possible, and will not remain the fruits of love, unless you remain firmly attached to Christ like the vine branch to the stem of the vine, like the branch to the trunk of the tree. The sap that will produce in you the dynamism of love is the Love which dwells in the Heart of Christ, his love of the Father and his love of man. Without this love our efforts will be merely human activism like "a clanging cymbal" [1 Cor 13:1].

Dear brothers and sisters, persevere in Christ, by taking all the means to tighten your links with him. Abide in Christ by faith, a living faith, a faith which is nourished from the words of Christ—"May my words abide in you"—meditated upon personally or as a group, by demanding an authentic interpretation of them from the Church; in brief, a faith which seems to understand better the salvation and the will of God. The homily of the Mass, the catecheses, the meetings for revision of life, the retreats, the biblical groups are powerful occasions for this revitalization and this mutual spiritual help.

Abide in Christ by prayer: prayer maintains links of love with God. It expresses the acknowledgment of the child who gives thanks, the daring of the child who asks, the availability of the child who says, "Lord, what do you wish me to do?"

Abide in Christ by receiving his sacraments, which are the efficacious signs of his presence. Prepare yourselves to receive them. Ask the Lord to purify you and to lift you up by the sacrament of reconciliation. Ask him to nourish you with his life through the Eucharist, especially in the Sunday assembly. Ask him to transfigure human love by the sacrament of Marriage. ✠

AIRE 1985

On 15 August 1985, the Solemnity of the Assumption of Mary, Pope John Paul II beatified Marie-Clementine Anwarite, the first sister of Zaire to be beatified. Later that same evening, the Pontiff met with the bishops of Zaire in Kinshasa, addressing them on the relationship between the sacraments and holiness. He also reflected on Blessed Marie-Clementine and her path to holiness initiated in her baptism. Born Anwarite Nengapeta, she was a convert to Christianity, together with her mother. She joined the Sisters of the Holy Family, a teaching order native to Zaire. In 1964 she was murdered by rebels in the uprisings against the postcolonial government and the Church. She died defending her virginity. Days before her death, she wrote in her retreat journal: "Our vocation is love, to serve God. The Lord Jesus, when he called us, demanded sacrifice from us—sacrifice of the things of this world, the sacrifice of human love, the sacrifice of our very own person."

Yes, the first Zairean raised to the altars inspires us with profound thankfulness. Here is presented to the eyes of her brothers and sisters the wonderful fruit of the baptism of this people. See, here at the end of more than a century of patient efforts by the builders, the Church built on this land finds itself consolidated. The labors of evangelization, accomplished with patience and a supernatural generosity by so many men and women, come from elsewhere, come to a head in the vitality of a community to the heart of which the Lord has called his pastors. I heartily associate myself with the homage which you have paid to the pioneer missionaries, come from afar, and I appreciate your determination to unite, in the same body of apostolic workers, priests, religious men and women, Africans or not, because they serve the one faith and the one Lord and Savior Jesus Christ. Is it not impressive that Anwarite should have been successively guided in the religious life by a mistress of novices come from Belgium, then by a superior, a native of her own country, while a missionary bishop who counseled her and listened to her with confidence was deprived of his life some days before her!

Quite close to the present generations, this humble religious of the Jamaa Takatifu takes to the heart of her people the relay of the saints whom she herself venerated. By her balanced and generous religious life, by her fidelity until death to the virginity offered to the Lord, Anwarite is a providential sign among you of God's presence in his Church; she witnesses to the greatness of the faith, she displays what a wonderful transfiguration the grace of God accomplishes in the human being who is united to him in holy baptism. Having been buried with Christ in death and having entered with him into the new life of his Kingdom, may she be able to draw her brothers and sisters in the wake of her sanctity! May this martyr, chosen by God, be able to shine her light vigorously over all your dioceses! ✠

KENYA 1985

THE IMPETUS FOR THE POPE'S VISIT was the first Eucharistic Congress ever to be held in Africa, the Forty-third International Eucharistic Congress, to be held in Nairobi, Kenya. After the *Statio Orbis* Mass, the Pontiff reflected on the Eucharist in the context of Mary as part of the Angelus for Sunday, 18 August 1985.

When Mary first agreed to be the Mother of God, when she said, "Let it be done to me according to your word" [Lk 1:38], the Word was made flesh, the divine and eternal word of God became man in her womb. And the history of humanity was absolutely changed. The world could never be the same again. God was now living in human flesh. Jesus had become our brother, a man like us in every way except sin.

The mystery of the Incarnation, the mystery of God becoming man, helps us to understand the mystery of the Eucharist. For what began in the town of Nazareth through the Blessed Virgin's generosity did not come to an end with the death and Resurrection of Christ. No, Christ continues to be in the world through the Church, and especially through the Sacred Liturgy. When God's word is read at Mass, it is Christ himself who speaks to his people. And Saint Paul tells us: "The blessing cup that we bless is a communion with the blood of Christ, and the bread that we break is a communion with the body of Christ" [1 Cor 10:16].

So if we wish to be close to Jesus, we must draw near to the altar of Sacrifice; we must love Christ in the Eucharist fervently and reverently. The Eucharist is the fountain of all virtues. It is spiritual food for daily living. It is the main source for light and love for the Christian family. It gives us a foretaste of the eternal happiness we shall share one day when we finally enter into the Kingdom of Heaven.

How wonderful is this mystery of God dwelling in our midst! The mystery of the Incarnation, the mystery of the Eucharist! The mystery of Christ among us makes us want to glorify God's name. We gladly join the Virgin Mary in her hymn of praise: "My soul proclaims the greatness of the Lord and my spirit exalts in God my savior" [Lk 1:46–47]. Together with Mary and all the angels and saints, we thank God for the Holy Eucharist. ✠

MOROCCO 1985

AT THE REQUEST OF KING HASSAN II, the Pope accepted the invitation to speak to Muslim youth in Casablanca, Morocco, on 19 August 1985. This marked the first time that a Roman Pontiff spoke directly and exclusively to the followers of Islam. In the presence of the king, Pope John Paul addressed the young people on moral issues, faith in God, and responsibilities to the larger community: "common witness." This term formed a special part of the pontifical vocabulary. He used it among bishops and in ecumenical gatherings. Now he applied it to an interfaith assembly.

Dialogue between Christians and Muslims is today more necessary than ever. It flows from our fidelity to God and supposes that we know how to recognize God by faith, and to witness to him by word and deed in a world ever more secularized and at times even atheistic.

The young can build a better future if they first put their faith in God and if they pledge themselves to build this new world in accordance with God's plan, with wisdom and trust.

Today we should witness to the spiritual values of which the world has need. First, of our faith in God.

God is the source of all joy. We should also witness to our worship of God, by our adoration, our prayer of praise and supplication. Man cannot live without prayer, any more than he can live without breathing. We should witness to our humble search for his will; it is he who should inspire our pledge for a more just and more united world. God's ways are not always our ways. They transcend our actions, which are always incomplete, and the intentions of our heart, which are always imperfect. God can never be used for our purposes, for he is above all.

This witness of faith, which is vital for us and which can never tolerate either infidelity to God or indifference to the truth, is made with respect of the other religious traditions, because everyone hopes to be respected for what he is in fact, and for what he conscientiously believes. We desire that all may reach the fullness of the divine truth, but no one can do that except through the free adherence of conscience, protected from exterior compulsions which would be unworthy of the free homage of reason and of heart which is characteristic of human dignity. There is the true meaning of religious liberty, which at the same time respects God and man. It is the sincere veneration of such worshipers that God awaits, of worshipers in spirit and in truth.

Normally the young look toward the future, they long for a more just and more human world. God made young people such, precisely that they might help to transform the world in accordance with his plan of life. But to them, too, the situation often appears to have its shadows.

In this world there are frontiers and divisions between men, as also misunderstandings between the generations; there are, likewise, racism, wars, and injustices, as also hunger, waste, and unemployment. These are the dramatic evils which touch us all, more particularly the young of the entire world. Some are in danger of discouragement, others of capitulation, others of willing to change everything by violence or by extreme solutions. Wisdom teaches us that self-discipline and love are then the only means to the desired renewal.

God does not will that people should remain passive. He entrusted the earth to them that together they should subdue it, cultivate it, and cause it to bear fruit.

You are charged with the world of tomorrow. It is by fully and courageously undertaking your responsibilities that you will be able to overcome the existing difficulties. It reverts to you to take the initiatives and not to wait for everything to come from the older people and from those in office. You must build the world and not just dream about it.

It is by working in harmony that one can be effective. Work properly understood is a service to others. It creates links of solidarity. The experience of working in common enables one to purify oneself and to discover the richness of others. It is thus that, gradually, a climate of trust can be born which enables each one to grow, to expand, and to "be more." Do not fail, dear young people, to collaborate with the adults, especially with your parents and teachers, as well as with the "leaders" of society and of the state. The young should not isolate themselves from the others. The young need adults, just as the adults need the young.

In this working together, the human person, man or woman, should never be sacrificed. Each person is unique in God's eyes. Each one ought to be appreciated for what he is, and, consequently, respected as such. No one should make use of his fellowman; no one should exploit his equal; no one should condemn his brother.

It is in these conditions that a more human, more just, and more fraternal world will be able to be born, a world where each one can find his place in dignity and freedom. It is this world of the twenty-first century that is in your hands; it will be what you make it. ✠

ℒIECHTENSTEIN 1985

IN A SPECIAL AUDIENCE ON 14 OCTOBER 1983, His Highness, Prince Franz Joseph II, invited Pope John Paul II to Liechtenstein. The Pope traveled to the tiny principality on the Feast of the Birth of Mary, 8 September 1985. In a Liturgy of the Word in St. Florian's Church in Vaduz, the Holy Father reflected on illness and on Mary under the title of Our Lady of Sorrows.

Mary stands by your side because she herself has suffered with her divine Son according to the prophecy which the aged Simeon had made to her in the Temple of Jerusalem: "A sword shall pierce through your own soul also" [Lk 2:35]. We are all well acquainted with the picture of the Mother of Sorrows and have it deeply engraved upon our hearts: the dead body of the divine Son lies on the lap of his sorrowful Mother, from whom he came. Mary's maternal heart is pierced with pain, for nobody is as close to the Son as his own mother. However, the heavenly Father, who does not desert people, even those suffering extreme affliction, gave the Mother of Jesus the strength to wait patiently under the Cross and to share the suffering of her Son.

The special devotion of the Seven Sorrows of Our Lady can be a source of strength for you, too, to accept in faith the burdens of your own life and to link them together by prayer and contemplation with the suffering and death of the Lord. By patient endurance of your daily burdens and troubles, you sanctify yourself and, at the same time, the Church and the world. Suffering accepted for the sake of Christ is always beneficial suffering. You know what Saint Paul—himself having had to bear much suffering and adversity—says to explain this beneficial power of suffering: "I rejoice in my sufferings for your sake, and in my flesh I complete what is lacking in Christ's afflictions for the sake of his body, that is, the church" [Col 1:24]. Yes, as believing Christians we must attempt to understand and to live the purpose and the dignity of human suffering. ✠

INDIA 1986

THE HOLY FATHER'S PILGRIMAGE TO INDIA, the world's largest democracy, occurred 1 to 10 February 1986. During his visit to Raj Ghat on 1 February, the Pope addressed an assembly at the shrine of Mahatma Gandhi, only two days after the thirty-eighth anniversary of his death. After speaking on peace and truth, the Pontiff planted a memorial tree.

My visit to India is a pilgrimage of goodwill and peace, and the fulfillment of a desire to experience personally the very soul of your country.

It is entirely fitting that this pilgrimage should begin here, at Raj Ghat, dedicated to the memory of the illustrious Mahatma Gandhi, the Father of the Nation and "apostle of nonviolence."

The figure of Mahatma Gandhi and the meaning of his life's work have penetrated the consciousness of humanity. In his famous words, Pandit Jawaharlal Nehru has expressed the conviction of the whole world: "The light that shone in this country was no ordinary light" [Homage to Mahatma Gandhi, New Delhi, 1948, pp. 9–10].

Two days ago marked the thirty-eighth anniversary of his death. He who lived by nonviolence appeared to be defeated by violence. For a brief moment the light seemed to have gone out. Yet his teachings and the example of his life live on in the minds and hearts of millions of men and women. And so it was said: "The light has gone out of our lives and there is darkness everywhere and I do not quite know what to tell you and how to say it. . . . The light has gone out, I said, and yet I was wrong. For the light that shone in this country was no ordinary light. The light that has illumined this country for these many years will illumine this country for many more years" [ibid.]. Yes, the light is still shining, and the heritage of Mahatma Gandhi speaks to us still. And today as a pilgrim of peace I have come here to pay homage to Mahatma Gandhi, hero of humanity.

From this place, which is forever bound to the memory of this extraordinary man, I wish to express to the people of India and of the world my profound conviction that the peace and justice of which contemporary society has such great need will be achieved only along the path that was at the core of his teaching: the supremacy of the spirit and *Satyagraha,* the "truth-force," which conquers without violence by the dynamism intrinsic to just action [John Paul II, Apostolic Letter to Youth, n. 41].

The power of truth leads us to recognize with Mahatma Gandhi the dignity, equality, and fraternal solidarity of all human beings, and it prompts us to reject every form of discrimination. It shows us once again the need for mutual understanding, acceptance, and collaboration between religious groups in the pluralist society of modern India and throughout the world. ✠

COLOMBIA 1986

RESPONDING TO AN INVITATION extended to him from both its civil authorities and its bishops, Pope John Paul II visited Colombia from 1 to 6 July 1986. Although the Pontiff went, as he did in almost all his journeys, as a "messenger of evangelization," he also noted for this visit that the fourth centenary of the restoration of the venerated image of Our Lady of the Rosary of Chiquinquirá was an appropriate occasion for the Pope to take up again the "Shepherd's crook" (radio address of 30 June 1986 to the people of Colombia). On this third day of pilgrimage, therefore, the Pope celebrated Mass at Chiquinquirá for the *campesinos* and preached on Mary and her role in salvation.

B lessed are you who have believed!" [see Lk 1:45].
I prostrate myself before you, O Mother of Jesus, as a pilgrim at your Sanctuary of Chiquinquirá, pronouncing the words with which Elizabeth, the wife of Zechariah, greeted you on the threshold of her house.

"Blessed are you who have believed!"

Blessed because, under the impulse of faith, in response to the message of the angel, you received in your womb the Word of the living God.

Blessed are you, for, having given your *Fiat,* you were changed, because of your ineffable virtue, from the Handmaid of the Lord to the Mother of the Eternal Word: God from God, Light from Light, made man in your virginal womb. The Word became flesh! [see Jn 1:14].

Blessed are you because, thanks to your acceptance of the Word of God, there was accomplished in the fullness of time that was then at hand the event that was most powerfully indicated by the prophets for the life and the history of mankind: "The people that walked in darkness saw a great light" [Is 9:1]: your Son Jesus Christ, the Son of man, the Redeemer of the world.

"Blessed are you who have believed!"

There are many places in the world from which the children of the people of God, born of the new covenant, repeat unceasingly to you the words of this beatitude: "Blessed are you among women, and blessed is the fruit of your womb; to what do I owe the visit from the Mother of my Lord to me?" [Lk 1:42–43].

And one of these places which you have wished to visit, like the house of Elizabeth, is this place: the Marian sanctuary of the People of God in the land of Colombia.

Here at Chiquinquirá, you wished, O Mother, to establish forever your dwelling place. For four centuries, your vigilant and efficacious presence has unceasingly accompanied the messengers of the Gospel in these lands, to give birth in them, with the light and the grace of your Son, to the immense richness of the Christian life. We may well recall today the words pronounced by my venerated predecessor Pope Pius XII, that "Colombia is a garden of Mary, among whose sanctuaries there dominates, like the sun among the stars, Our Lady of Chiquinquirá."

Beloved brothers and sisters: I join you with joy in this pilgrimage of faith and love as the fourth centenary of the renewal of this venerated image draws to its close. I have come to this place to prostrate at the feet of the Virgin, desiring to strengthen you in the faith, that is, in the truth of Jesus Christ, which includes the truth of

Mary and true devotion to her. I also wish to pray with you for the peace and prosperity of this beloved nation, to her whom you acclaim as Queen of Peace, invoking her with filial affection as Queen of Colombia. ✠

$\mathscr{S}$AINT LUCIA 1986

THE HOLY FATHER MADE A BRIEF PASTORAL VISIT to the island nation of St. Lucia on his return from Colombia on 7 July 1986. In a Mass for the faithful which he celebrated in Reduit Park, the Pope preached on the blessing of the gift of faith in this new nation.

God's grace has indeed been at work in your midst. The history of the Church of Saint Lucia bears witness to the goodness and mercy of God, to "the immeasurable greatness of his power in us who believe" [Eph 1:19].

The gift of faith "enlightens the eyes of our hearts" [see Eph 1:18], giving us a new vision of life and of the world. Every human event takes on a new perspective when we know that God is our loving Father, who watches over us with gentleness and compassion. And having been "sealed with the promised Holy Spirit" [Eph 1:14] in Baptism and Confirmation, we are sent forth to live our faith, to "employ it for one another, as good stewards of God's varied grace" [1 Pt 4:10].

The first response to the gift of faith is praise and gratitude, and this is accomplished especially in the Church's greatest act of worship: the Eucharist. A deep faith always expresses itself in a fervent love for the Eucharist, for it is at Mass that we hear the Word of Life and share in the Body and Blood of Christ our Lord. I urge you therefore to make Sunday Mass and frequent Communion a regular part of your lives, in fact the center and summit of all you are and do.

Faith, which we have received as a gift, must in turn be put into practice. Saint James tells us that "faith by itself, if it has no works, is dead" [Jas 2:17]. That is why I am so pleased at all the efforts you are making to practice your faith. An excellent example of this is the Pastoral Theme which you have chosen for the Archdiocese this year: "Strengthen our faith, Redeemer." I am confident that this deserving initiative will bring you many graces as you continually practice your faith through prayer and good works. ✠

FRANCE 1986

FROM 4 TO 7 OCTOBER 1986 Pope John Paul II made his third pilgrimage to France in order to confirm the French people in their faith. He also venerated several of France's saints. Among these were Saint Jean Vianney, the Curé of Ars; Saint Margaret Mary Alacoque, Blessed Claude de la Colombière, Blessed Pauline Garicot, and Blessed Claudine Thevenet. On 4 October, the Feast of Saint Francis of Assisi (whose mother was French), the Pope presided at the beatification of Father Antoine Chevrier. This beatification was the principle reason for his visit to France. The beatification was held at Lyon at an outdoor ceremony. In his homily, the Pontiff praised Blessed Antoine, a protégé of Saint Jean Vianney, for his humility and his dedication to work with the poorest of the poor. In his own writings, Father Chevrier left a motto which the Pontiff was to cite: "We must represent Jesus Christ in the poverty of his crib, Jesus Christ suffering in his passion, Jesus Christ letting himself be eaten in the Holy Eucharist." The Pope's homily reflected the need for imitation of such a saintly hero in the context of modern-day France.

L et us take a special look at Antoine Chevrier: He is one of those "little ones" who cannot be compared with the "wise" and the "learned" of his own day or of other centuries. He constitutes a class of his own, with a greatness that is wholly evangelical. His greatness shows itself in what one can call his lowliness or poverty. Living humbly, with the poorest of means, he is the witness of the hidden mystery of God, a witness of love that God bears for the masses of "little ones" who are like him. He was their servant, their apostle.

For them, he was the "priest according to the Gospel"—to use the first title of his collected exhortations on "the true disciple of Jesus Christ." He is an incomparable guide for the many priests present here, beginning with those of Prado whom he founded. But all the lay Christians who make up this assembly will likewise find a great light in him, because he shows to each of the baptized how to proclaim the Good News to the poor, and how to make Jesus Christ present through one's own existence.

An apostle—yes, this is what Father Chevrier wanted to be when he was preparing for the priesthood. "Jesus Christ is the one sent by the Father: the priest is the one sent by Jesus Christ." The poor themselves enlivened his desire to evangelize them, but it was Jesus Christ who "took hold of him." He was particularly affected by his meditation before the Crib at Christmas 1856. From then on, he always sought to know Jesus Christ better, to become his disciple, to be conformed to him, in order to proclaim him better to the poor. He relived especially the experience of the Apostle Paul, whose testimony you have just heard: "Whatever gain I had, I counted as loss . . . because of the surpassing worth of knowing Christ Jesus my Lord" [Phil 3:7–8]. What a radical message these words contain! This is what characterizes the apostle. In Christ, "sharing in the communion of his sufferings" and "experiencing the power of his resurrection," he finds the divine "justice" that is offered to sinful humanity, offered to each person as the gift of justification and reconciliation with the God who is infinitely holy.

DURING HIS APOSTOLIC JOURNEYS, the Pope often engaged in question-and-answer sessions with the youth of the country. The questions would be solicited by the Bishops Conference and submitted to the Pope, who would then prepare his answers. At Lyon on 5 October, John Paul engaged in just such a question-and-answer session with fifty thousand young people at the Gerland Stadium. The various questions or problems stated included the following:

(1) It is not easy to bear witness; (2) How can we share our faith with others?; (3) Our friends laugh at us if we talk about God; (4) By means of the sciences and technology, the world unceasingly calls our faith into question; (5) We have always a thirst for God: but what is the use of believing?; (6) How can one live God today?; (7) How can one rediscover his first fervor? The Holy Father was even asked if he had ever had doubts. The Pontiff responded to all of these in terms of the structures of faith. He first replied to the question: Is it useful to believe?

I would first say to you: What "usefulness" do you mean? If you try directly to utilize God and religion as something extra that will help you to achieve a happiness that can be felt, or to serve your own interests, or to ensure the effectiveness of undertakings that depend on the nature, the intelligence, and the heart that God has given you so that you may dominate the world, or even as a means to perfect your moral stature, you risk disappointment. God is not an instrument to make up for our defects. He is Someone. He exists for himself, above everything. He deserves to be known, adored, served, and loved gratuitously, for his own sake. It is also true that he wills that we reach full realization of ourselves.

Irenaeus, the successor of Pothinus and second bishop of Lyon, said, "The glory of God is the living man, and the life of man is the vision of God." Some have asked me to speak about eternal life. Dear friends, do you desire truly to see God? Face-to-face in the next world, after having encountered him in faith in this world? Do you desire to share even now in his divine life, to be saved from what separates you from him, to be forgiven your sins? Such graces do not lie in your own power. God alone can grant you them. Starting from this point, he will do many other things too. You ask him to change things; better than this, he will change you. By looking at God, by giving him your faith, by praying, by nourishing yourselves on him, by "doing the truth" with him, and in particular by responding to the commandment of love, you will no longer be the same persons. In this sense, indeed, faith is very effective. These are the paths to live God, as you put it. God is greater than our heart.

God does not cease to be *present to this world*. He is the source of all that exists, of all that lives, of all that is Spirit and love. His presence *cannot be wiped out*. In A.D. 177, the pagans of Lyons believed that they had eliminated the faith in Jesus when they went to the length of throwing the ashes of the martyrs into the Rhone. The Resurrection of Christ has a different power. The Holy Spirit does not let himself be quenched. In point of fact, Lyons as a whole became Christian, and all of Gaul. In our time, some countries believed that they had destroyed the attraction of Jesus and wiped out the name of God. Much has been said about "the death of God," but he does not cease to rise up, astonishingly alive in consciences.

Dear friends, Christ looks intently on each one of you, whoever you may be, as he looked on the young man in the Gospel. Your letters speak of the good fortune of knowing Jesus Christ. I would define this more precisely: It is the good fortune of knowing that he is present, of becoming aware that one is joined to him like a member to the Head of the Body. This is what is effected by baptism, which configures us to Christ. For you who believe, it is Christ who lives in the Church, as in the time of the martyrs. You are the Church that bears witness that Jesus Christ is alive.

God is present, but it is true that *we can be absent*. It is not God that fails to turn up at the rendezvous; the risk is that we have *failed to meet him*. We have just celebrated the anniversary of the conversion of Saint Augustine in 386. After he had looked for happiness on many false paths, he confessed to God: "Late have I loved thee, O beauty ever ancient, ever new! . . . You were within me when I was outside myself and it was outside that I sought you. . . . You were with me, and I was not with you." Many of our contemporaries too live in *religious indifference,* forgetful of God, organizing our lives without him; they try all the paths to happiness, without daring to believe that Christ is the Truth, the Way, and the Life. May they have the strength to wake up, "to rekindle the gift of God that is in them," to pay attention to the One who is knocking at their door, who indeed is more intimate to their being than they themselves are! You are not indifferent. You recognize that in your depths there is the thirst for God, but you suffer from today's indifference.

On 6 October Pope John Paul delivered a meditation during a retreat for clergy and seminarians at Ars, the town where Saint Jean Vianney ministered through the middle of the nineteenth century. Noting that priests of today are often overlooked in their dignity and in the character of their vocation—even taken for granted by Church and society alike, the Pontiff spoke of the special grace inherent in their call. He held up the Curé of Ars as a model. Quoting him, he said, "The priesthood is the love of the heart of Christ."

I t is Christ who chooses us; he sends us as he was sent by the Father, and he imparts the Holy Spirit to us. Our priesthood is rooted in the missions of the divine Persons in their mutual Gift in the heart of the Holy Trinity. "The grace of the Holy Spirit . . . continues to be transmitted by episcopal ordination. Then, through the sacrament of Orders, the bishops make the sacred ministers sharers in the spiritual gift" [Encyclical *Dominum et Vivificantem*, n. 25]. Priests and deacons, too, share in this grace.

Our mission is a *mission of salvation*. "God sent his Son into the world, . . . so that the world might be saved through him" [Jn 3:17]. Jesus preached the Good News of the Kingdom; he chose and formed his apostles; he accomplished the work of Redemption by the Cross and the Resurrection; following the Apostles we are associated in a particular manner with his work of salvation, to make it present and effective everywhere in the world. Saint Jean-Marie Viannay went so far as to say: "Without the priest, the death and passion of our Lord would be of no use. It is the priest who continues the work of redemption on earth" [*Jean-Marie Vianney, Curé d'Ars: Sa Pensée, Son Coeur*, presented by Father Bernard Nodet, Le Puy, 1958, p. 100].

It is this that we must put into effect: it is, accordingly, not our work, but the design of the Father and the salvific work of the Son. The Holy Spirit makes use of our mind, of our mouth, of our hands. It is our special task to proclaim the Word unceasingly, in order to spread the Gospel, and to translate it in such a way that we touch people's hearts, without altering it or diminishing it; and it is ours to perform once again the act of offering which Jesus made at the Last Supper and his act of pardon for sinners.

In the Curé of Ars, we see precisely a priest who was not satisfied with an external accomplishment of the acts of Redemption; he shared this in his very being, in his love of Christ, in his constant prayer, in the offering of his trials or his voluntary mortifications. As I said already to the priests at Notre-Dame in Paris, on 30 May 1980, "The Curé of Ars remains for all countries an unequaled model both of the carrying out of the ministry and of the holiness of the minister." ✠

ℬANGLADESH 1986

FROM 19 NOVEMBER TO 1 DECEMBER 1986, Pope John Paul visited Asia and Oceania, with his first stop in Bangladesh. At E'rshad Stadium in Dhaka, he presided at the ordination of the largest class of priests in Bangladesh's history. While his theme for this visit was "communion and fraternity," he also spoke of their ordination to the service of human dignity, perseverence, and accomplishment.

Who is it that gives praise and glory to God? It is the entire universe, every creature. But above all it is man who acknowledges and adores his Creator. For this very purpose all things have been put under his control. As the Psalm says: "You have made him little less than a god; with glory and honor you crowned him, gave him power over the works of your hand, put all things under his feet" [Ps 8:5–6].

Commenting on this idea, the Second Vatican Council teaches that "man, created in God's image, received a mandate to subject to himself the earth and all that it contains, and to govern the world with justice and holiness, a mandate to relate himself and the totality of things to him who was to be acknowledged as the Lord and Creator of all. So, by the subjection of all things to man, the name of God would be wonderful in all the earth" [*Gaudium et Spes,* 34].

Man's task in this world, therefore, is "to make life more human and to render the whole earth submissive to this goal" [ibid., 38]. In this sense man is lord of all material reality. Indeed, he is the "priest" of the cosmos, whose duty it is to proclaim, in the name of all creatures, the adorable greatness of the Almighty and to give the entire universe back to the Creator as a pleasing sacrifice.

In this universal religious perspective man's great and inalienable dignity is immediately recognizable. Where this dignity is marred by poverty, hunger, and disease, a lack of proper living conditions and of opportunities for education and work, the conscience of the world needs to be alerted to the duty of defending God's image in man. In Bangladesh, too, professionals and leaders have ample scope for the service of their fellow citizens, in building a just society and in responding to the urgent needs of so many people. Motivated and inspired by true human, moral, and religious values they can give new direction and impulse to the task of development and progress.

What does Christ expect from you, his friends? He looks for your love. "This is my commandment, that you love one another as I have loved you" [Jn 15:12]. And then he shows how far this love should go: "Greater love has no man than this, that a man lay down his life for his friends" [v. 13]. Of this love Jesus himself gave the perfect example, and every time that you celebrate the Eucharist you will recall and renew his saving Sacrifice for the glory of the Father and the salvation of the world.

Your service to the community will take many forms, and all of them must express this love. When you preach the word of life and administer the sacraments of faith, when you travel up and down this land to reach your brothers and sisters in need, when you heal the soul, when you educate and encourage the young, when you help to consolidate development and peace with justice and compassion for all, let love be your inspiration and your strength. Then you will bear "fruit that abides," which nurtures the divine life of souls and the vitality of the community of God's people, the "Body of Christ," to which [today's] second reading refers.

Saint Paul's exhortation in that reading—"to live a life worthy of the calling to which you have been called, with all lowliness and meekness, with patience, forbearing one another in love" [Eph 4:1–2]—is directed to the "building up of the body of Christ, until we all attain to the unity of the faith and of the knowledge of the Son of God, to mature manhood, to the measure of the stature of the fulness of Christ" [vv. 12–13]. In other words, the life of the Church in Bangladesh is intimately linked to the strength of your love for Christ. ✠

INGAPORE 1986

ON 20 NOVEMBER 1986, the Holy Father arrived in Singapore. The Pontiff celebrated a Mass along with twenty bishops and 150 priests in the National Stadium of Singapore. Delivering a homily for all those gathered, Pope John Paul II highlighted Singapore's duty to foster world peace in the context of Christian love and justice. This same obligation is both worldwide and personal.

P eacemaking is a task that is never finished, but always in progress, always in need of being confirmed and strengthened. We must constantly work for peace.

True peace begins in the mind and heart, in the will and soul of the human person, for it proceeds from genuine love for others. Indeed it is true to say that peace is the product of love, when people consciously decide to improve their relationships with others, to make every effort to overcome divisions and misunderstandings, and if possible even to become friends.

As Christians, we know that we can love others only because God has first loved us. We find inspiration and strength in the words of today's first reading, from the Prophet Jeremiah, where God says to us: "I have loved you with an everlasting love, so I am constant in my affection for you" [Jer 31:3]. The everlasting love of God spurs us on in our efforts at peacemaking.

Peace requires justice, an attitude which recognizes the dignity and equality of all men and women, and a firm commitment to strive to secure and protect the basic human rights of all. Where there is no justice there can be no peace. Peace is possible only where there is a just order that ensures the rights of everyone. World peace is possible only where the international order is just. ✠

ℱIJI 1986

THE HOLY FATHER'S THIRD STOP DURING HIS PILGRIMAGE was the Fiji Islands where, on 21 November 1986, the Pope was received in a traditional welcoming ceremony.

In a Mass at Albert Park, the Pope reflected in his homily on Mary and her single-hearted dedication to the Lord. He also spoke on mercy and compassion in the context of Fiji's cultural, racial, and religiously diverse environment. Above all, he stressed the life of each individual as constituted by a true call from God.

You can be sure that the word of Christ dwelling in your hearts will bear abundant fruit, especially in acts of mercy and compassion. When he tells his disciples to love one another, Jesus emphasizes that he has chosen them and not the other way round, and that they are to go forth and bear fruit: "It was not you who chose me, it was I who chose you to go forth and bear fruit. Your fruit must endure, so that all you ask the Father in my name he will give you" [Jn 15:16].

The Lord's command of love has been proclaimed to the people of Fiji from the arrival of the first Christian missionaries. I invite all of you to become more aware of Christ's call to spread the Gospel to others as well as to pray and work together for Christian unity. I encourage you in your esteem and friendship for your Hindu and Muslim brethren, so that respectful dialogue may bring about better mutual understanding.

It is my fervent prayer that my pastoral visit to Fiji will help you to dedicate yourselves ever more to doing the Father's will and to sharing in the mission of his Son. For this reason:

I call upon you to love one another as Jesus has commanded.

I call upon you to renew your efforts to appreciate and respect each other's cultural diversity.

I call upon you to show special concern for the poor and those who are pushed to the margins of society.

I call upon you to work for a more just society, in which wealth will be more equally divided and in which it will be possible for all to live a life in keeping with their human dignity.

I call upon you, especially the young people, to respond to the Lord's love and to share his joy with others.

I call upon you who are sick to offer your sufferings for the growth of the Kingdom of God.

And I commend all of you to the intercession of the Blessed Virgin Mary, the perfect example of dedication to the Lord, the Mother of him who says: "This is my commandment: Love one another as I have loved you." Amen. ✠

NEW ZEALAND 1986

ON 22 NOVEMBER, Pope John Paul arrived in New Zealand, where he was welcomed in a traditional Maori ceremony. The next day, the Pope presided at Mass in the Athletic Park in Wellington, the capital. His words were a call to peace—which can only come from a heart at peace.

Peace, as well as love, is born from a new heart, a heart made new by God's gift of reconciliation. A new heart is the foundation of peace in the world. All truly human actions proceed from the heart, the innermost center of the human person, the dwelling place of our conscience and of our deepest convictions. This is why peace of heart is the heart of peace—peace inside families, peace within villages, towns, and cities, peace between nations and in international life. Peace anywhere in the world is possible only if there is first of all peace of heart.

But this inner peace is continually threatened in our modern world. It is disturbed by human passions: by hatred, envy, lust for power, pride, prejudice, and an uncontrolled desire for wealth. Violence and war come from our blindness of spirit and the disorder in our hearts. These lead to injustice, which in turn causes tension and conflict. In addition, people's consciences are often confused today by an ideological manipulation of information.

Clearly it takes great courage to open ourselves to conversion of heart and to maintain this conversion in humility and freedom. The obstacles to peace are many. "They are grave, they present serious threats. But since they depend on the spirit, the will, the human 'heart,' with the help of God, people can overcome them. They must refuse to give in to fatalism and discouragement. Positive signs are already piercing the darkness" [1984 World Day of Peace Message, 5]. And let us never forget that the final triumph over darkness has already been won by Jesus Christ, the Light of the World. ✠

AUSTRALIA 1986

POPE JOHN PAUL ARRIVED IN CANBERRA on 24 November 1986 for the Australian leg of his pilgrimage. This was his first visit to Australia as Supreme Pontiff, since he had visited as Cardinal Wojtyla in 1973 to participate in the International Eucharistic Congress in Melbourne. During his pilgrimage, the Pope stopped in Alice Springs and addressed the Aborigines and the Torres Strait Islanders. The Pope revered their native relationship to the land. His words were poetic.

The rock paintings and the discovered evidence of your ancient tools and implements indicate the presence of your age-old culture and prove your ancient occupancy of this land.

Your culture, which shows the lasting genius and dignity of your race, must not be allowed to disappear. Do not think that your gifts are worth so little that you should no longer bother to maintain them. Share them with each other and teach them to your children. Your songs, your stories, your paintings, your dances, your languages, must never be lost. Do you perhaps remember those words that Paul VI spoke to the aboriginal people during his visit to them in 1970? On that occasion he said: "We know that you have a lifestyle proper to your own ethnic genius or culture—a culture which the Church respects and which she does not in any way ask you to renounce. . . . Society itself is enriched by the presence of different cultural and ethnic elements. For us you and the values you represent are precious. We deeply respect your dignity and reiterate our deep affection for you" [Sydney, 2 December 1970].

For thousands of years this culture of yours was free to grow without interference by people from other places. You lived your lives in spiritual closeness to the land, with its animals, birds, fishes, water holes, rivers, hills, and mountains. Through your closeness to the land you touched the sacredness of man's relationship with God, for the land was the proof of a power in life greater than yourselves. You did not spoil the land, use it up, exhaust it, and then walk away from it. You realized that your land was related to the source of life.

The silence of the bush taught you a quietness of soul that put you in touch with another world, the world of God's spirit. Your careful attention to the details of kinship spoke of your reverence for birth, life, and human generation. You knew that children need to be loved, to be full of joy. They need a time to grow in laughter and to play, secure in the knowledge that they belong to their people.

You had a great respect for the need which people have for law, as a guide to living fairly with each other. So you created a legal system—very strict, it is true, but closely adapted to the country in which you lived your lives. It made your society orderly. It was one of the reasons why you survived in this land.

You marked the growth of your young men and women with ceremonies of discipline that taught them responsibility as they came to maturity.

These achievements are indications of human strivings. And in these strivings you showed a dignity open to the message of God's revealed wisdom to all men and women, which is the great truth of the Gospel of Jesus Christ. ✠

 EYCHELLES 1986

AFTER HIS VISIT TO AUSTRALIA, the Holy Father made a brief stop in the Seychelles, where he celebrated the Eucharistic Liturgy in Port Victoria. Directing his words to the many different peoples in attendance, he highlighted in his homily the wonderful gifts which God has bestowed on his peoples.

Yes, dear brothers and sisters, we can thank God for all the gifts he has given to us, starting with the sight of nature which is before us. Do you not have here a very beautiful land, bathed by the sun and made fertile by the rain, with its mountains, the splendor of its rocks, its lush forests, its lovely beaches? Here we are moved to praise from the depths of our hearts the Creator of the world!

But the most beautiful of divine creations is the human heart: from the beginning God created the human being—man and woman—in his own image and likeness [see Gen 1:26]. And God has not stopped loving his people. Despite their refusal, their sin and misery, God leads them freely back to himself, he pardons and reconciles them, he makes a covenant with them.

In Jesus Christ the covenant between God and man becomes something unheard of: The Son of God is himself made man; by his Cross and Resurrection he saves his people and restores their union with God; he gives to people his own life, the life of God; he gathers them into his Church to share in the love of the Father and the riches of the Spirit.

This is the Good News which has spread throughout the world from Jesus onwards, through the Apostles and the missionaries of the Gospel, the Good News which was brought to your islands and which you have believed.

For all the gifts of nature and of grace we are to give thanks. Today, the Successor of Peter comes to confirm you in your faith, to encourage your community in order to give it new energy in building up the Church. ✠

RUGUAY 1987

ON 31 MARCH 1987, Pope John Paul II began his eighth apostolic visit to the Latin American continent, with a brief stop in Uruguay, to which he would return for another visit thirteen months later. On the evening of his arrival, the Pope visited the Palacio Taranco in order to commemorate the "Treaty of Montevideo," which effectively avoided serious conflict between Chile and Argentina through the peaceful mediation of Uruguay. The treaty, initially signed on 8 January 1979, therefore held a prominent place in the Holy Father's wishes to visit Uruguay, if only briefly.

I n this Palacio Taranco where the seed was sown which would produce such seasoned fruits of peace and cooperation, it gives me pleasure to highlight, in the presence of such distinguished representatives of the international community, the twofold exemplary value of that Treaty with which the interested parties were able to resolve a difficult and longstanding difference and, in addition, set down the guidelines for solving those which might arise in the future. Here and now I would like to renew the urgent appeal that no one should waver in the determined search for peaceful means of resolving effectively and honorably the conflicts—open or latent, national or international—which are present in our world today. To those who think that they could be solved apart from dialogue and reason or through the use of force, I repeat now the fervent wish which I expressed the day that the Treaty went into effect: namely, that the way of dialogue and negotiation be the "pathway taken by the countries which, for one reason or another, now find themselves in dispute."

May those who are tempted to use force for ends which may well be legitimate, have no doubt that there are always possibilities for negotiation with a view to true and honorable solutions which can be acceptable to all. ✠

*C*HILE 1987

THE POPE CONTINUED ON TO CHILE, where for several days he would reflect, in particular, on peace and the many social conditions of that country. On 2 April 1987, he met those who inhabited the slums of Santiago and, after the Liturgy of the Word, he preached on poverty and its unjust causes.

A short time ago the twentieth anniversary of the publication of Pope Paul VI's encyclical on the development of people, *Populorum Progressio,* occurred. It is with some regret that we must admit that that prophetic voice still resounds in the world without ever having found an adequate response. Therefore, today, here in this continent of hope, in your midst, people of Santiago, I want to repeat for all men and women of goodwill in Latin America and everywhere the words of Paul VI, in the same spirit in which they were spoken by him: "May individuals, social groups, and nations join hands in brotherly fashion, the strong aiding the weak to grow, exerting all their competence, enthusiasm, and disinterested love. More than any other, the individual who is animated by true charity labors skillfully to discover the causes of misery, to find the means to combat it, to overcome it resolutely" [*Populorum Progressio, 75*].

The Church, recognizing that we form a single family, the great family of the children of God, repeatedly calls upon each person to dedicate himself to the task of removing from your land the causes of unjust poverty, using whatever means, great or small, at his disposal in his own social situation and surroundings. Work together to build a world that is more just and fraternal, whose foundations are set "in truth, built according to justice, vivified and integrated by charity, and put into practice in freedom" [*Pacem in Terris, 167*]. ✠

ARGENTINA 1987

AT THE INVITATION both of the bishops as well as the president of the Republic of Argentina, the Holy Father visited Argentina for the second time 6 to 13 April. His first visit, in June 1982, was as a "messenger of peace" to help calm its relationship with England. This second visit, however, saw the Pope in a pastoral role. On 8 April, the Pope went to Salta, where, as a part of the Liturgy of the Word, he again discussed "evangelization" in Argentina as well as the Church universal.

Throughout the almost two thousand years of her pilgrimage on earth, the whole Church has continually proclaimed to all humanity that message of repentance and conversion to God. It is a message that is divinely efficacious, because through the strength of the word and the sacraments, the power of Christ, the Son of God made man, operates. The command and the divine assurance with which the Gospel of Saint Matthew ends, is addressed to all generations of evangelizers who continue the Lord's mission: "All authority in heaven and on earth has been given to me. Go, therefore, make disciples of all nations; baptize them in the name of the Father and of the Son and of the Holy Spirit, and teach them to observe all the commands I gave you. And know that I am with you always: yes, to the end of time" [Mt 28:18–20].

The command to evangelize embraces "all nations," and extends "to the end of time." Hence, with the approaching celebration of the fifth centenary of the discovery of America by Christopher Columbus in 1492, the Church could not refrain from making the celebration of this event her own, since she has also fulfilled that command of Christ in the vastness of this continent during these five hundred years.

On seeing how the command to preach and baptize has been fulfilled in this continent, the Church humbly confesses that she has received the mission and authority of Christ to continue his work of Redemption through the centuries. As I said in Santo Domingo, "So far as the Church is concerned, she wants to approach the celebration of this centenary with the humility of the truth, without triumphalism or false modesty" [Homily of 12 October 1984, 11, 3]. The truth about what America is, and is called to fulfill, makes me affirm with renewed conviction that it is a continent of hope, not only because of the quality of its men and women, and the possibilities of its rich natural resources, but principally by reason of its response to the Good News of Christ. Hence, with the third millennium just around the corner, America should feel called to present itself to the universal Church and to the world with a renewed activity of evangelization, which shall reveal the power of the love of Christ to all people, and sow Christian hope in their hearts which are thirsting for the living God. ✠

*W*EST GERMANY 1987

FOR FIVE DAYS, beginning 30 April 1987, the Holy Father visited West Germany for a second time. In each of the three cities that he visited, he held up a model of courage in three outstanding opponents of the Nazi philosophy. In Münster, he recalled Cardinal Clemens August von Galen (1878–1946), who defended the rights of the mentally impaired. He held him up as a model "for life!" In Cologne, he beatified Edith Stein (1891–1942). A famous philosopher of the phenomenology school, she was a convert to the Church from Judaism. She and her blood sister, Rosa, were gassed at the Auschwitz Concentration Camp. On 3 May the Pontiff also beatified Father Rupert Mayer, S.J. (1876–1945) at Munich. This priest opposed everything in Hitler's political program as atheistic and evil. Arrested and confined to prisons and concentration camps, he was eventually released in a weakened condition to a Benedictine abbey in the final months of the Second World War. He died of a stroke in 1945. In regarding Father Rupert among "the Blessed," the Pontiff spoke of the extraordinary love seen in the example of "martyr saints."

Dear brothers and sisters, the saints and the blessed of the Church are God's message, past and present, to us. Hence they are there for us to venerate and imitate. Let us therefore today open our hearts to the message which Rupert Mayer has proclaimed so vividly with his words and deeds. Let us, like him, see in God the essence and source of our life. He had a child's unshakable trust in God. "Lord, let thy will be done. Let me act in accordance with your will. Only help me to understand your will" was the first verse of his favorite prayer. God our Lord was the source from which, in long hours spent in prayer, during Mass, and in fulfilling his daily duties, he drew the strength for his amazing life's work.

Let us, too, draw from the same source of power in shaping our lives and our environment. Blessed Rupert Mayer is a model for us all; his life is an appeal to us to lead a holy life. Holiness is not reserved for a few chosen ones. We are all, without exception, called upon to be holy. He himself tells us what we have to do to lead a holy life: "No extraordinary work, no extraordinary religious experiences, no manifestations. Merely heroic virtue." This means faithfully and unerringly doing God's will day by day, deriving strength from his presence, each of us personally and in the family. We know how much Blessed Rupert cherished the Christian family and how, together with two other priests, he even founded a sisterhood to promote Christian family life.

The many divorces and the small number of children indicate the great burdens on and threats to family life in the modern society. Yet decisions affecting the future of your nation, and the future of the Church in your nation, lie in your families.

> **On 4 May 1987** Pope John Paul beatified Edith Stein, known in religion as Sister Teresa Benedicta of the Cross. The beatification was controversial, and it was protested by many Jewish organizations. But the Pontiff was personally consistent in his decision to beatify this woman who had influenced his life by her writings and her example. Two quotes from his beatification homily stand out: "Edith Stein's entire life is characterized by an incessant search for truth and is illuminated by the blessing of the cross of Christ." He also said: "Her own life and the cross she had to bear were intimately connected with the destiny of the Jewish people." In a radio address delivered at that time to the whole of the German nation, the Pontiff spoke of the personal significance of Edith Stein's elevation to the altar as a beata.

Rejoice and be glad, for your reward is great in heaven" [Mt 5:12]. Blessed also is the philosopher Edith Stein. She came from a Jewish family in Breslau and spent several years in the Cologne Carmel as Sister Teresa Benedicta of the Cross. She believed in Jesus, in Jesus as Messiah and Savior, the Redeemer of the world. She sought and found the ultimate meaning of her life in him; she saw her life and death as a sharing in the cross of Christ.

Like Jesus she surrendered herself unreservedly to the Heavenly Father and trusted in his love. As a Catholic Jewess she was killed in the concentration camp of Auschwitz, Birkenau; my countryman Maximilian Kolbe was also murdered in Auschwitz.

As Archbishop of Kraków, I often stood before the wall of the dead and walked among the ruins of the crematorium at Birkenau. I have asked myself again and again: "Where are the frontiers of hate—the frontiers of the destruction of people by people—the frontiers of atrocity?" [Homily, 7 June 1979].

Edith Stein said that "hatred must never have the last word in the world!" ✠

OLAND 1987

THE PONTIFF'S THIRD VISIT TO POLAND, from 8 to 14 June 1987, occurred during a time of great national transition. The issues of human rights, raised by the labor struggles of 1981, continued to prevail and, before long, the Marxist government would collapse. While in the course of this visit he would beatify Karolina Kozka, a young Polish martyr, for the sake of chastity, as well as open the Polish Eucharistic Congress. His most important address was delivered to President Wojciech Jaruzelski and the members of the government.

Today's meeting, on the occasion of my third pilgrimage to our homeland, is taking place in the Royal Castle of Warsaw. This castle, destroyed along with the entire capital during the Second World War, was rebuilt and can continue to witness to the traditions of Poland as a state, and to the history of the independent and sovereign homeland.

The Royal Castle of Warsaw rose from the ruins. They have disappeared, but there has not vanished from the minds of Poles—nor, for that matter, from the minds of many other European peoples— the memory of the Second World War. If in the pronouncements of statesmen, including those of the president of the state council, the word "peace" resounds so frequently, it remains linked first of all with that war, which caused so many victims. I remember being on the soil of the concentration camp of Auschwitz in 1979, and the words I pronounced then as I stopped before the gravestones with inscriptions in nineteen languages. Each gravestone remains, as it were, a mute witness to the terrible slaughter. I remember noting gravestones with inscriptions in Hebrew, Russian, and Polish. Those gravestones testified to the horror of the Second World War and constitute a warning! . . .

This warning echoes in the consciences of peoples, especially of those who in a particular way suffered the atrocities of the war, and among them the Polish nation certainly occupies one of the foremost places. If I recall it today, I do so also with the aim of emphasizing once again the great affirmation of conscience, in a certain sense common to all men, expressed in the Charter of Human Rights. This document forms almost the very basis of the United Nations, whose purpose it is to watch over the peaceful coexistence of nations and states throughout the world.

The last time I was in the homeland, during the difficult days of 1983, my salutation was expressed in these words: "Peace to you, Poland, my homeland!"

Addressing you today, in the Royal Castle of Warsaw, I have before the eyes of my soul the whole history of our homeland, so often marked by the stain of war and destruction. These historical experiences, and especially the experiences of the last war, constitute for us a particular challenge to undertake the "struggle for peace" also in our nation. Can we do so in any other way than by referring to the Charter of Human Rights? In fact, peace between nations and the heart of a society is always the mature fruit of social justice: *opus iustitiae pox*.

Therefore one must begin with society: with men and women who constitute the Poland of the second half of the twentieth century. The Poland of the 1960s, '70s, and '80s!

If each of these human beings possesses his own personal dignity, he has rights that correspond to it. In the name of this dignity, it is right that each and all seek to be not only the object of the directives of state authority and institution, but also their subject. To be a subject means to participate in the management of the public affairs of all the Polish people.

The nation lives its own life authentically only when it experiences its own subjectivity in the whole life of the state. When it is aware of being the master of its own house, of participating in decisions through its work, through its contribution. How essential it is for the life of a society that man not lose faith in his own work, that he not suffer disillusionment because of this work!

I say this because the aforementioned truth is part of the Church's message in the contemporary world, part of the message of peace and justice. I speak in this way also because I am profoundly aware of the difficult period that the life of the nation and the state is passing though: difficult in a socioeconomic sense. ✠

UNITED STATES 1987

FROM 10 TO 20 SEPTEMBER 1987, Pope John Paul responded to an invitation from the bishops of the southern and western regions of the United States, where he addressed the issues of pluralism, migration, and secularism. In a historic visit to Columbia, South Carolina, on 11 September, the Pope met with twenty-seven leaders of Orthodox and Protestant denominations. The Pontiff conferred privately with them about contemporary ecumenical issues. Later, at a prayer vigil in Williams-Brice Stadium at the University of South Carolina, he addressed the challenges of family life in the United States. The twenty-seven religious leaders likewise participated in the service. The ceremonies were concluded by Joseph Cardinal Bernardin, a native son of Columbia, South Carolina. The Pontiff chose the theme of "family as domestic Church" to underscore a major point of ecumenical consensus.

Christian families exist to form *a communion of persons in love.* As such, the Church and the family are, each in its own way, living representations in human history of the eternal loving communion of the three Persons of the Most Holy Trinity. In fact, the family is called the Church in miniature, "the domestic church," a particular expression of the Church through the human experience of love and common life [*Familiaris Consortio,* 49]. Like the Church, the family ought to be a place where the Gospel is transmitted and *from which the Gospel radiates to other families and to the whole of society.*

In America and throughout the world, *the family is being shaken* to its roots. The consequences for individuals and society in personal and collective instability and unhappiness are incalculable. Yet, it is heartening to know that in the face of this extraordinary challenge many Christians are committing themselves to the defense and support of family life. In recent years the Catholic Church, especially on the occasion of the 1980 Synod of the world's bishops, has been involved in an extensive reflection on the role of the Christian family in the modern world. This is a field in which there must be the maximum collaboration among all who confess Jesus Christ.

So often the pressures of modern living separate husbands and wives from one another, threatening their lifelong *interdependence in love and fidelity*. Can we also not be concerned about the impact of cultural pressures upon *relations between the generations*, upon parental authority and the transmission of sacred values? Our Christian conscience should be deeply concerned about the way in which *sins against love and against life* are often presented as examples of "progress" and emancipation. Most often, are they not but the age-old forms of selfishness dressed up in a new language and presented in a new cultural framework?

Many of these problems are the result of a *false notion of individual freedom at work in our culture,* as if one could be free only when rejecting every objective norm of conduct, refusing to assume responsibility, or even refusing to put curbs on instincts and passions! Instead, *true freedom* implies that we are capable of choosing a good, without constraint. This is the only human way of proceeding in the choices—big and small—which life puts before us. The fact that we are also able to choose *not* to act as we see we should is a necessary condition of our moral freedom. But in that case we must account for the good that we fail to do and for the evil that we commit. This sense of moral accountability needs to be reawakened if society is to survive as a civilization of justice and solidarity.

It is true that our freedom is weakened and conditioned in many ways, not least as a consequence of the mysterious and dramatic history of mankind's original rebellion against the Creator's will, as indicated in the opening pages of the book of Genesis. But *we remain free and responsible beings* who have been redeemed by Jesus Christ, and we must *educate our freedom* to recognize and choose what is right and good, and to reject what does not conform to the original truth concerning our nature and our destiny as God's creatures. *Truth*—beginning with the truth of our redemption through the Cross and Resurrection of Jesus Christ—*is the root and rule of freedom, the foundation and measure of all liberating action* [cf. *Instruction on Christian Freedom and Liberation,* 3].

It would be a great tragedy for the entire human family if the United States, which prides itself on its consecration to freedom, were to lose sight of the true meaning of the noble word. America: You cannot insist on the right to choose, without also insisting on *the duty to choose well, the duty to choose the truth!*

Toward the end of his visit, on 17 September, Pope John Paul visited the historic Mission Dolores Shrine in San Francisco. Founded by Blessed Junipero Serra, this church and the Franciscan convent attached to it, remain a memorial to the evangelical efforts of the early Spanish friars who spent themselves in the service of God in the eighteenth century. Here, in a Franciscan-like context, the Pope spoke on the love of God for those who suffer.

I t is also true to say that *God's love for us is like that of a mother.* In this regard, God asks us, through the prophet Isaiah: "Can a mother forget her infant, be without tenderness for the child of her womb? Even should she forget, I will never forget you" [Is 49:15]. God's love is tender and merciful, patient and full of understanding. In the Scriptures, and also in the living memory of the Church, the love of God is indeed depicted and has been experienced as *the compassionate love of a mother.*

Jesus himself expressed a compassionate love when he wept over Jerusalem, and when he said: "O Jerusalem, Jerusalem. . . . How often would I have gathered your children together as a hen gathers her brood under her wings" [Lk 13:34].

Dear friends in Christ: The love of God is so great that it goes *beyond the limits of human language,* beyond the grasp of artistic expression, beyond human understanding. And yet, it is *concretely embodied in God's Son, Jesus Christ,* and in his Body, the Church. Once again this evening, here in Mission Dolores Basilica, I repeat to all of you the ageless proclamation of the Gospel: God loves you!

God loves you all, without distinction, without limit. He loves those of you who are elderly, who feel the burden of the years. He loves those of you who are sick, those who are suffering from AIDS and from AIDS-related complex. He loves the relatives and the friends of the sick and those who care for them. He loves us all with an unconditional and everlasting love.

In the spirit of Saint Francis, then, I urge you all to open your hearts to God's love, to respond by your prayers and by the deeds of your lives. Let go of your doubts and fears, and let the mercy of God draw you to his heart. ✠

ANADA 1987

FOLLOWING HIS TRIP TO THE UNITED STATES, Pope John Paul spent a day with the Native American peoples of Canada. His address was delivered in French and in English. With this visit he wanted to show that the nature of his global travels was not only as a pilgrimage but as a missionary journey. He placed himself in the footsteps of the great missionaries to Canada in the sixteenth and seventeenth centuries.

I come to you, then, like so many missionaries before me who have proclaimed the name of Jesus among the native peoples of Canada—the Indians, Inuit, and Metis—and have learned to love you and the spiritual and cultural treasures of your way of life. They have shown respect for your patrimony, your languages, and your customs [*Ad gentes,* 26]. As I remarked on the occasion of my previous visit, the "rebirth of your culture and traditions which you are experiencing today owes much to the pioneering and continuing efforts of missionaries" [address at Yellow Knife, 18 September 1984, n. 2]. Indeed, the missionaries "remain among your best friends, devoting their lives to your service, as they preach the Word of God" [ibid.]. I too come to you as a friend. ✠

BOLIVIA 1988

THE HOLY FATHER ARRIVED IN BOLIVIA on 9 May 1988 at La Paz, where he greeted both civil and religious leaders. Visiting many cities over five days, he arrived in Tarija on 13 May, where he celebrated the Liturgy of the Word at the airport. The Pope directed his homily to children, stating the need for health and education for them, as well as encouraging them to grow and develop in the faith.

My dear *"changuitos"*: The Lord chose to become a child like you, and to grow "in wisdom, stature, and grace before God and men" [see Lk 2:52]. He wanted his arrival to be announced first of all to shepherds who were watching their flocks at night [see Lk 2:8–20], and to be known as the carpenter [see Mk 6:3] or "the son of the carpenter" [Mt 13:55]. He traveled on foot the great distances of Palestine [see Jn 4:6], and many times "he did not even have a place to lay his head" [Mt 8:20].

Jesus hopes that you will grow up like him, "in wisdom," by not leaving school, by studying and fulfilling your school duties. The Pope knows that it involves sacrifice on your part, because many times you have to go through rain or snow, covering great distances on foot through very cold regions, and even after a day of tiring work. Continue your efforts and do not be discouraged, because the Lord is pleased with what you are doing.

Learn the catechism well. In this way you will be able to know the Child Jesus better each time; make him your best friend, and you will learn to love God above all things.

Jesus wants you, like him, to grow also "in grace." For this you have to fulfill the Sunday obligation, whenever circumstances do not prevent you from doing so, and grow in grace by receiving the sacraments. Prepare yourselves well for First Confession and First Communion, and continue to receive Jesus often. Afterwards, when you grow a little bigger, prepare yourselves to receive the Sacrament of Confirmation, which will help you to be witnesses of Christ.

Like him, who "grew in stature," you should develop yourselves in body and spirit as perfect men and women. Obey your parents, loving and helping them, as is the tradition among your people. Share your play and your work with your brothers, sisters, and friends. Always tell the truth. Do not take what does not belong to you. Be strong in your tasks, in your studies, and in recreation.

Children of Bolivia, the Pope prays for you, but he also relies on you. Therefore, I ask you to accompany me with your prayers, and with that part of the Lord's burden which he has permitted you to take upon your shoulders. Continue on this path of love, and Jesus will always fill you with happiness [see Mt 11:28–30]. ✠

*U*RUGUAY 1988

THE HOLY FATHER CONSIDERS HIS VISIT TO LATIN AMERICA from 7 to 9 May 1988, a continuation of the brief visit he made only thirteen months earlier. Well aware that his arrival closely coincided with the fifth centenary of the arrival of Christianity to the South American continent, the Pope underscores evangelization, justice, and human dignity as he travels and greets. This excerpt comes from a Mass in Salto, Uruguay, on 9 May:

My brothers and sisters, the year is approaching when the American continents, and particularly Latin America, will give thanks to the Blessed Trinity for five hundred years of evangelization—that is, for the five hundredth anniversary of the arrival of the "Good News" to what was at that time "the end of the earth." Disciples of Christ proclaimed the Gospel in the lands recently discovered. Then, as now, the words which the Master spoke still applied: "He who believes and is baptized will be saved; but he who does not believe will be condemned" [Mk 16:16]. The first evangelizers, conscious of that precept and moved by faith in those words of

Christ and by the love of souls, worked in an admirable way to bring Christ to the recently discovered peoples. At the same time, they carried out a prodigious work of social and cultural advancement, which today is the pride and patrimony of the entire continent, and forms part of the national identity of all these countries. Some of the fruits of this work of civilization include outstanding examples of artistic and literary work, grammars and catechisms in the main indigenous languages, the ordinances and laws of the Indies.

The resolute work of so many priests, religious, and laypeople, and the flame of the faith which is always alive in Christian families, true domestic churches, have made possible the continuity of that first evangelization and the joyful reality of Christian life which I have experienced during my stay among you. Your presence here is a clear sign of this "fruit" [Ps 84 (85):13], which the "earth" [ibid.], watered by the rain of the Lord, has yielded. All of you who join me in this Eucharist are part of that garland and those jewels [see Is 61:10] with which God adorns those who are faithful, those who do not cease in their effort to maintain the faith in this country. ✠

$\mathscr{P}$ERU 1988

POPE JOHN PAUL II'S ARRIVAL IN PERU coincided with the closing of the fifth Eucharistic and Marian Congress of the Bolivian nations. The following day in Lima, on the Feast of the Ascension, the Holy Father celebrated the Mass for the official closing of the Congress and preached on the relationship of the Eucharist to the mission of witnessing to Christ.

Every time that we participate in the Eucharist, we are more closely united to Christ, and in him, to all people, with a more perfect bond then any natural union. Thus united, we are sent into the whole world to bear witness to God's love through faith and works of service to others, preparing for the coming of his Kingdom and anticipating it in the shadows of this present time. We also discover the profound sense of our action in the world in favor of development and peace, and we receive from him the energy to pledge ourselves to this mission more generously each time [cf. *Sollicitudo Rei Socialis,* 48]. Thus, we will construct a new civilization: the civilization of love. A civilization which, here in Peru, has formed chosen souls such as Saint Turibius de Mogrovejo, Saint Rose of Lima, Saint Martin de Porres, Saint Francis Solanus, Saint John Marcias, Blessed Ann de Los Angeles, and many other exemplary Christians who, through the testimony of their lives and their works of charity have given us a shining way of authentic preferential love for the poor according to the Gospel. A civilization which, on this basis of love of the person who is near us—our neighbor—will transform structures and the whole world. ✠

PARAGUAY 1988

THE SIXTEENTH OF MAY 1988 marked Pope John Paul's first visit to Paraguay, at the invitation of both its president and its episcopacy. On that same day in Asunción, the Holy Father celebrated a Mass of Canonization for three Jesuit martyrs—Father Rogue Gonzalez de Santa Cruz, the first native saint, and two companions, Father Alfonso Rodriguez and Father Juan del Castillo, both from Spain.

A ll of them spent their lives fulfilling Christ's command to announce his message "to the ends of the earth" [Acts 1:8]. The saving and liberating force of the Gospel became alive in these selfless Jesuit priests, whom the Church presents today as model evangelizers. Their unshakable faith in God, nourished at all times by a deep interior life, was the great force that sustained these pioneers of the Gospel here in these American lands. Their zeal for souls led them to do everything they could to serve the poorest and most abandoned. All their exemplary activities in favor of those peoples—so much in need of spiritual and human help— all their hardships and sufferings had as their sole objective the transmission of the great treasure of which they were the bearers: faith in Jesus Christ, Savior and Liberator of humanity, conqueror of sin and death.

The pastors and the entire People of God dwelling in Paraguay, as well as the other sister nations of the basin of the River de Plata whose worthy representatives are among us, will find in these new saints models and sure guides in their pilgrim journey to Jerusalem, the heavenly homeland. The fact that they are venerated in all the countries of the south of this continent of hope not only reveals the presence of a faith that knows no frontiers, but should also encourage you to promote in these nations an ever more living and practical consciousness of the Christian ideal of fraternity, based on common religious, cultural, and historical roots. ✠

AUSTRIA 1988

AT THE INVITATION OF ITS BISHOPS, Pope John Paul II made his second apostolic visit to Austria, commencing on 23 June 1988. The next day, the Feast of the Birth of John the Baptist, the Holy Father celebrated Mass for the faithful of the Diocese of Eisenstadt. In his homily on this occasion, he reflected on the sacredness and dignity of human life within the context of John the Baptist's miraculous conception.

M an is that being which God calls by name. For God he is the created "you."

Dear brothers and sisters, how do we people answer this, our divine calling? How does modern man understand his life?

In no other time has there been a greater effort in technology and medicine to protect human life from illness, to prolong it and to save it from death. At the same time, there has hardly been another age which has seen as many places and methods of contempt for and annihilation of human life as the present one. The bitter experiences of our century, with the death machinery of two world wars, the persecution and annihilation of whole groups of people because of their ethnic or religious origin, the atomic arms race right up to the present hour, the helplessness of people faced with poverty in many parts of the world, could mislead us into doubting or even denying God's concern and love for mankind and all creation.

Or should we not, precisely because we are faced with these terrible events which have befallen the world through man, and with the many threats of our time, ask just the opposite? Has man not distanced himself from God, his origin; has he not turned away from him, and made himself the center and measure of life? Do not the experiments with human life which violate human dignity, the attitude of many toward abortion and euthanasia, reveal an alarming loss of respect for life? Is it not increasingly clear in your society, from the fate of many individuals, characterized by emptiness, anxiety, and escape, that man has cut himself off from his own roots? Must we not recognize sexualization, alcoholism, and drug consumption as alarms? Do they not indicate the great loneliness of the person of today, a longing for care, a hunger for love which a world turned in on itself cannot satisfy?

In fact, without connection to his root, which is God, man becomes impoverished of inner worth and gradually succumbs to the many threats. We learn from history that individuals and peoples who believe they can do without God always surrender to the catastrophe of self-destruction. The poet Ernst Wiechert said it so well: "Rest assured, no one turns away from the world who has not first turned away from God."

From a living relationship with God, on the other hand, grows an awareness of the uniqueness and value of one's life and personal dignity. Amid his concrete life situations, man knows he is called, sustained, and spurred on by God. In spite of prevailing injustices and personal suffering, he realizes that life is a gift. He is grateful for it and feels responsible to God for it. Thus God becomes the source of power and trust from which the person is able to shape a life of human dignity and selfless service to others. ✠

IMBABWE 1988

ON 10 SEPTEMBER 1988, Pope John Paul concluded his summer vacation at Castel Gondolfo and traveled immediately to Zimbabwe to begin a nine-day tour of Southern Africa, where he would visit five countries. On 11 September, the Pope celebrated Mass in Harare and delivered a homily on baptism and reconciliation. There he gave a brief description of his own role as Bishop of Rome, Successor to Peter.

Today, I stand in your midst as the Bishop of Rome and I make this joyful proclamation: "The Lord is my Shepherd."

I make it together with you, with the whole Church, and with all the People of God who dwell in your country, Zimbabwe.

"The Lord is my Shepherd."

I come to you as a pastor. I come in the name of the Lord who is our Shepherd. I come in the name of Jesus Christ, the Good Shepherd, the Eternal Pastor of our souls. And in his name I extend most cordial greetings to all those who constitute the Church in Zimbabwe.

At your invitation I have willingly come to Zimbabwe. I have come as the Successor of Peter and Bishop of Rome, who has inherited a particular mission and responsibility, linked with the witness of the Apostles Peter and Paul. For Peter and Paul strengthened the very foundation of the Church by their apostolic service, and above all by their death as martyrs, giving their lives for Christ, for the truth which is Christ himself. This truth they have faithfully handed on to all generations of the Church. This same truth I come to proclaim to you, as the Successor of Peter in the last part of the twentieth century. Ever since the time of the Apostles, the Church has built on this truth, not only in Rome but throughout the entire world. In your country, too, the Church of Christ builds on this truth, in communion with the Apostolic See of Rome. ✠

BOTSWANA 1988

THE HOLY FATHER ARRIVED ON 13 SEPTEMBER 1988 in Botswana. Later that same day, the Pope celebrated Mass in Gaborone Stadium and gave a discourse on the demands of love and the sacraments in the lives of the faithful.

The reconciliation of all human beings with God and with each other which Christ accomplished on the Cross is at the heart of every celebration of the sacraments. As we read in one of our liturgical texts, "From [Christ's] wounded side flowed blood and water, the fountain of sacramental life in the Church" [Preface of the Sacred Heart]. Dear brothers and sisters, we cannot emphasize enough the importance of this sacramental life. Sacraments make us sharers in the reconciliation and communion that are essential for our own peace and for the peace of the world. They strengthen us for the daily struggle to turn away from sin and to believe in the Gospel. They nourish us with the very life of God. For the Christian community the forgiveness of Christ comes to us in a special way through baptism and the sacrament of Penance.

Sacramental life, in its deepest sense, is the very heart of the Church in Botswana, as it is for every local Church. The first missionaries had a burning desire to bring to this land a new life, in Christ, both by word and sacrament. Their witness to the Gospel was inseparable from their commitment to justice and peace and from their vision of a world reconciled and redeemed. The sacraments not only sustained them, but also made their labors fruitful in the lives of your forebears and in the lives of each of you today, for we know that as actions of Christ, sacraments bring about what they signify; they are alive with the power of God. Each of you has responded to God's offer of reconciliation and peace by your faith and baptism and by your commitment to participate in the Church's sacramental life. ✠

OUTH AFRICA 1988

ARRIVING IN LESOTHO ON 14 SEPTEMBER, the Feast of the Triumph of the Cross, the Pope proceeded directly to the cocathedral of Roma. In the context of the feast, he preached a homily on the Cross and the salvation it brings. The Pontiff beatified the Venerable Father Joseph Gérard, a French missionary of the nineteenth century, noted for his piety and his zealous foundation of many missions in Lesotho. The message of the Holy Cross dominated the duration of the Pope's visit.

Yes, it is through the Cross that Christ is exalted. Today's feast of the Church speaks to us of this mystery. At the same time, it speaks of Christ, who by means of the Cross lifts up humanity, lifts up all humanity and indeed all creation. "For God sent his Son into the world, not to condemn the world, but so that through him the world might be saved" [Jn 3:17].

Being "saved" means that every man and woman can be healed of the sin that poisoned the human family and all history. Jesus says to his Apostles after his Resurrection: "Those whose sins you forgive, they are forgiven" [Jn 20:23]. And as he says it he shows them the wounds of his crucifixion, to let them know that it is precisely in the Cross that the power to forgive sins is hidden, the power to heal consciences and human hearts.

Generation after generation passes. And in the midst of this passing, the Cross of Christ remains. Through the Cross, God continuously proclaims to the world the infinite love which no created evil is able to overcome. Yes, the Cross remains, so that in it the world, indeed every human person, may find the way of salvation. For it is by this Cross that the world is saved! ✠

WAZILAND 1988

THE HOLY FATHER MADE A BRIEF STOPOVER IN SWAZILAND on 16 September where, after being greeted at the Matsapha International Airport, he went to the Somhlolo Stadium to celebrate Mass for the faithful. Preaching his homily on the individual's obligation to strive for peace, the Pope also remarked on the peace that should exist within each family and which is founded on marital love and fidelity.

Like the Holy Family of Nazareth, every family in Swaziland, every family in the world, is built on love and exists for love. As I stated in my Apostolic Exhortation on the Role of the Family in the Modern World, "the family has the mission to guard, reveal, and communicate love, and this is a living reflection of, and a real sharing in, God's love for humanity and the love of Christ the Lord for the Church his Bride" [*Familiaris Consortio,* 17].

In family life, the love between husband and wife is of primary importance. For if a family is to be true to its own nature as an intimate community of life and love, then husband and wife must form a loving communion of total and mutual self-giving. God our Creator has established natural complementarity and equal dignity between man and woman, which facilitate and favor this communion. Furthermore, as a special source of grace, Christ instituted the sacrament of Matrimony, in which the Holy Spirit is poured forth on a couple to be their light and wisdom, to give them the strength to remain faithful for all of life to their marriage vows. Christian marriage, then, is characterized by a special bond of unity and indissolubility, for Christ gives to each couple the grace to overcome all obstacles to a lifelong and exclusive union in love.

For this reason, Christians find that a monogamous marital union provides the foundation upon which to build a stable family, in accordance with the original plan of God for marriage. "From the beginning," God founded the marriage covenant on the equal personal dignity of men and women, "who in matrimony give themselves with a love that is total and therefore unique and exclusive" [*Familiaris Consortio*, 19]. Hence, all forms of disregard for the equal dignity of men and women must be seen as serious contradictions of the truth that Christ, the King of Peace, has brought into the world.

At the same time, it is important to recognize the positive practices and values which strengthen and support marriage and family life. These include the worthy traditional Swazi values and practices that have come down to you. It has been a constant tradition of the Church to receive from various cultures everything that helps to express better the unfathomable riches of Christ. Your culture can enrich the whole Church to the degree that it is filled with human wisdom and enlivened by moral values [*Familiaris Consortio*, 10]. ✠

*M*OZAMBIQUE 1988

POPE JOHN PAUL II CONCLUDED HIS PILGRIMAGE to Southern Africa in Mozambique, spending three days there beginning 16 September. On 18 September, the Pontiff went to St. Anthony Church in Maputo where, during evening prayer, he spoke to priests, religious, seminarians, and committed laypeople on consecrated life.

The maturity and continuity of a particular Church depend also upon the consecrated life. In Mozambique, it is now a time of great hope: a consoling time that sees the flowering of women's vocations in the dioceses and the appearance of new institutes also. These hopes will be confirmed if there is a profound and careful formation of the new Mozambican religious within the right framework: a vision of faith, which nourishes generosity and perfection in charity, continued prayer-dialogue with God [Jn 15:5], and a bond with a certain institute and its charism, despite immediate concerns.

The concrete model of life that you offer is, in itself, valuable, most of all for the young people—with your availability, your detachment, your competence, and your diligence—in the community, in teaching, in caring for the sick, and in assistance to the poor of every kind, in your promotion of women and literacy. Always remember that, in all this, you must let the gift of Redemption, which is expressed in the evangelical counsels, shine forth, as "living hosts, holy and pleasing to God" [cf. Rom 12:1], in a constant attitude of praise. Be persevering in prayer, joyful in your dedication, and enthusiastic in your vocation! ✠

FRANCE 1998

POPE JOHN PAUL II VISITED FRANCE FROM 8 TO 11 OCTOBER 1988, for the specific purpose of addressing the parliamentary assembly of the Council of Europe in Strasbourg. In his speech the Pontiff looked forward in hope to a united Europe, and he praised forty years of cooperation between the Western European nations, which he saw as a cornerstone to a bright and hopeful future. He singled out the vision of those whom he called the "fathers of modern Europe": Jean Monnet, Konrad Adenauer, Alcide De Gasperi, and Robert Schuman.

After greeting President Mitterand, he proceeded to the headquarters of the Council of Europe. This address was the first on his agenda.

I t is true that the men and women of this old continent with such a tormented history need to regain the awareness of that which forms their common identity, of that which dwells in their vast collective memory. Indeed, the European identity is not a reality that is easy to understand. The distant springs of that civilization are many, coming from Greece and Rome, from Celtic, Germanic, and Slavic sources, from Christianity, which profoundly shaped it. We know what a diversity of languages, cultures, and juridical traditions mark the nations, regions, and also the institutions. However, in the eyes of the other continents, Europe is a single unity, even if its co-hesiveness is less clearly perceived by those who constitute it. This viewpoint can aid it in rediscovering itself.

In almost twenty centuries Christianity has contributed to the shaping and understanding of the world and the human person which today still have a fundamental relevance, despite the divisions, weaknesses, and even abandonment by Christians themselves. Please allow me to recall here some of the essential characteristics. The Christian message translates such a close relationship of the human being with his Creator that it enhances all aspects of life, beginning with physical life: the body and the cosmos are God's work and gift. Faith in God the Creator has demythologized the cosmos in order to open it up to mankind's rational investigation. Mastering his body and exercising dominion over the earth, the human person uses his "creative" capacities; in the Christian vision the human being, far from scorning the physical universe, has it freely and fearlessly at his disposal. This positive vision has greatly contributed to the development of science and technology among Europeans.

At peace with the cosmos, the Christian has also learned to re-spect the inestimable value of each person created in God's image and ransomed by Christ. Gather together in families, cities, and peo-ples, human beings do not live and suffer in vain: Christianity teaches them that history is not a meaningless cycle in perpetual repetition, but that it finds meaning in the covenant that God offers to people to invite them to accept freely his Kingdom.

The biblical concept of man has permitted Europeans to develop a lofty understanding of the dignity of the person, which retains an es-sential value even among those who do not adhere to a religious faith.

The Church affirms that in man there is an indomitable awareness of the conditions that affect him, a consciousness capable of recognizing his true dignity and being open to the absolute, a consciousness that is the source of fundamental choices guided by the search for good for others as well as for self, a consciousness that is the place of a responsible freedom.

It is true that there has been a lot of drifting away, and Christians know that they have played a part in it. The person as the unique subject of rights and duties has often been replaced by the individual, a prisoner of his own selfishness, who thinks he is an end unto himself. On the other hand the exaltation of the group, nation, or race has led to totalitarian and murderous ideologies. Everywhere pragmatic or theoretical materialism has threatened the spiritual nature of man and tragically reduced his reasons for living. Democracies have the honor of looking for an organization of society that will enable the person to be not only respected in all that he is, but also to participate in the common task in the exercise of his free will.

Your Council has been faithful to this heritage of the European conscience in taking as its main task the proclamation and protection of human rights. By ratifying the Convention for the Safeguard of Human Rights and Basic Freedoms the member states decided to strengthen their union around the most noble Christian principles and values of the European tradition. In order to ensure their application everywhere, they instituted the European Court and Commission for Human Rights, recognizing in them a competence and juridical authority that is unique among international organizations.

Ladies and gentlemen, if Europe wants to be faithful to itself, it must be able to gather all the living forces of this continent, respecting the original character of each region but rediscovering in its roots a common spirit. The member countries of your Council are aware that they are not the whole of Europe. In expressing the ardent wish to see intensified the cooperation, already taking shape, with other nations, particularly those of the center and east, I have the feeling of gathering together the desire of millions of men and women who know that they are bound together by a common history and who await a destiny of unity and solidarity on the scale of this continent.

Over the centuries Europe has played a considerable role in other parts of the world. We must admit that while it has not always given its best in the encounter with other civilizations, no one can deny that it fortunately shared many of the values which it had developed over the years. If Europe wants to play a role today, it must, in unity, clearly base its action on that which is most human and most generous in its heritage.

ON 11 OCTOBER, the Pope again addressed the issue of European unity before the entire European Parliament. Following the style of Pope Paul VI, he cited the "signs of the times." Among them he listed an atmosphere of peace and cooperation; a common sensitivity to human rights and the value of democracy; an economic cooperation that crosses the frontiers of nations. He praised the Single European Act which facilitates new common political structures, allowing for easier communication and transportation. This was to go into effect in 1992. He also spoke of the role of the Church in encouraging such positive action in building the peace.

Since the end of the last World War, the Holy See has not ceased to encourage the development of Europe. Assuredly, the Church's mission is to make known to all people their salvation in Jesus Christ, whatever the conditions of their present history, since this is her inalienable task. In addition, without departing from her own area of competence, it is the Church's duty to clarify and accompany the initiatives people develop which are in accord with the values which she must proclaim; at the same time she must remain attentive to the signs of the times which call for the permanent demands of the Gospel to be translated within the changing realities of existence.

How could the Church not be interested in the development of Europe, a Church which for centuries has been implanted in the people that constitute it and brought them to the baptismal fonts, people for whom the Christian faith is and remains one of the elements of their cultural identity?

After Christ, it is no longer possible to idolize society as a collective greatness that devours the human person and his inalienable destiny. Society, the state, and political power belong to the changing and always perfectible framework of this world. No plan of society will ever be able to establish the Kingdom of God, that is, eschatological perfection on this earth. Political messianism most often leads to the worst tyrannies. The structures that societies set up for themselves never have a definitive value; they can no longer seek for themselves all the goods to which man aspires. In particular, they cannot be a substitute for human conscience or for the search for truth and the absolute.

Public life and the good order of the state rest on the virtue of the citizens, which invites them to subordinate their individual interests to the common good, to establish and recognize as law only that which is objectively true and good. The ancient Greeks already discovered that there can be no democracy without the subjection of all to law, nor can there be any law that is not based on a transcendent norm of the true and just. ✠

PART III

NEW EVANGELIZATION: TOWARD THE MILLENNIUM AND BEYOND

MADAGASCAR 1989

THE TWENTY-EIGHTH OF APRIL 1989 marked the beginning of Pope John Paul's forty-first apostolic visit, an eight-day pilgrimage through four countries of Africa: Madagascar, Réunion, Zambia, and Malawi. Always aware of the social and material needs of the peoples he visited, the Pope often stressed the importance of dialogue and justice. In Madagascar, on 30 April, he addressed various diplomats accredited to that country on issues of development, drug control, and the environment.

More and more, world opinion is becoming aware of the precious good that the earth is, together with all that it contains and produces. People speak of the "environment"; it is a matter of the context in which man must live; it involves nature, which has been entrusted to him. We know the threats which weigh upon entire regions because of thoughtless exploitation or uncontrolled pollution. To protect against the erosion of the soil, to avoid the spread of toxic substances which are dangerous to man, animals, and plants, to safeguard the atmosphere, all these imperatives can be taken into consideration only by an active and informed cooperation, for which frontiers must be crossed without obstacles, and struggles for influence must be overcome.

Welcomed on a "Great Island" where such difficulties are felt, I deem it necessary to recall the seriousness of the situation. It is urgent that the international community create the juridical and technical means to guarantee the protection of the environment, to prevent abuses inspired by what must be acknowledged as selfishness, to the detriment of others.

The Christian faith believes that God made man the master of the earth. That means that he is responsible for it, that he is more the steward than the discretionary owner. He must pass it on, living and fruitful, to the coming generations. ✠

RÉUNION 1989

ON 1 MAY 1989, Pope John Paul arrived for a brief visit in Réunion, where he was welcomed by civil and religious authorities at Gillot Airport in Saint-Denis. Later in the day, at the Cathedral of Saint Denis, the Pope delivered an address to priests and pastoral representatives on the topic of the mission of the local church and its parishes.

Having invited you to breathe new life into the family apostolate, I should like to encourage you to rediscover the true image of the parish, that is, the very mystery of the Church, living and acting in the parish. Before ever being a structure, the parish is "a family home, fraternal and welcoming, in which the baptized and those who are confirmed are aware of being God's people. Therein the bread of true doctrine and the Bread of the Eucharist are abundantly broken before them . . . : from it, daily, they are sent out on their apostolic mission into all the workplaces of the world's life" [*Cathechesi Tradendae*, 67].

The participants at the last Synod of Bishops expressed the wish that the parishes would more resolutely renew themselves by encouraging the participation of laity in pastoral responsibilities. The action of lay men and women is, in fact, so necessary in the parishes that without it the apostolate of pastors cannot have its full effect. We return once again, my brothers and sisters, to what is to be the theme of this meeting, the ecclesiology of communion. Because they are diverse and complementary, ministries and charisms have each their proper part to play in the growth of the Church.

The parish, which represents the Church's presence amid the dwellings of men, provides the possibility of experiencing and cultivating, day after day, more fraternal relations between faithful of diverse origins and circumstances. It is the first place for community celebration of the Lord's presence acknowledged in faith. It is the pole of the apostolate, and it awakes missionary drive toward the unbeliever or the half believer. It is open to everyone, at everyone's service, or—to take up again a phrase of John XXIII—it is the "village fountain" to which all come to slake their thirst.

The Second Vatican Council encouraged the examination and the search for answers to pastoral problems with the participation of all the parishioners. Here we have the *raison d'être* of the parish pastoral council, on which the Fathers at the latest Synod rightly insisted and which must be strengthened. I encourage you to keep working to set up "parish councils for pastoral animation" so as to reinforce the cohesion of all those among you who work in the apostolate and to put the parish in a state of mission. ✠

AMBIA 1989

ON THE AFTERNOON OF 2 MAY 1989, the Pope flew from Réunion to Lusaka, Zambia, where he was greeted by civil and religious authorities. On 3 May, Pope John Paul II addressed a gathering of diplomats in Mulungushi Hall, Lusaka, on the issues of racism, international debt, and solidarity.

The problem of international debt is a clear example of the interdependence which characterizes relations between countries and continents. It is a problem which cannot be solved without mutual understanding and agreement between debtor and creditor nations, without sensitivity to the real circumstances of indebted nations on the part of creditor agencies, and without a wise and committed policy of growth on the part of the developing nations themselves. Is it merely a rhetorical question to ask how many infants and children die every day in Africa because resources are now being swallowed up in debt repayment? There is no time now to lament policies of the past or those elements in the international financial and economic picture which have led to the present situation. Now is the time for a new and courageous international solidarity, a solidarity not based on self-interest but inspired and guided by a true concern for human beings.

Recent moves on the part of the developed and creditor countries to lessen the burdens of repayment on the economies of debtor nations are obviously a step in the right direction. Such moves deserve to be encouraged. But much more remains to be done. It is to the ethical and moral values involved that the Church primarily directs her attention. Her appeal is to the conscience and the heart of those who can bring about a just solution to the problem, in respect for the equal dignity of all people. It is her task, in obedience to the Gospel, always and everywhere, to emphasize justice, reconciliation, and love. It has become more and more evident that measures of solidarity are imperative so that hope may be restored to many sorely tried peoples. I pray that those in a position to influence events will truly express that solidarity in a new and generous approach to the problems of the international debt. ✠

MALAWI 1989

WITH HIS ARRIVAL AT CHILEKA AIRPORT IN MALAWI on 4 May 1989, Pope John Paul II began the final phase of his eight-day pilgrimage. The following day at Our Lady of Wisdom School in Blantyre, the Holy Father addressed lay leaders on the issues of the apostolate of witness and of holiness.

B ut the lay apostolate here and throughout the world has been given fresh vigor and renewed meaning by the Second Vatican Council. In the spirit of the Council, I urge all of you to continue growing in the knowledge of the new life of grace that is yours by baptism, and to let that new life transform your thoughts, words, and actions for the glory of God and the salvation of the world, so that you may participate fully in the Church's life and mission.

The heart and soul of this participation is the universal call to holiness, the perfection of charity, which is central to the Council's teaching [*Lumen Gentium*, ch. 5]. Holiness is our vocation. Holiness is the fulfillment of our dignity as persons created in God's image and likeness and redeemed by the blood of the Lamb. It is the saints who are the flowering of the Church and her greatest treasure. In every age God renews the Church "by raising up men and women outstanding in holiness, living witnesses of his unchanging love" [Preface II for Holy Men and Women].

Holiness is the fruit of "life in the Spirit" [Gal 5]: a life which impels the baptized person to follow and imitate Christ by living the Beatitudes, by heeding God's word, by taking part in the Church's sacramental and liturgical life, as well as by personal prayer, and above all by practicing the commandment of love and service, especially to the poor and suffering [*Christifideles Laici*, 16]. "Life in the Spirit" touches every aspect of human existence, from the inner shrine of personal conscience to the most visible of public acts. ✠

NORWAY 1989

THE VISIT OF POPE JOHN PAUL II TO SCANDINAVIA from 1 to 10 June 1989 was ecumenical and devotional. In a certain sense it could be said that the two motives were but one expression of piety, whereby he recognized authentic centers of spirituality and ecclesial identity in the Church life of the Scandinavian nations. The Pope's itinerary included Norway, Iceland, Finland, Denmark, and Sweden. The Pope spoke of his intentions when he landed in Norway to be greeted by the prime minister, Mme Gro Harlem Brundtland, on 1 June 1989.

My visit to the Nordic countries is a confirmation of the Catholic Church's commitment to the ecumenical task of fostering unity among all Christians. Twenty-five years ago the Second Vatican Council clearly impressed the urgency of this challenge on the Church. My predecessors have pursued this goal with persevering attention to the grace of the Holy Spirit, who is the divine source and guarantor of the ecumenical movement. From the beginning of my pontificate I have made ecumenism a priority of my pastoral concern and action. God grant that my visit will bring us ever closer to that full fellowship in faith and love which Christ himself wished for his followers [Jn 17:21].

I have come to the Nordic countries as a spiritual pilgrim to honor the memory of the saints who called your ancestors to the faith, led them to baptism, and bore valiant witness to Christ, even at times to the shedding of their blood for his sake. The great saints of the North were men and women rooted in their own historical context, individuals who knew how to apply the message of God's eternal love— revealed in Jesus Christ—to the important questions affecting their peoples and the world around them. Their example still speaks to us today about the profound truths and values on which the whole of European civilization is built and in which your own Norwegian culture developed—truths and values which have lost nothing of their relevance for contemporary society, since they reveal "man's deepest sphere" and give back "meaning to his life in the world" [*Redemptor Hominis*, 10]. To remember the events and influences which have shaped a nation is to understand better the sources of its present historical direction. ✠

ICELAND 1989

ON 3 JUNE 1989, the Pontiff traveled to Iceland, where he was greeted by the president of the republic, Mme Vigdís Finnbogadóttir. While in Norway he had cited contemporary issues such as the United Nations peacekeeping force and the safe haven for refugees afforded by all the Scandinavian countries. In Iceland he firmly held to the ecumenical context and to the spirituality of the Norsemen. He gave the world a small lesson in history.

The Christian religion was brought to Iceland by missionaries who responded to the words of Christ which we have just heard from the Gospel according to Saint Matthew: "Go therefore and make disciples of all nations, baptizing them in the name of the Father and of the Son and of the Holy Spirit, teaching them to observe all that I have commanded you" [Mt 28:19–20]. Your ancestors answered this call by accepting Christ and striving to forge a society based on his teachings. A great Christian era of religion, culture, and sanctity began, so that the words of the Psalmist can well express what was accomplished by faith for centuries afterwards: "O Lord, you have been our refuge from one generation to the next" [Ps 90:1].

More than five hundred years later the divisions which shook Christian Europe were brought here. A painful time in Christian history had begun, and the effects of it persist to this day. The staunch Bishop Jon Aranson resisted the shifts taking place in Icelandic faith and culture and gave his life for his beliefs. Frail and human though he was, he showed the typical courage of an Icelander, a churchman, and a bishop by shedding his blood at Skalholt.

Yet the changes became accepted. In this new context, too, many Icelanders served the Lord in holiness and were generous in works of evangelical love and mercy. To mention one example, the great Hallgrimur Petersson called the nation to the Lord through his *Hymns of the Passion*. A prayer which he wrote fits well the spiritual hopes and struggles of many in our own times:

> Oft am I unbelieving—
> Thou knowest me, my Lord,
> Fast to my error cleaving
> Unmindful of thy word.
> Yet I would now seek truly
> Thy counsels to obey,
> Turn from my ways unruly;
> Grant me thy grace, I pray.

Deep wounds were inflicted on the Western Christian world, wounds which are still in need of healing. We must persevere on the path to unity, not for reasons of convenience, but because this is the declared will of Christ, "the head of the Church, his body" [Eph 5:23].

It is important to remember that down the centuries Lutherans and Catholics and other Christians have continued to have much in common.

We know that it is not ourselves who will heal the wounds of division and reestablish unity—we are merely instruments that God can use. Unity among Christians will be God's gift in his own moment of grace. Humbly we strive toward that day, growing in love, in mutual forgiveness, and trust. ✠

$\mathcal{F}$INLAND 1989

FROM 4 JUNE TO 6 JUNE 1989 the Holy Father visited Finland. On the evening of 5 June, he addressed the assembly at the Finlandia Hall in Helsinki. Here he addressed his remarks to the so-called Helsinki Accord, which came from the International Conference for Security and Cooperation of 1975. At that particular conference the Holy See had made an intervention asking that religion be recognized as a fundamental human right. In this statement the Pope, once again, speaks of the importance of human rights and religious freedom.

R eligious freedom has become a common theme within the context of international affairs. The subject has become part of the culture of our times, for our contemporaries have learned from the excesses of the recent past, and have come to realize that believing in God, practicing a religion, and joining with others in expressing one's faith is the special expression of that freedom of thought and expression which takes its source not from a concession granted by the state but from the very dignity of the human person.

In any event, the developments of these recent years, and the progress made in drawing up the various texts issued by the Conference, show ever more clearly that religious freedom can exist in various social systems. What the Church has asked for is that religious life should not be denied the freedom it needs. What the state owes itself to guarantee, as the Second Vatican Council's Declaration on Religious Freedom clearly indicated, is the protection of this freedom for all its citizens, by means of just laws and by ensuring favorable conditions for the development of their religious life [*Dignitatis Humanae,* 6]. The idea that religion is a form of alienation is no longer fashionable, because, fortunately, the leaders of the nations and people themselves have come to realize that believers constitute a powerful factor in favor of the common good. Hatred and fanaticism can find no justification among those who call God "Our Father." Who in fact could deny that the commandment of charity, forgiveness of offenses, a sense of duty, concern for the neglected—all of which is at the heart of the message of many spiritual families—constitute a priceless asset for society? At any rate, these are among the values which Christians have to offer as their specific contribution to public and international life. Moreover, from the very fact that they come from all social classes, cultures, and nations, the members of religious denominations constitute an effective force for union and cooperation.

Let us help Europe to discover its roots, to become more closely identified with its past. For religious life is not threatened merely by vexing restrictions; it can also be threatened by the spread of false values—such as hedonism, power seeking, greed—which are making headway in various countries and which in practice stifle the spiritual aspirations of large numbers of people. This is why it is vital for believers to be able to share freely in public debate, and thus put forward another view of the world—the one inspired by their faith. In this way they contribute to the moral uplift of the society in which they live. European nations have become more and more aware that the honest confrontation of ideas and convictions has been an indispensable condition for their overall development. For this reason, Europe and the world can rightly expect from religions an effective contribution to the search for peace. ✠

*D*ENMARK 1989

THE PONTIFF CONTINUED HIS THEME OF ECUMENISM throughout his stay in Denmark (6 to 8 June 1989). On 7 June he addressed an ecumenical gathering at the Moltke's Palace in Copenhagen. He focused on the importance of reading and praying the Bible.

All Christians "seek God" in his own written word. We are convinced that our Lord Jesus Christ reveals himself to us, today and always, in the Scriptures. The Incarnate Word of God continues to speak to the Church through the sacred books. In reading and studying the Scriptures, then, Christians seek to know God and to understand his plan for the human family. Technical and scientific study is only an instrument of this larger aim. Primarily, the word of God is intended to build up and sustain the Church, to provide strength for her children, food for the soul, and to be a pure and lasting source of spiritual life [*Dei Verbum,* 21]. That is why Catholics and Lutherans as well as the members of other ecclesial communities make the word of God a fundamental component of the liturgy, which, according to the Fathers of the Church, consists in the "table of the Word" as well as the "table of the Eucharist."

The extent of our growing convergence is attested by the fact that we use the same critical methods, and often arrive at the same exegetical conclusions, that more and more we listen to the voice of Tradition in the interpretation of the word of God, and that, on the practical level, collaboration has increased among us in the translations, publication, and diffusion of the Sacred Texts.

However, we are all well aware that much remains to be done to make of Scripture that instrument of unity which the Lord wills for it—and for us. And it is said to acknowledge that the interpretation of Scripture sometimes remains a factor of division and therefore of disunity among Christians. This is not so much because we read in different, or divergent, ways certain particular texts or passages. Rather, it is because we hold different views of the "relationship between the Scriptures and the Church" and the role of the Church's authentic teaching office in their interpretation [*Unitatis Redintegratio,* 21].

These differing views are now an important subject on the agenda of our dialogue. I am convinced that it is by pursuing this dialogue with confidence and perseverance and above all with prayer, that we shall be able to overcome our differences, without being unfaithful to what belongs to the integrity of the Christian faith. We shall be led to strengthen our faithfulness to the revealed word of God with the assistance of the Holy Spirit, who "guides us into all the truth" [Jn 16:13]. It is precisely in this endeavor, difficult as it is, that the "powerful instrument" of God's sacred word can serve to build that "peace" between us which "surpasses all understanding" [Phil 4:7].

Thus the road ahead of us is clearly indicated. We are all called to continue and deepen our common study of Holy Scripture, our dialogue on its content and interpretation, and our collaboration in making it more accessible and understood.

Dear brothers and sisters in Christ: In the Holy Scriptures all Christians have been given a common treasure, a rule of faith, a source of spiritual growth and encouragement to know and serve one true God. ✠

SWEDEN 1989

ON 8 JUNE 1989 Pope John Paul II landed in Sweden, where he was greeted by Prince Bertil and Princess Liliane of the Swedish royal household as well as Bishop Hubertus Brandenbrug of Stockholm and his Auxiliary Bishop William Kenney, C.P. The following day he addressed the venerable university community at Uppsala which was established in 1477.

As I had the occasion to state last year, on the ninth centenary of the University of Bologna, one of the richest legacies of the Western university tradition is precisely the concept that a civilized society rests on the primacy of reason and law. As Bishop of Rome, a son of Poland, and once a member of the Polish academic community, I wholeheartedly encourage all the representatives of intellectual and cultural life who are engaged in revitalizing the classical and Christian heritage of the university institution. Not all teachers, not all students are equally involved in the study of theology and the liberal arts, but all can benefit from the transmission of a culture by the great common tradition.

Your university system has kept alive the teaching of theology, and this offers an open forum for studying the word of God and its meaning for the men and women of today. Our times are in great need of interdisciplinary research in meeting the complex interdisciplinary challenges brought by progress. These problems bear on the meaning of life and death, the threats involved in genetic manipulation, the scope of education, and the transmission of knowledge and wisdom to the younger generation. We certainly have to admire the marvelous discoveries of science, but we are also aware of the devastating power of modern technology, capable of destroying the earth and all it contains. A mobilization of minds and consciences therefore is urgently needed.

WHILE IN SWEDEN Pope John Paul honored the memory of Dag Hammarskjöld and Raoul Wallenberg, noble sons of Sweden. At the same time he used the Swedish environment with its scholarly and cultural atmosphere to call for a new humanism. At the end of his visit, he visited Vadstena, where the relics of Saint Bridget are enshrined. He recalled her memory and those of other Scandinavian heroes and heroines. The Mass was celebrated for a congregation of young people.

In the Gospel of today's mass, Jesus says the following words in the house of Zacchaeus: "Today salvation has come to this house" [Lk 19:9]. I wish to repeat these words of Jesus in this house, in the courtyard of Vadstena Castle. For all of us—both in Sweden and in Rome—this castle is associated with the memory of Saint Bridget. In her lifetime Sweden was a Catholic country. Christianity was still new to the region. Living on the far edge of the Christian world of that time, she felt called by God to renew the Church, which she saw was turning away from the center, away from Christ. She went to Rome, and there she worked bravely for the unity of the Church. She was a woman strong in character, and heroic in faith, hope, and love.

Together with Saint Bridget, I wish to mention some of the first apostles and missionaries in Scandanavia and elsewhere in northern Europe, holy men and women who were living witnesses of Christ: Young people of Sweden, do you remember the personality of Saint Bridget and the example of her daughter Catherine, both of whom found purpose for their lives in the Christian faith? Saint Ansgar also traveled these regions, planting the seeds of faith. His courageous missionary work led him to be called "the Apostle of the North." King Eric IX is your patron saint and the symbol of national unity. These men and women are a part of your heritage. In the Gospel they discover the great adventure which gave meaning to their lives. Through their prayers may they help you to do likewise.

I greet young people of Finland who have come here to celebrate with the Pope. For you Saint Henrik, your patron saint, is a reminder that following Christ requires courage and a great sense of confidence in God's loving presence in your lives.

Dear young people of Denmark: Your traditional patron saint is the beloved King Canute, but Denmark also produced many other holy men and women. Less than a year ago I had the happiness of declaring Blessed the great Danish scholar and bishop, Niels Stensen. May his example teach you to be fully at peace in your Catholic faith.

Young people of Norway: The memory of Saint Olaf is still very much alive in your country. You have to translate the example of his faith and dedication into present-day forms of Christian service. Be strong in your love of God and see Him in each of your brothers and sisters throughout the world who need your support and solidarity.

Young friends from Iceland: Do you know the story of Saint Thor-lac Thorhallsson, Bishop of Skalholt? He was a native of your country, famous for his learning, piety, and zeal. He did much to improve the Christian life of his people. I am confident that you too will find the strength for your lives in knowing and loving Jesus Christ.

Today at Vadstena we are celebrating our unity. It is unity and diversity. It is authentically Nordic and is authentically Catholic! With different talents and different hopes, you are one in Jesus, one in the ideal of Christian service, one in pursuing justice, one in proclaiming the equal human dignity of all people.

A special characteristic of the young people of our time is openness—openness to the great cultural diversity of our world. But you must also be open to Christ. Just as he did in the case of the rich young man in the Gospel [Mk 10:17 ff.], Jesus looks on you who are rich in talents and material things and he looks on you with love. He asks you to be completely open to him. He will never disappoint you! ✠

$\mathscr{S}$PAIN 1989

WORLD YOUTH DAY 1989 was held 19 to 21 August in Santiago de Compostela, Spain. Pope John Paul was invited by the Spanish Hierarchy to attend and address the young adults from all over the world. France, Australia, Vietnam, Brazil, the United States, Japan, Canada, and many other countries were represented.

The theme for this World Youth Day was "The Way, the Truth and the Life." The Pope attended the various ceremonies, which often included elaborate performances by the young people. At Monte del Gozo (Mount of Joy), the Pontiff reflected upon God's specific call to today's new generation.

B ut, more than one of you is asking himself or herself: What does Jesus want of me? To what is he calling me? What is the meaning of his call for me?

For the great majority of you, human love will present itself as a way of self-realization in the formation of a family. This is why, *in the name of Christ,* I want to ask you:

Are you prepared to *follow the call of Christ through the sacrament of Marriage,* so as to be procreators of new life, people who will form new pilgrims to the heavenly city?

In the history of salvation, Christian marriage is a *mystery of faith.* The family is a *mystery of love,* because it collaborates directly in the creative work of God. Beloved young people, a large sector of society does not accept Christ's teachings, and consequently it takes other roads: hedonism, divorce, abortion, birth control, and contraceptive methods. These ways of understanding life are in clear contrast to the law of God and the teachings of the Church. To follow Christ faithfully means *putting* the Gospel message *into practice,* and this also implies chastity, the defense of life, and also the indissolubility of the *matrimonial bond, which is not a mere contract* which can be arbitrarily broken.

Living in the "permissiveness" of the modern world, which denies or minimizes the authenticity of Christian principles, it is *easy and attractive to breathe in this contaminated mentality* and give in to the passing desire. But, bear in mind that those who act in this way *neither follow Christ nor love him.* To love means to walk together in the same direction toward *God,* who is the *Source of Love.* In this Christian framework, *love is stronger than death* because it prepares us to welcome life, to protect it and defend it from the mother's womb until death. Therefore, I ask you again:

Are you prepared to *protect human life* with the maximum care at every moment, even in the most difficult ones? Are you prepared as young Christians *to live and defend love through indissoluble marriage,* to protect the stability of the family, a stability which favors the balanced upbringing of children, under the protection of a paternal and maternal love, which complement each other?

This is the Christian witness that is expected of the majority of you, young men and women. To be a Christian means to be a witness to Christian truth, and today, particularly, it is to put into practice the authentic meaning which Christ and the Church give to life and to the full realization of young men and women through marriage and the family. ✠

South Korea 1989

From 6 to 16 October the Pontiff paid another visit to Asia. This time his itinerary included South Korea, Indonesia, Mauritius, and Timor. On 7 October 1989, Pope John Paul II touched down in South Korea. He was greeted by President Roh Tae Woo. The occasion of this visit was the closure of the International Eucharistic Congress, which had been held at the Youido Plaza in Seoul. In his homily the following day, the Pope referred to the division of Korea into northern and southern realms.

The words "Christ our Peace" have been chosen as the theme of this Congress. We have heard what the Apostle proclaims: "In Christ Jesus, you who once were far off have been brought near in the blood of Christ. For he is our peace, who has made us both one, and has broken down the dividing wall of hostility" [Eph 2:13–14].

The Apostle is perhaps thinking of the wall in the Temple of Jerusalem, which divided Jew from Gentile. But how many walls and barriers divide the great human family today? How many forms of conflict? How many signs of mistrust and hostility are visible in countries all over the world?

East is divided from West; North from South. These divisions are the heritage of history and of the ideological conflicts which so often divide peoples who otherwise would wish to live in peace and brotherhood with one another. Korea, too, is marked by a tragic division that penetrates ever more deeply into the life and character of its people. The Korean nation is symbolic of a world divided and not yet able to become one in peace and justice.

Yet there is a way forward. True peace—the shalom, which the world urgently needs—springs eternally from the infinitely rich mystery of God's love, *"mysterium pietatis"* [1 Tm 3:16], about which Saint Paul writes: "God was in Christ reconciling the world to himself" [2 Cor 5:19].

As Christians we are convinced that Christ's Paschal Mystery makes present and available the force of life and love which overcomes all evil and all separation. Your admirable ancestors in the faith knew that "in Christ" all are equal in dignity, and all are equally deserving of loving attention and solicitude. ✠

NORTH KOREA—RADIO TALK—1989

LATER THAT SAME DAY, 8 OCTOBER, Pope John Paul spoke directly through the radio to the peoples of mainland China and North Korea. He did this in order to show his personal solidarity with what was termed "the Church in chains."

Today in Seoul we offer a fervent prayer that the peace of Christ will descend upon all nations and peoples. Allow me to mention in particular two peoples who are very close to my heart. Confident of Mary's tender concern for all her children, we cannot fail to recommend to her, with deep affection, hope, and sorrow, the people of North Korea and especially its Catholic community. We pray for those parents and children, brothers and sisters, friends and relatives who are separated but wait with undiminished hope to be reunited as one family. May Jesus, through the intercession of his blessed Mother, the Queen of Peace, hasten the day when all Koreans will be reconciled in mutual trust and respect, and reunited in the joy of brotherly love. ✠

$\mathcal{I}$NDONESIA 1989

ON 10 OCTOBER 1989 Pope John Paul arrived in Jakarta in Indonesia. The Roman Catholic Church in Indonesia has grown rapidly since the conclusion of the Second World War. It is one of the leading nations today in the development of vocations to the priesthood and to the religious life. In his homily at the Cathedral of the Assumption in Jakarta, the Pontiff spoke briefly of the rich history of missionary activity in these islands and then spoke of vocations as a blessing from the Lord. The purpose of this visit to Indonesia was to foster vocations and to encourage the many young priests and religious in their ministry and in their formation.

Y ou who are today's generation of priests are heirs to the high ideals of the great missionaries who selflessly laid the foundations of the Church in Indonesia. Many of them were personally known to you. You were confirmed by their faith and led to the Lord's service through their example. Our thoughts turn to those "faithful stewards," who have now been called to their eternal reward but whose memory lives on. The example of their Christian life and witness is their legacy, and even now they are interceding with God for the continued fruitfulness of that part of the Lord's vineyard which they cultivated with such loving care. One thinks of Father van Lith of Java, as well as of intrepid pastors of more recent times, such as the renowned Bishop Thijssen, who labored in Lesser Sunda, and Archbishop van den Hurk, so recently taken from us.

The high esteem in which you are held today by the Indonesian people, including those who are not Christian, is due in great measure to the dedication and moral integrity of those who have gone before you. But their powerful example also constitutes a challenge, since your Churches continue to need holy and wise priests who are able to show the right path, however daunting or difficult.

Vocations are a sign of the healthy state of religious life as well as the result of the dedicated ministry of bishops and priests. It is preaching by good example that leads young people to embrace a life of total consecration and of ministry. Both foreign missionaries and Indonesian-born clergy, working closely together, have given a shining example of Christian life and service. Although there have been obstacles to the continued presence of the missionaries, this very problem has been turned to the Church's good: such is the power of faith.

Since the building up of the Church is the work of God, we must never cease to pray for vocations and ask others to do the same.

Dear brothers and sisters, we must also look to the future even as we give thanks for the blessings of the past and the graces of the present. Once initial evangelization has been completed, a new task begins: the task of forming consciences and of interiorizing the faith. This calls for a renewed commitment on your part, a commitment which is absolutely necessary if the Gospel is to strike deep roots in Indonesian life and culture. Formation serves to nurture the fragile, and still vulnerable, plant from its early stages of growth. ✠

 Timor 1989

On 12 October 1989 Pope John Paul visited the troubled island of Timor, where there had been widespread suffering due to ethnic discrimination. He brought a word of comfort and acknowledgment of the rights of those whose origins are in East Timor.

Let us consider the meaning that Jesus attaches to the images "salt of the earth" and "light of the world." In Timor you are very familiar with salt. You extract it along the coastal plains of Cassaid, Tibar, Manatuto, Sical, and from the salt lake at Laga. Salt preserves food and enhances its flavor. In the Gospel "salt" refers to preservation from the corruption of sin and death. It refers to the spiritual wholeness of every disciple whose duty it is to enliven and elevate humanity with the assistance of divine grace.

The image of "light" refers not only to the wisdom that comes from the revelation of divine truth, but also to everyday wisdom in action. It is the wisdom that comes from the experience of life as well as the wisdom that gives life—the wisdom that enlightens those who live by faith. Wherever this "light" is found, it shapes human life and conduct, and leads people to God.

What does it mean to be "the salt of the earth" and "the light of the world" in East Timor today? For many years now, you have experienced destruction and death as a result of conflict; you have known what it means to be the victims of hatred and struggle. Many innocent people have died, while others have been prey to retaliation and revenge. For too long you have been suffering a lack of stability, which has rendered your future uncertain. This distressing situation causes economic difficulties which, in spite of some relief, still exist, preventing the development needed to alleviate the burden which still weighs heavily on the population.

Respect for the rights which render life more human must be firmly ensured: the rights of individuals and the rights of families. I pray that those who have responsibility for life in East Timor will act with wisdom and goodwill toward all as they search for a just and peaceful resolution of present difficulties, in order to bring about a speedy improvement of conditions of life which will permit you to live in social harmony, according to your own traditions and requirements, in serene and fruitful productivity. ✠

MAURITIUS 1989

FROM 14 TO 16 OCTOBER 1989 Pope John Paul visited the island nation of Mauritius. Situated in the Indian Ocean, it is considered a meeting place between both North and South, and East and West, from a global perspective. Ten years before, the Pontiff had beatified Blessed Jacques Laval, the Apostle to Mauritius. This beatification, held in Rome, was the first of Pope John Paul's pontificate. The island nation was obviously very important to him for many reasons. He spoke of it upon landing, where he was greeted by the prime minister and members of the government.

D ue to its location at the crossroads between the Orient and Occident, the island of Mauritius has the vocation to bring about a synthesis of the finest values of the East and West through the commitment of the major religions, whose members enjoy cordial relations in this country. It is my hope that your society will not hesitate to cast aside certain idols such as materialism and hedonism, and that it will, on the contrary, continue to value moral fiber, which liberates and pacifies, and continue to foster tolerance, patience, and moderation.

In the wake of what has been undertaken and achieved in the past, may all Mauritians continue to acknowledge and accept one another in the diversity of their cultures, beliefs, races, and languages, so as to provide the image of a society where all live together in peace, foreshadowing in some way, on a smaller scale, an international community which will be a homeland for all peoples. To attain this end, Mauritius has its own role to play, especially at the regional level, as can be seen from the recent decisions of the Indian Ocean Commission. It is called to help strengthen the bonds between the islands of this region of the world and, together with them, to look beyond, so that the North-South dialogue may not be the exclusive prerogative of Europe.

As he left the island nation of Mauritius, Pope John Paul celebrated with the children of that land the eleventh anniversary of his election as Pontiff. He spoke of himself in his address to the youth of Curepipe. In so doing, he defined his role as Successor to Saint Peter.

Y ou called me "the Pilgrim of Peace." Yes, I would like to be just that wherever I go, because Jesus, when he gave his own life for the world, gave us a deep peace, which never left his heart that was full of love, his heart as the Son of God and brother of all people.

Thank you for your anniversary wishes. Eleven years ago today I received the mission of succeeding Saint Peter, the capital Apostle whom Jesus asked to strengthen the faith of his brethren. In response to your wishes, I ask you to continue faithfully to know Jesus Christ better, to prepare yourselves well to receive him in the Eucharist, to pray every day, to show those around you your joy at being Christian. ✠

APE VERDE 1990

POPE JOHN PAUL JOURNEYED TO CAPE VERDE to commence his sixth pastoral visit to Africa, 25 January to 1 February 1990. In this address, the Pope identified the very force that compelled his travel around the world to see God's people. The nations he visited included Cape Verde, Guinea-Bissau, Mali, Burkina Faso, and Chad.

I come, then, joyfully, *once again to sow a seed* of faith, hope, and love in a furrow which has been open for quite some time, trusting in the "early and late rainfall" of God's grace, which makes this soil fertile. That is to say, I come *to strengthen* in a faith that is both courageous and resplendent these brothers and sisters of mine and these children of God through baptism; and *to encourage* their witness to and proclamation of the "reasons for their hope" in eternal life; and finally, *to urge* them to show in word and deed that they are good sisters and brothers in Christ, loving God above all things and loving their neighbor, as Jesus himself loved us.

This is always the *reason for the pastoral visits* which I have been making to various countries of the world: to pass on the news of the unfathomable riches of the divine and human dimensions of Christ the Redeemer, so that all may be saved and know the truth [1 Tm 2:4], as God wills.

LATER DURING THIS SAME VISIT, the Pope addressed the youth of Cape Verde at the Sports Palace in Praia. This discourse on "faith" is considered an important pastoral address, for its clarity.

D ear young people, welcome Christ into your lives! If you walk with him, if you take him as a traveling companion who points the way, you will not go searching for false values, nor will you follow after the idols of personal success, power, wealth, or eroticism; rather, you will head in the direction of the true values upon which real freedom is based. That does not come from *having more,* but from *being more:* being real men and women.

You already know that true freedom requires self-control, mastery of one's self: thanks to that, it is possible to live a perfect life, holy and victorious over the demeaning kingdom of sin [see Rom 6:12].

These words of mine, dear young people, are situated within a faith context, as you can see. I know the objections raised by today's world against faith. You have heard them, too. People who live next door, your classmates, people at work, and those you go out with raise these objections. Do not let yourselves become fearful, nor renounce your beliefs; do not sell out your ideals, passed on to you by those who, in the light of what they have been through, have experienced that faith is real.

Faith does not debase human dignity. On the contrary, it fills our minds with the right amount of understanding in order to reach a full answer to the questions which trouble us. Faith leads us to know the final truth about things, about people, about God. Faith does not separate us from the world, or from our brothers and sisters. Rather, it brings us even closer to their problems and hopes. True faith in the Redeemer does not isolate us or alienate us from the world or the human race; rather, "it contributes greatly to the promotion of this communion among persons and at the same time leads to a deeper understanding of the laws of social life which the Creator has written into man's spiritual and moral nature" [*Gaudium et Spes,* n. 23]. ✠

GUINEA-BISSAU 1990

ON 27 JANUARY 1990, Pope John Paul II landed in the nation of Guinea-Bissau for a one-day stay. In his homily during his Eucharistic liturgy celebrated on 27 January in the Bissau National Stadium, he spoke of African identity and the need to avoid temptation to materialism.

True human development requires man to rediscover the plan of God, who entrusted him with the created world so that he would know it and master it in the context of the wisdom of God's law. God wants man to know and make use of the goods and energies of nature, considering them as a gift necessary to personal realization, without the values of the spirit being obscured.

In order to achieve a harmonious relationship between man and the created universe, the paths of cultivating thought and love must be traveled. It is through these dimensions that man is elevated to his supreme dignity, that of being a spiritual and free being. This product is achieved by developing a body of knowledge and a vocabulary springing out of an appreciation for one's own cultural heritage and without admitting the dialogue that the modern world favors.

Our vocation in Jesus Christ is a vocation for eternal life in God: "Be glad and rejoice, for your reward is great in heaven" [Mt 5:12]. This is what our Savior tells us. This is what the Redeemer of the world teaches us: the One who has words of eternal life! ✠

MALI 1990

ON 28 JANUARY 1990 Pope John Paul visited the African nation of Mali for one day. There he praised the Catholic community for its centenary celebration of evangelization. He incited the youth of the country to avoid "idols of false happiness" and encouraged them to be "children of the Beautiful Names": mercy, understanding, pardon, and reconciliation. Most interesting were his impromptu and humorous remarks to the young adults.

In a less formal vein, I want to express my appreciation and my admiration for the program you have prepared. I followed your rather brief but very meaningful presentation with great interest. I have frequently met with young people—almost every Sunday in Rome and then during my visits to other countries. It is interesting to note a common feeling among young people the world over, as I watch the presentations they use to speak to the Pope and ask the Pope questions.

These presentations are very similar everywhere, not in terms of details but rather the general latitude . . . they show a great sense of the human family. I am privileged to be able to meet young people in different places; but I am not so young myself now. When I entered the building, I met the organizers of this meeting and I asked them: "Up until what age can a person be considered young?" They answered, "Up until age forty." I responded, "Then for me there is no hope." Nevertheless, I keep repeating my meetings, and to this very day I have never been rejected by youth! ✠

$\mathcal{B}$URKINA FASO 1990

THE POPE VISITED THE AGRICULTURAL NATION OF BURKINA FASO (formerly Upper Volta) from 29 to 30 January. There he again spoke of indigenous evangelization and enculturation. His presence called attention to the drought of Sahel. In his departing remarks he summed up his love for Africa and his concern. Again these sentences were spontaneous and referred to current events.

This has been a spiritual gathering, because there was a fervent discussion of many of the issues in our mission; not all of the possible issues, but many of them. We see the importance of collegiality; I believe this is important for your country, for the Episcopal conference of Burkina with the participation of the bishop of Niger, but it is also important for the continent. I must say that this initiative of an African continental Synod was considered several times, discussed, and it had to be liberated from certain preconceived ideas. When we were freed of these preconceived ideas, then it was decided to take this initiative which seems to be very important. Thus it will indeed be able to develop stronger collegiality on the continental level; and continents also need to be collegial. At the moment it seems to me that there are two continents which have need of greater collegiality. That is, Africa and Europe. However, we are going to see how the Good God, the Good Shepherd, will help us to promote it. In every case, I must always thank Providence that ten years ago I was led to Ouagadougou and to pronounce this appeal, the first appeal, appeal number one, for the Sahel. This is one of the appeals which, I feel, belongs to the job, to the responsibility of being Pope. Without making this appeal, it would be hard for the Pope to stand before the Lord. ✠

CHAD 1990

THE PONTIFF ARRIVED IN CHAD ON 30 JANUARY, prior to departing for Rome the next day. This nation has been characterized by its scarcity of clergy, by developing relations between the Christian and Muslim communities, and also by a struggle against poverty and famine. Here, in an address to the Diplomatic Corps assembled at N'Djamena on 1 February, he spoke pointedly to the leadership of the African nations.

Here on African soil, since I am seeing firsthand the admirable qualities of its peoples, I cannot help but mention also the conflicts which are afflicting them in several regions of this continent. It is a source of what seems to be endless suffering. I am thinking of Ethiopia, the Sudan, other peoples exposed to racial discrimination, and others whom endemic ethnic rivalries sometimes led to violent conflicts.

It is true that all areas of the world have known the fires of war. Changes are occurring; positive signs are also appearing. I recently had the opportunity to express my views on these subjects. However, since no human suffering can leave us indifferent, I want to say forcefully to the international community that solidarity among peoples has no borders; that the great changes taking place in Eastern Europe must not distract our attention from the South, and from the African continent in particular.

One must agree that, very often, it is not clear what causes peace to break down. It is necessary for both local authorities and those who have influence in international relations to have the courage to be clear: What is at stake in the confrontations? Who is stirring them up? What rights are in the balance?

One should come to understand what minorities want to defend, even at the cost of their lives; their traditions, culture, and convictions, their dignity in the face of the powers which barely tolerate them and reject their legitimacy. One should also have the courage to shed light on the role being played by all parties, beginning with the more powerful ones who control the economy, military aid, and alliances.

It is up to political leaders and diplomats to heed the appeals addressed to the international community. People should begin to acknowledge errors, the abuses of power, the injustices, the exploitation which they may have caused, because it is more important to serve the progress of peace for the good of entire peoples than to defend one's own prestige. There could be even further success if the first objective is always respect for the rights and dignity of every person. ✠

CZECHOSLOVAKIA 1990

THE HOLY FATHER ARRIVED IN PRAGUE, CZECHOSLOVAKIA, for a two-day visit on 21 April 1990. This was the first visit ever by a Roman Pontiff, coming only five years after the eleventh centenary of the evangelization of that country. The evening of his arrival, the Pope met with leaders of the cultural and academic world, as well as non-Catholic Church leaders, in Hradcany Castle in Prague, where he delivered an address on the freedom recently acquired by its citizens, as well as the call to unity among Christians.

A united Europe is no longer only a dream; it is not a utopian memory from the Middle Ages. The events which we are witnessing show that this goal can be actually reached. Europe, ravaged by wars and wounded by divisions which have undermined its free development, is searching for a new unity.

This process is not and cannot be only a political and economic event; it has profound cultural, spiritual, and moral dimensions. Europe's cultural unity lives in and from different cultures, which blend and enrich one another. This particular quality characterizes the uniqueness and the independence of life on our Continent. The search for a European identity leads us to the sources.

If Europe's historical memory fails to go beyond the ideals of the Enlightenment, its new unity will have superficial and unstable foundations. Christianity, brought to this continent by the Apostles and carried into its various parts by the activity of Benedict, Cyril, Methodius, Adalbert, and innumerable ranks of saints, is at the very roots of European culture. The process toward a new European unity will have to take this into account!

What would happen to the fascinating panorama of this "City of a Hundred Towers" if the outlines of the Cathedral and that of many other monuments which constitute so many jewels of Christian culture were to vanish? How poor would your nation's spiritual, moral, and cultural life be if all that was, is, and will be inspired by Christian faith were excluded from it! ✠

MEXICO 1990

FROM 6 TO 13 MAY 1990, the Pope visited Mexico and Curaçao. During his trip, he beatified three children and two men at the Mass of the Fourth Sunday of Easter on 6 May.

The children, Cristóbal (1514–27), Juan (1516–29), and Antonio (1516–29), attended a school opened by Franciscan missionaries. Cristóbal was murdered by his father, after pointing out the wrong in his father's polygamous and idolatrous ways. Juan and Antonio died while on a difficult mission to Oaxaca.

José María de Yermo y Parres (1851–1904) was ordained a diocesan priest in 1879. After working with mission churches on the outskirts of León, José realized his true calling. He founded the hospice of the Sacred Heart and a charitable work called Christian Mercy that gave Christian formation to former prostitutes. Blessed José served the poor until his fatal illness in 1904.

In December of 1531, Juan Diego was witness to the apparition of our Lady on Tepeyac hill. A beautiful woman asked Juan to deliver a message to the bishop. Juan relayed the message, telling the bishop to build a church on the site of Tepeyac hill. The bishop, being understandably reluctant, paid no heed to Juan's words. A few days later, the woman approached Juan again, urging him to deliver the message once more. This time, Juan carried with him some roses he picked from the site of their meeting. The bishop looked at the rare roses and in them saw a vision of the woman that Juan described. This woman's image, with native features and dress, can be seen today in the third Basilica of Our Lady of Guadalupe in Mexico City. Blessed Juan Diego lived a life of holiness and humility from that day forward in a hut, near the new chapel.

A large banner of Our Lady of Guadalupe was hung from scaffolding near the dry bed of the Santa Catarina River in Monterrey, where Pope John Paul celebrated Mass on 10 May. During the homily, the Pontiff used the words of the Sermon on the Mount (Mt 5–7) to fully express his feelings concerning materialism in today's society.

Today I wish to meditate along with you on the message which the Lord offers us in this Eucharistic celebration. "Do not worry about your life, what you will eat, or about your body, what you will wear. . . . Look at the birds in the sky. . . . Learn from the way the wild flowers grow" [Mt 6:25–26, 28].

What do these words spoken by Jesus Christ in the Sermon on the Mount mean? What was their significance for those who heard them for the first time? What meaning do they encompass for us today?

Truly *these words of the Gospel seem to contradict so many criteria and attitudes which we see in the modern world.* In reality, productivity, earnings, and economic progress seem to be considered as the ultimate and definitive criteria governing human behavior for humanity and today's society. And it is in relation to these criteria that persons and peoples are judged and evaluated and given a place on the social scale, according to the importance paid to them and the power they possess.

If this hierarchy of values is accepted, the human being would be obliged to seek possessions continually as life's only goal. Therefore the person would be evaluated not for what he or she *is,* but for what he or she *has.*

Jesus, the Master of the Sermon on the Mount, *the one who proclaims the Beatitudes, teaches us first of all that the Creator and creatures stand above the works of man.* Man and society can produce industrial commodities which advance civilization and progress to the degree that they find in the created world the resources which allow them to carry out their work.

To you, humanity, gazing contentedly at the works of your hands, the fruit of your genius, *Christ says: Do not forget the One who gave origin to everything!* Do not forget the Creator! And further, the more deeply you come to know the laws of nature and the more you discover its wealth and potential, so much the more do you have to be mindful of him. ✠

CURAÇAO 1990

On 13 May 1990, Pope John Paul II visited the island of Curaçao, which is part of the Netherlands Antilles. He was greeted by the governor-general, Jamie Saleh, and the prime minister, Maria Liberia Peters. He referred to the unique character of this island nation, a dependent territory of Holland.

I have kissed the soil of Curaçao as a sign of my cordial esteem and friendship toward all the peoples of this region. As Bishop of Rome and the Successor of Peter, I have done so in homage to all those who have testified here, in words of truth and deeds of love, to the power of the Gospel of our Lord Jesus Christ.

As a fellow pilgrim with the rest of the human family, living in a world which is witnessing dramatic social and political changes, my visit is meant to be an expression before you and before all men and women of goodwill of the Church's profound solidarity with developing peoples. Individuals and peoples everywhere aspire to be truly free. They seek support in overcoming the obstacles that stand in the way of their full development. They are willing to undertake and endure much in order to achieve a more human way of life.

The real challenge facing developing nations is as much spiritual as material. It is the challenge of enabling the sense of human dignity to develop and flourish. It is the task of building into the very fabric of society a profound sense of human rights and of the corresponding personal and social responsibilities of every citizen. In a word, it is the ever-present duty of considering and treating each human being according to his or her unique worth as a beloved child of the Creator. ✠

MALTA 1990

SAINT PAUL WAS SHIPWRECKED ON THE MEDITERRANEAN ISLAND OF MALTA while being transported to Rome as a prisoner. On 25 to 27 May 1990, Pope John Paul traveled to Malta to retrace his patron's footsteps.

At the Shrine of Our Lady Ta' Pinu in Gozo, the Pope turned his homily toward Mary, reminding his listeners that the Virgin Mother's protection and care are abundant and steadfast.

In the Gospel of today's Mass, we are invited to reflect on Mary's maternal cooperation in the divine mission of her Son. Saint John tells us that at the *wedding feast of Cana,* when Jesus began his public ministry by turning the water into wine, he worked the miracle at the urging of his Mother, who was concerned for the needs of the guests. Meditating upon this passage of Scripture down the ages, the Church has come to understand that the confident words which Mary spoke to the servants—"Do whatever he tells you" [Jn 2:5]—are a mysterious indication of *Mary's unique maternal role in the entire economy of Christ's grace.* As a mother, "Mary places herself between her son and mankind in the reality of their wants, needs and suffering" [*Redemptoris Mater,* 21]. Out of loving concern for others, she brings all mankind's needs within the radius of Christ's saving power.

Toward the end of John's Gospel, Mary appears once again, this time standing *at the foot of the Cross.* What more powerful image could the Evangelist have given us of Mary's profound spiritual union with the redemptive mission of her Son? When from the Cross Jesus says to the Beloved Disciple, "Behold, your mother!" [Jn 19:27], he entrusts Mary to us, to each one of his disciples, to be our Mother too. At the foot of the Cross, Mary is fully revealed as Mother of the Church, *Mater Ecclesiae,* inviting each of us to trust in her prayers. Let us never hesitate to turn to her!

How often, in your families, do you feel powerless in the face of painful and apparently insoluble situations? How many people find it a constant struggle to forgive long-standing grudges, or to overcome deeply rooted feelings of anger, hostility, jealousy, or resentment? How many people desperately long for someone they love to abandon a way of life or a course of action which they know will only lead to frustration and unhappiness? And how frequently do our hearts go out to someone who is caught up in the toils of mental anguish or a bitter grief which knows no consolation? At moments like these, should we not trust in Mary's loving intercession, confident that *the most hopeless of human situations can be transformed by the saving power of Jesus,* who in answer to her request turned water into wine, who died on the Cross that we might live forever? ✠

Tanzania 1990

From 1 September until 10 September 1990, Pope John Paul visited the continent of Africa. During the journeys of this seventh apostolic visit to Africa, the Pope spent some time in Tanzania, a country he had never before visited, as well as the nations of Rwanda, Burundi, and the Ivory Coast.

On 2 September, the Pontiff met with various religious leaders in Dar es Salaam, Tanzania, and spoke on the importance of dialogue between Christians and Muslims. Respecting the religious beliefs of one another is crucial to world peace. Tanzania has a relatively equal compliment of populations: Muslims (25 percent) and Catholics (21.5 percent).

I extend warm greetings and good wishes to the members of other religions, Hindus, Buddhists, and especially to the followers of Islam. I pray that this encounter will serve to strengthen the good relations which exist in Tanzania between the religious groups represented here. May our faith in One God be the very source of our love and esteem for each other!

It must be acknowledged that dialogue between Christians and Muslims is increasingly important in today's world. It is also a very delicate question, since both religions are deeply committed to the spread of their respective faiths. But, objectively speaking, there is a firm foundation on which mutual respect and cooperation can be built. It is the recognition that every person has an inalienable right and a solemn duty to follow his or her upright conscience in seeking and obeying the truth. The Lord of heaven and earth cannot be pleased with a religious observance that is somehow imposed from without. What would then become of the wonderful gifts of reason and free will which make individuals privileged to bear personal responsibility and which constitute the worth and glory of the Creator's beloved sons and daughters [see *Dignitatis Humanae, 2*]?

Dialogue, as I described it a moment ago, does not attempt to produce an artificial consensus with regard to our faith convictions, but rather helps to ensure that in our zeal to proclaim our beliefs, and in the methods used, we respect every person's right to religious freedom. By cultivating positive and constructive relations between our communities and their individual members, we can arrive at a mutual understanding and respect which guarantees the exercise of this fundamental human right and opens the way to building a society in which all can contribute to the common good.

Christians and Muslims can live in harmony and show their solidarity with one another in all the joys, sorrows, and challenges that mark the life of a local community. As experience in many parts of the world shows, religious differences of themselves do not necessarily disrupt life together. Indeed, Christians and Muslims in Tanzania can be partners in building a society shaped by the values taught by God: tolerance, justice, peace, and concern for the poorest and weakest. May both religions work closely to ensure that these values and the right to religious freedom be enshrined in civil law, thus safeguarding a true equality among all Tanzania's citizens. ✠

$\mathscr{B}$URUNDI 1990

ON 5 SEPTEMBER 1990 Pope John Paul II met with the bishops of Burundi in Bujumbura to discuss the international AIDS pandemic, but with a particular emphasis on the African experience of this tragedy. The Pope referred to an "immune deficiency of values."

Society in Burundi, just as society in many other parts of the world, is exposed to a grave danger. I am thinking of the AIDS pandemic, which is affecting a growing number of your citizens, above all young adults and, it is sad to see, little children. That calls you to lavish your pastoral care on all, and it leads you to deepen your reflection about the origins and consequences of this disease.

I should like to remind you that the gravity of this illness has to do not only with the suffering and death it inexorably provokes, but also with its implications in the anthropological and moral orders. This epidemic differs from so many others that mankind has known by reason of the fact that forms of deliberate human conduct play a role in its spread.

Changing mentalities have been tending to make us lose sight of the dreaded moment of death, the place of which in everyone's destiny cannot be denied. However, the threat of AIDS now confronts our generations with the end of earthly life in a way that is all the more striking because it is directly or indirectly related to love and the transmission of life. One senses that the life-giving powers of our being are in danger of becoming fatal powers.

It is therefore necessary to understand what this illness reveals to us: alongside the biomedical problem, there appears what I have termed "a kind of immune deficiency at the level of essential values." To inform about the risks of infection and to organize a prevention program from a purely medical point of view would not be worthy of man if he were not called upon to rediscover the demands of emotional maturity and well-ordered sexuality. In that same discourse I said: "It is for that reason that the Church, as sure interpreter of the Law of God and 'an expert in humanity,' does not want only to say 'no' to certain forms of conduct, but above all to propose a style of life that is totally meaningful for the person. She vigorously and joyfully points out a positive ideal" [Rome, 15 November 1989, n. 5].

Confronted with AIDS, the Church's apostate faces an array of challenges. It is necessary to inform and educate, not accepting the problem's being handled with no regard for ethics, for in that case the origin of the illness is neither understood nor combated.

There is also the duty of assisting the people affected by AIDS. I know how difficult care can be in the situation of poverty in which you find yourselves. I hope and request once again that unlimited help may be given to you in this field where Catholics are collaborating effectively with institutions and persons devoted to the same medical tasks.

But I am also thinking of the psychological and spiritual assistance that the seriously ill or seropositive person should not lack. The latter often tend to retreat into themselves in anguished silence. They need fraternal companionship to have the courage to face their condition. We must firmly cast aside all temptations to discriminate against them.

We are dealing here with the difficult problem of the meaning of suffering and the value of every life, even that of the sick and weak period. May the disciples of Christ Crucified remain lovingly at the foot of the cross that is carried by these poor people with whom our Savior has also wished to be identified. The Christian communities will need great generosity to sustain the families worn out by the illness of one of their members and to look after the children who have lost their parents.

We hope that the day is near when this scourge will be conquered. In the face of the present trial, however, let us be living witnesses to the merciful love of God. Let us be bearers of hope, in faith in Christ who gave his life for the salvation of the many. ✠

$\mathscr{R}$WANDA 1990

IN THE COURSE OF A TWO-DAY VISIT TO RWANDA on 8 and 9 September 1990, the Pontiff made a terse and comforting radio broadcast to the entire nation. His concern was the threat of drought, famine, and disease, which is perennial to this nation.

Today I want to give a special message to the men and women of the countryside, who constitute the great majority of the population. I would have liked to go to your hillsides, visit your fields, be welcomed into your homes, but my stay in your country is too short and does not allow me to do so.

Dear men and women of Rwanda's countryside, be assured that I am aware of your situation. You keep this country alive; you are its great strength. Thanks to you, Rwanda forges ahead. It is you who are the ones most responsible for the progress of your country through your work and your agricultural production. You are to be complimented for what you do! You should be proud of what you are!

However, I also know the many difficulties which you encounter. Your work is not easy, and your efforts are often frustrated by unfavorable material and economic conditions. There are many of you living on land that is wearing out more and more. The soil which you cultivate is depleted from years and years of erosion and lack of fertilizers. Sometimes the rain is too plentiful and at other times it is cruelly lacking. Disease can attack your crops and animals alike. The price you receive for your produce is not always proportionate to your work and needs. The international environment is also unfavorable to you. With great sadness I learned of the food shortage which has been afflicting your country these last few months. Know that the Pope admires your courage in your daily struggle to improve the standard of living of your families and your country.

The problems which confront you are complex. There is no simple solution. In order for your situation to improve, the concerted effort of everyone is needed. But it is up to you first of all, Rwanda's rural men and women, to be the agents of your own development. It is important for you to know how to organize in order to make your voice heard, to express your expectations. I know that in Rwanda's tradition, solidarity played a great role in the countryside. Now that you are in difficult straits, understanding becomes more difficult. Each person, having reached the limits of his or her own ability to survive, finds it more difficult to help others. I invite you to make an effort to rediscover and intensify your rural solidarity, in order to develop a sense of sharing among yourselves.

To be in solidarity means to be involved personally and along with others in a common project. Together you could see to it that your rights are respected and that you are assured greater room for your freedom. Your land is your most important wealth, and it allows you to live. You most protect it from damage and depletion. Undertake joint initiatives to improve its yield. The Gospel is good news for everyone . . . also for the rural people of the Thousand Hills who work for the development of their country. In the eyes of God you are great, you are important. Throughout his whole life Jesus was close to the simple people. He was a part of their lives. His sermons and parables are marked by an easy familiarity with farming. Following Jesus' example, the Church must be close to the rural people. ✠

IVORY COAST 1990

ON 10 SEPTEMBER 1990 Pope John Paul II addressed the General Secretariat of the Special Synod for Africa, which was to be conducted between 1993 and 1995. By the time of this visit to the Ivory Coast the guidelines for the Synod had been distributed and were the topic for discussion. The Pope's purpose in this discourse was to encourage optimism for a widening and deepening evangelization on the African continent. His words, while theological and historical, were also enthusiastic.

The Synod assembly which we are preparing will mark, I am truly convinced, a new and shining step in the two-thousand-year-old course of the Gospel on this continent. With admiration we recall the birth and growth of the first Churches of Africa, in close relationship with the primitive Church and the apostolic tradition. We recall the illustrious Fathers and the flourishing communities of ancient Christian Africa, which have a place of honor in the history and doctrine of the universal Church. The synods and councils of these Churches have received the *sacra traditio;* by their ancient search for an understanding of the faith, they enriched our common heritage in an irreplaceable manner. A precious part of their heritage comes to us in a living manner through the witness of the Churches of Oriental rites: we give thanks for their presence.

At the cost of centuries of mysterious silence and later through the generosity of missionaries and the fidelity which moved them to devote their lives to the Church in Africa, the Church edifice raised in every region. Christ, who lays its foundation and builds it with the living stones which are his disciples, is raising up in this land the sign and sacrament of salvation [*Lumen Gentium,* 1]. The rivers of living water, promised by the Son of God made man, are satisfying the thirst of the men and women who are waiting to see the face and learn the name of the living God. The inscrutable mystery of the love of the Blessed Trinity gives life to the people of God, whose numbers are growing.

A Synodal Assembly cannot be reduced for consultation under practical matters. Its true *raison d'être* is the fact that the Church can move forward only by strengthening communion among her members, beginning with her Pastors. We are always conscious of the teaching of the Second Vatican Council, which highlighted the Church's vocation to be, by divine institution, a *communio.* Using the words of an African—Saint Cyprian—the Council fittingly described the Church as a "people brought into unity from the unity of the Father, Son, and Holy Spirit" [*Lumen Gentium,* 4]. Indeed, it is out of the fruitful and essential reality of *communio,* characteristic of the Church, that the institution of the Synod of Bishops was born. This institution is meant to manifest and develop solidarity among the heads of particular Churches in the fulfillment of their mission beyond the boundaries of their individual dioceses.

The present session of your Council follows the publication of the *Lineamenta* which you had prepared. This text develops the theme "The Church in Africa and Her Evangelizing Mission Toward the Year 2000: You Shall Be My Witnesses" [Acts 1:8]. The synodal process has thus entered a new phase, one which directly involves the bishops of Africa and the whole people of God. Here again, it is communion that must express itself. Dear sons and daughters of Africa, pray and reflect.

By entering into the many cultural, spiritual, and ecclesial situations of the continent and revealing the bounty of Christ's meeting with the people of Africa, you will discern a better course for evangelization and will make apparent contemporary requirements for priestly ministry, for the consecrated life, and for monastic life which is rapidly developing on your continent, as well as requirements regarding local assemblies and their celebration of the Christian mysteries, the role of movements, the education of youth, an open and sincere dialogue with Christians of other confessions and with believers of other spiritual traditions, the presence of Christian values in society, and the human development which your brothers and sisters are waiting for. ✠

$\mathscr{P}$ORTUGAL 1991

FROM 10 TO 13 MAY 1991, Pope John Paul once again rendered thanks to Mary for his protection against an assassination attempt ten years before. Quoting the Ave Maria, the Pope professed his personal devotion to Mary and made reference to the motto of his coat of arms: *Totus Tuus*. He also made reference to the forthcoming European Synod and the need in Europe and in Portugal, in particular, for a "new evangelization." But his primary theme was Mary.

O Mother of Emmanuel, "Show us Jesus, the blessed fruit of your womb!" The entire life of Mary, from whose womb came and shone "the true light which enlightens every person" [Jn 1:9], was spent in intimate communion with that of Jesus. "While on earth her life was like that of any other, filled with labors and the cares of the home: always, however, she remained intimately united to her Son" [*Apostolicam actuositatem,* 4], remaining in intimacy with the mystery of the Redeemer. During this journey of collaboration in the work of Redemption, her motherhood "itself underwent a singular transformation, becoming ever more imbued with 'burning charity' toward all those to whom Christ's mission was directed" [*Redemptoris Mater,* 39]. He consecrated her at the foot of the Cross: "Behold your son!" In fact, since she gave birth to Christ, the Head of the Mystical Body, she also had to have given birth to all the members of that one Body. Therefore, "Mary embraces each and every one in the Church, and embraces each and every one through the Church" [*Redemptoris Mater,* 47]. The Church, for her part, does not cease consecrating herself to Mary. ✠

POLAND 1991

From 1 to 9 June 1991, Pope John Paul again visited Poland. The theme of his visit was morality and the Ten Commandments. With the transfer of government and the downfall of communism, the Pontiff urged the Church of Poland to remain faithful to the tradition of Catholicism. He was concerned that the faithful not give themselves over to materialism and to dissipation among idle pleasures. To emphasize this point he beatified three Polish Servants of God. The first was Mother Boleslawa Lament, foundress of the Missionary Sisters of the Holy Family. She died in 1946 after dedicating her life to the work of unity in the Church. Her Beatification Ceremony was held on 5 June at Bialystok. In the course of his visit to Poland, the Pope also beatified Bishop Jozef Sebastian Pelczar, who had served the Diocese of Przemyśl from 1900 to 1924. Finally, on 9 June, he beatified Rafal Shylinski, O.F.M., an eighteenth-century mystic who dedicated his life to the service of the poor. This Beatification ceremony was conducted in Warsaw. The following citation is taken from the Liturgy for Blessed Boleslawa Lament, where he combined the themes of unity and morality. His message was not lost on his audiences.

Morality is a just measure of humanity. Man fulfills himself in it and through it when he does good. When he performs evil, he destroys the order of morality within himself as well as in the interpersonal and social aspect of his existence.

During this Mass special mention must be made of one of those happy people who followed the ways of the ancient wisdom and found life and favor with God. Forty-five years ago, the Servant of God, Boleslawa Lament, died in Bialystok. She was the founder of the Missionary Sisters of the Holy Family. Today she will be beatified. God called this daughter of the city of Lodicz to establish Catholic organizations designated to care for and educate the needy, as well as to found other organizations concerned with spiritual well-being in faraway St. Petersburg, Mohilev, and Zytomierz. After World War I she carried her work to the areas of Pinsk, Bialystok, and Vilnius. She carried on her work in spite of difficult times and constant obstacles. Twice she witnessed the loss of the entire assets of her order. She and her fellow Sisters were forced, on numerous occasions, to work hungry and homeless. She was known to draw her strength from Ignatius's famous motto, "All for the greater glory of God." She exhibited great patience and godliness during the last five years of her life, when she was paralyzed.

Throughout her life she set herself apart by showing particular sensitivity to human misfortune. She was particularly concerned with the fate of those people living on the margins of society, or even those who belonged to the criminal underworld.

With great emotional pain Boleslawa witnessed the breakup of the Church's unity, because she always felt a profound sense of responsibility *for the whole Church*. She personally witnessed many divisions and even ethnic and religious hatreds, deepened ever more by the political circumstances of the times. That is why the chief goal of her life as well as that of the order which she founded became the unity of the Church. It was that unity which Christ prayed for on Holy Thursday during the Last Supper. "Father, keep in your name those whom you have given me, that they may be one, even as we are one" [Jn 17:11]. Mother Lament particularly served the cause of unity in cases of severe division. She did not spare anything in her pursuit to strengthen the faith and increase love of God in order to bring about the improvement of relations between Catholics and Orthodox. She did this, she said, "so that we may all love each other and become one." She considered her opportunity to work for the unity of the Church, especially in the Eastern areas, to be a particular grace of Divine Providence. Long before Vatican II she became a driving force for spreading *ecumenism through love in daily life*.

The faithful in Poland and in the areas of her apostolate will henceforth be able to acclaim her in liturgical prayer and to follow the example of her life.

My pilgrimage to the homeland this year is closely linked to the Ten Commandments. An enormous wealth is contained in the ten commandments which the God of the Old Testament conveyed to his "people" through Moses. A great wealth is contained in these Ten Commandments and incomparable synthesis of the wisdom of salvation. Every commandment requires thorough reflection. There is no need to add that the historical context in which our society finds itself requires this. If it is recognized that this society is living in a period of profound *economic crisis,* then the equally important *ethical crisis* must also be recognized. What is more, to a large extent the latter conditions the former. ✠

POLAND 1991 (SECOND VISIT)

ON WHAT WAS TRULY A "PASTORAL VISIT," the Pope visited Poland
from 13 to 16 August 1991. This was his second visit to Poland
within three months. He presided at a World Youth Day at the shrine
of Our Lady of Czestochowa. He visited hospitals and seminaries. He
also beatified Miss Angela Salawa (1881–1922), a consecrated lay-
woman who dedicated herself to the poor and who was especially
active in her care of the wounded during the First World War. The
Pope was most at home in addressing the members of the International Theological Congress at the monastery of Jasnà Góra. This assembly included two hundred scholars from Central and Eastern
Europe. Organized by the Catholic University of Lublin, this gathering was the first of its kind since the Second World War. In his
lengthy address the Pontiff emphasized the importance of language,
including the Slavic tongue, in disclosing the mystery of God. This
discourse, both pastoral and philosophical, is deemed an important
address. In it, he speaks of "witness" as the foundation of morality.
He brings together Eastern and Western thought on this matter.

Theology is the fruit of an intimate relationship through faith
with the mystery of God, when this intimacy assumes the
form of methodical thought. Nevertheless, witness is prior to
the same methodical thought of the theologian. *Theology derives from
witnessing,* and especially from the witness which comes from the
Son, from Christ. He is the eyewitness of the mystery of God, and is,
at the same time, the "faithful witness" [Rv 1:5]. *Christ is the witness
of the mystery of God,* since he is both the subject and the definitive
revelation, rather, since he himself is this revealed mystery.

From the fullness of his witness *Christ calls witnesses.* He says to
the Apostles, "You will be my witnesses" [Acts 1:8], announcing to
them that the Spirit of truth is coming: "He will testify to me. And you
also testify, because you have been with me from the beginning"
[Jn 15:26–27]. Being present at the side of Christ and sharing in the

events of his life, death, and Resurrection constitute the human qualifications of the witness. However, this is not sufficient when it is a matter of witnessing the mystery of the living God. The witness of the Apostles must be rooted in the witness of the Holy Spirit, the Spirit of truth, because he alone scrutinizes the depths of God [1 Cor 2:10]. This was confirmed on the day of Pentecost; and from that time on it continues in the apostolic mission of the Church. All the baptized are called to this witness, especially through Confirmation, the sacrament which enables them to give witness in the power of the Holy Spirit. The history of the Church is the history of Christ's witnesses. Some of them were particularly important in presenting at different historical periods the mystery of the living God, revealed in Christ.

The Congress of theologians from the countries of Central and Eastern Europe held in Lublin has above all been *recording testimonies*: testimonies regarding the life of the Church under conditions of oppression which, according to the theological premises of Marxist philosophy, fought religion with the intention of eradicating it, considering it a basic form of human alienation. It fought religion and the Church (the Churches) to free the human person. This was an "administrative" program (as Cardinal Stefan Wyszyński defined it) for making society atheistic. Under these conditions, which limited and violated religious freedom as a fundamental human right, the *only possible attitude was one of apostasy or conformity* for the individuals living in the midst of their respective societies. Under the same conditions, however, it was also possible to make a *conscious choice* of Christ's truth; this stance was in the nature of a special witness. It is well known that the Greek term for giving witness, the word: *"martyrion"* (eventually, *"martyria"*)—in Latin, *"martyrium"*—also denotes persecution for the truth even to the sacrifice of one's life. This was, first of all, the witness—the *martyrium*—of Christ himself. Precisely in the sacrifice of his life on the cross there is the fullness of the revelation of God, who is love. This contained "the fullness of God's self-revelation." Human *martyrium,* or *the witness given to Christ at the price of persecution and even death,* possesses a fundamental significance for the life of the Church; it makes the divine mystery present in a special way, the mystery by which the Church lives and with which she brings life to the world. This is also confirmed in that particular "site" of *martyrium* which has involved the European continent during recent decades. Parallel to the "Eastern" *martyrium*, there has also been a "Western" one, connected with Hitler's racism, which did not last as long, but was just as cruel.

The Congress of theologians, which has focused on recording these testimonies, assumes a basic function from the theological point of view as well. Witness is a particular knowledge, an intimacy with mystery, in the global and existential sense. Let us not forget that *among the written sources of Christianity there is the "martyrologium,"* which during the course of the Church's history is constantly updated according to various geographical areas. Our century needs a new martyrology, for our continent perhaps first of all. In it many Christians (along with others who gave their lives for the truth they professed) will be found who are united to the recognized Tradition of the East and West. Even if the martyrology in its external form is an elementary register of persons and events, nevertheless its deep theological content allows one *to discover the very roots of every theology*. The martyrology speaks of the facts of Christian experience which are especially filled and permeated by contact with the divine mystery and the presence of this same mystery.

Christ, in telling his disciples about the persecutions waiting for them because of his name, added "Take courage, I have conquered the world" [Jn 16:33]; and John the Evangelist writes that *this victory is "our faith"* [1 Jn 5:4]. This victory consists above all in the very experience of witnessing ("martyrium"). It is the experience of God's activity in man, of the power of the Holy Spirit, who "comes upon" him [Acts 1:8]. In some way the reflection of this victory is externalized and recorded in the history of the Church and in the life of societies. ✠

UNGARY 1991

POPE JOHN PAUL II MADE A PASTORAL VISIT TO HUNGARY from 16 to 20 August 1991, during which he encouraged a revival of the faith at every level. His principal reason for selecting these dates was the celebration of the Feast of Saint Stephen the King on 20 August. On that date the Pontiff celebrated Mass in Budapest's Heroes' Square. He addressed the nation by identifying the significance of King Stephen (977–1038).

Your Holy King, dear brothers and sisters of the Hungarian nation, left you as an inheritance *not only the royal crown which he received from Pope Sylvester II*. He left you *the spiritual testament, a heritage of fundamental and indestructible value*: The true house built upon the rock. This edifice built upon the rock is not only a doctrine of a compilation of laws and counsels or a human institution: above all, it is *a solid testimony of Christian life*. Saint Stephen is a Christian who believes in the revealed truth, fixes his heart on Jesus, true God and true man, and follows his words without hesitation. Indeed, it is on Christ that the Church and the life of every Christian are built: on Christ the cornerstone [Eph 2:20], the same yesterday and today and forever [Heb 13:8], who is with us until the end of time [Mt 28:20].

We are firmly set upon this rock when we live *through* Christ, *in* Christ, *for* Christ. To live *through Christ* is to count on the power of his grace; to live *in Christ* is to strive to have his own mind [Phil 2:5], unconditionally obeying the Father and generously loving our neighbor; to live *for Christ* is to be committed to building the Kingdom of God in the world.

This is your vocation, dear brothers and sisters, this is your commitment, if you wish the house of your nation to continue to stand firm amid the changing fortunes of history.

None of you is ignorant of the many attacks which at different times this house has had to endure from foreign enemies, and how many difficulties it has likewise had to face as a result of internal tensions and divisions. Today Hungary is on the way toward a new situation and at present there are no threats from foreign enemies. This offers her a unique opportunity to strengthen the house built by her forebears. For the success of this enterprise, however, her citizens must be able to restrain excessive impulses toward the selfish pursuit of individual comfort, as well as the temptation of a mentality of conflict which would systematically set citizens, groups, and social classes at odds with one another.

The solid rock upon which it is possible to build in a lasting way is Christ the Lord, the way, the truth, and the life. Hungary has been liberated from external oppression; the hour has come when she must free herself from the inner chains of the various forms of spiritual slavery. The name of peace is justice, solidarity, and love. The nation can hope for a better future only if its citizens assume their own responsibilities in a joint effort aimed at the common good.

Saint Stephen recognized that the true way to survive and form from various tribes a single nation was conversion to Christianity. Only Christian values, in fact, can offer a solid basis for a truly human culture. At present, Hungary has become a pluralistic society in which citizens and groups follow different value systems. But history teaches that fundamental Christian values have been assimilated into modern humanism: the dignity of the person, solidarity, freedom, and peace. The Church is present among you to continue to proclaim the Kingdom of God, showing therein the foundation of human dignity and the transcendent horizon within which every human value takes on its full meaning. ✠

BRAZIL 1991

POPE JOHN PAUL II SPENT NINE DAYS TOURING BRAZIL, 12 to 21 October 1991. Speaking to countless numbers of faithful across the country, he praised ongoing apostolic activity while also reminding listeners of their duties toward ecology. His never-ending theme throughout Latin America is always the significance of evangelization.

On 15 October the Pope celebrated Mass in the Archdiocese of Brasília. Fittingly, he blessed the cornerstone of the new Cathedral during the ceremony; the Pope's homily spoke of faith as a cornerstone of the Church. Faith is always a dialogue.

W*hat is faith?* The Apostle replies: "Faith is the realization of what is hoped for and evidence of things not seen" [Heb 11:1]. That is why, through faith, in a certain manner, we overcome the limits of visible reality, to enter into the invisible reality. *The visible is,* in a certain way, *the proof of the invisible.* The universe bears witness to God as its Creator. We read in the Letter to the Hebrews that "by faith we understand that the universe was ordered by the word of God, so that what is visible came into being through the invisible" [Heb 11:3]. The testimony of the word of God the Creator is thus written in all creation.

Apart from this testimony, which is accessible to everyone, *faith finds support in human testimonies of divine revelation.* . . .

Faith is a gift of God which reaches man through the message of absolute truth, but it is, at the same time, *the response of the person* who sincerely seeks an encounter with God.

ON 18 OCTOBER THE HOLY FATHER VISITED FLORIANÓPOLIS and Santa Catarina to beatify Mother Pauline of the Heart of Jesus in Agony (Amabilis Visintainer, 1865–1942), foundress of the Daughters of the Immaculate Conception and the first native Brazilian to be beatified. Her religious community cared for the sick. An often misunderstood and misjudged leader in religious life, she remained faithful.

The ceremony of Blessed Mother Pauline's beatification was an acknowledgment of the Communion of Saints. The Pope's remarks magnified her charism.

I n what way was Mother Pauline, whom we proclaim blessed today, clothed in love?

What most distinguishes the life of the saints is their *ability to awaken the desire for God* in those who have the joy of being around them. Their generous correspondence to divine grace is therefore rewarded with a constant inclination toward God, who is desired, known, loved, and praised. It is precisely in this light that the Servant of God is presented to us as we prepare to recognize her solemnly among the blessed in the kingdom of heaven.

"Think of what is above" [Col 3:2].

This was precisely the gift lived to the highest degree by Mother Pauline. She was able to convert all her words and actions into a continual act of praise to God. In her youth she asked God for the grace to enter religious life with *the single goal of loving and serving him* in the best way possible. . . .

It was this ability to be constantly united to God and, at the same time, to work intensely for the good of souls that characterized the life of Blessed Pauline of the Heart of Jesus in Agony. From today on the Church proposes her as an example of life to be admired and imitated.

Holiness is shown in everyday life, in work on behalf of one's brothers and sisters, as a result of union with God. It is connected to an active, effective love for Christ's Church, which is represented by her pastors who, within the Episcopal College, are united to the Successor of Peter. Holiness, then, is the expression of this faith profoundly lived through charity, *"Fides operatur per caritatem,"* which is capable of giving a new breath of hope and an answer to the society which seems to want to live in an atmosphere of hedonism and consumerism. ✠

$\mathcal{S}$ENEGAL 1992

POPE JOHN PAUL VISITED THREE COUNTRIES IN WESTERN AFRICA during his eighth apostolic journey to Africa, 19 to 26 February 1992. He arrived in Senegal, the country he called a "pioneer on the paths of African democracy." The Pope addressed the Diplomatic Corps at the Apostolic Nunciature in Dakar on 22 February.

Various types of tension and conflict often result from offenses against human rights. When the simple right to life is threatened, when the minimum of material means is lacking, when the legitimate aspirations for a family life, education, and work are not satisfied, a society cannot live in peace. The primary goal of the organization of society is to respond to these demands. The juridical definition of rights has value only if it is based on respect for the human being, the subject of rights. The dignity of peoples presupposes that their just aspirations, their traditions, and their beliefs can be expressed freely.

In a society which respects the rights of each person, responsibilities are shared and social relationships are constructive initiatives and associations. Freedom of conscience is truly granted in the freedom to express one's religion publicly. Everyone has the same opportunity and the same open future.

Ladies and gentlemen, if I mention these simple principles, it is because it seems to me they shed light on the immense democratic movement which we see spreading throughout the world at this time, and especially in Africa. ✠

AMBIA 1992

Pope John Paul then traveled to Gambia, where he identified the importance of mission and called on the youth of the nation to be "the salt of the earth," be "the light of the world!" [Mt 5:13–14]. He used the theme of salt and light throughout the entire apostolic journey into Western Africa. In Gambia, the Pontiff acknowledged the efforts of the Christian communities during evolving times.

Among the messages delivered to Catholic and Muslim audiences, which included gatherings of youth and the poor, was the importance of faith and prayer in the midst of change and unrest. However, he also said, "Your country needs you to strengthen family life." The following remarks were delivered at the Banjul Independent Stadium in Gambia immediately after his arrival on 23 February 1992.

Today our world cries out for salt and light from God. Africa needs this savor and fire in order to preserve what is good and just in its traditional culture and values; in order to direct its search for solutions to its pressing problems; in order to enlighten and guide with wisdom its efforts to achieve greater development and a better life for its peoples.

In a particular way, your nation needs the witness of strong Christian family life, for it is above all in the heart of a united and loving family that the young learn essential values and the Christian attitude to the realities and relationships through which we journey to our transcendent destiny. "The family is the first and fundamental school of social living" [*Familiaris Consortio,* n. 37]. It teaches the value of human dignity. It teaches respect for each one's rights. It teaches true justice and solidarity. The communion and constant sharing involved in everyday life in the home is the best training for an active and responsible sharing in the wider life of society.

The truth about the family receives a ready acceptance in the hearts of African men and women, because the strength of Africa has always been the family. Your society has been built upon the bonds which expand from the love of husband and wife to embrace children and all who make up the extended family. Your culture's respect for the family shows how you have always prized the family's fundamental role in God's plan. As Christian families, you are called to pass on to future generations this great inheritance, and to strengthen and ennoble it with the grace of the sacrament of Marriage. ✠

GUINEA 1992

THE POPE'S FINAL ADDRESS on this African journey was in the context of a Marian prayer service conducted on the grounds of the Archbishop's residence in Conakry, Guinea. The date was 25 February. During the vigil, he reflected upon the strengthening of faith that occurs through the recitation of the Rosary. His favorite prayer, Pope John Paul prays it daily. Every Saturday night the Pontiff recites the Rosary in the Hall of Benedictions of the Apostolic Palace with the faithful of Rome.

The Rosary is a marvelous prayer, simple and profound. We repeat the words of the Archangel Gabriel and those of Elizabeth to our Lady. Against this background of "Hail Mary," the main episodes of Jesus' life pass, united in joyful, sorrowful, and glorious mysteries. With Mary's help we enter into communion with the Lord. At the same time, we introduce into these decades of the Rosary the events about which we care most: those in our personal life, in our family life, and in our life as a nation. We offer to God, through Mary, "the joy and the hope, the grief and the anguish, of the people of our time, especially of those who are poor or afflicted in any way," which are "the joy and hope, the grief and anguish of the followers of Christ as well" *(Gaudium et Spes,* n. 1). I exhort you, dear brothers and sisters, to rediscover even more the values of the Rosary as a personal, family, and parish prayer, in order *to grow in faith.* ✠

NGOLA 1992

THE PONTIFF SPENT 4 TO 10 JUNE 1992 IN ANGOLA, with a one-day visit to the nation of São Tomé and Príncipe. The purpose of the visit was to provide comfort to a people who had known sixteen years of civil war. On 5 June he celebrated Mass in the city of Huambo. Here he spoke directly to the suffering caused by the tragedy of war. In this liturgy, the Pope prayed for justice and peace within Angola. He prayed together with "all the sons and daughters of this great nation. . . . In the Lord's presence we cannot fail to remember and to pray for those brothers and sisters who in this tormented part of Angola were the victims, often the innocent victims, of ideological conflict and war; they numbered tens of thousands." Below is the theme of his homily:

O*ur eyes are on the Lord, our God, till he have pity on us"* [Ps 123:2]. The family of Angola needs God's grace to heal the wounds caused by the sin of war and hatred. It needs God to receive the strength of heart necessary for overcoming the difficulties which lie in its way. For this reason, "ours eyes are on the Lord." Angola also needs the joint disinterested help of the international community. If in the past there were some who instilled dissension in the country, there were also countries and international organizations which generously alleviated the sufferings of the Angolan people. "Blessed are they who show mercy; mercy shall be theirs," the Lord said [Mt 5:7]. As I give thanks for the aid received in the past, I make an appeal that Angola may continue to be helped by the international community. But Angola must first of all help itself.

We must acknowledge the fact that the long years of war have introduced ways of acting which promote confrontation, when cooperation is needed. In addition, removing God from life, from the family, from education and society brings about a human impoverishment of the person. The introduction of foreign customs and behavior into your cultural identity, which is religious, has weakened the sense of the great moral values which are part of your tradition. *"To reestablish peace you must restore justice:* the justice of truth, the justice of social equality, and the justice of fraternal solidarity." ✠

$\mathscr{S}$ÃO TOMÉ AND PRÍNCIPE 1992

ON 6 JUNE THE POPE made a one-day visit to São Tomé and Príncipe. This territory is the oldest diocese of sub-Saharan Africa, having been established by Pope Paul III in 1534. Because of the strong tradition of faith, the Pope encouraged his listeners to be examples of faith and moral virtue. He addressed the lay leaders of the nation.

One of the temptations of our day is that people can become too secure and self-sufficient, and do not have their minds and hearts open to the word of God. It is "living and effective, sharper than any two-edged sword" [Heb 4:12], but it is necessary freely to open one's self up to the word in order to have life. The "narrow gate" and the "rough road" of the Gospel are, in fact, the path "that leads to life" [Mt 7:14]; the "broad road" of selfishness, hedonism, and eroticism ultimately leads to dehumanization without satisfying a person's deepest desires. Distancing one's self from God is a flight toward darkness and death, while the paths of the house of God are the paths which lead to life. ✠

DOMINICAN REPUBLIC 1992

THE HOLY FATHER celebrated the founding of America by Christopher Columbus with a trip to the Dominican Republic. For nine years the Catholic Church in all the American nations had been preparing for this event. The Pontiff remained on the island from 9 to 14 October 1992. In the course of his stay he canonized Blessed Ezequiel Moreno y Diaz, a nineteenth-century bishop of the order of Augustinian Recollects. This missionary labored in Colombia, where he served as bishop of Pasto. He died on 19 August 1905.

In the course of his remarks, the Pope addressed a constituency of all Americas. He offered a special message, which was delivered to the African-American community of the entire hemisphere on the date of the discovery itself.

The evangelization of America is a reason for giving heartfelt thanks to God who, in his infinite mercy, wanted the message of salvation to reach the inhabitants of this blessed land, made fruitful by the cross of Christ, which has left an imprint on the life and history of his people and has produced such abundant fruits of holiness and virtue throughout the span of these five centuries.

The date of 12 October 1492 marks the initial encounter of races and cultures that feature in the history of these five hundred years, during which the penetrating Christian gaze enables us to discover God's loving intervention, in spite of human shortcomings and faithlessness. In fact, in the course of history, there is a mysterious confluence of sin and grace, but in the long run grace triumphs over the power of sin. As Saint Paul tells us: "Despite the increase of sin, grace has far surpassed it" [Rom 5:20].

In these celebrations of the fifth centenary, I could not fail to bring my message of closeness and warm affection to the African-American peoples who are an important part of the population of the whole continent. They enrich the Church and society in so many countries with their human and Christian values as well as with their culture. In this context, the words of Simon Bolívar come to mind. He declared that "America is the result of the union of Europe and Africa with aborigine elements. That is why there is no room there for racial prejudice, and if it were to appear, the Americas would return to a state of primitive chaos."

ON 12 OCTOBER POPE JOHN PAUL once again opened a general assembly of the Latin American Bishops Conference (CELAM). Here is his most important address of the visit and it reflects the very first apostolic visit which he undertook, to Puebla in 1979. In this later address he developed the theme of the "new evangelization." He had coined this term in 1983, when he inaugurated a nine-year preparation of prayer to commemorate the discovery of the Americas. In this speech he developed the meaning of the term, placing it in the context of the needs of Latin America.

The *new evangelization* is the main idea of the whole theme of this conference.

Since my meeting in Haiti with the bishops of CELAM in 1983, I have placed particular emphasis on this expression, using it to indicate a new fervor and new desires for evangelization in America and the whole world; it is meant to give pastoral action a new stimulus, which would introduce the Church, now thoroughly imbued with the strength and power of Pentecost, into a new and more fruitful era of evangelization [*Evangelii Nuntiandi,* n. 2].

The new evangelization does not consist of a "new Gospel" which would arise from us, from our culture, or our analyses of the needs of mankind. In that case, it would not be the "Gospel," but a mere human invention, and salvation would not be found in it. Neither does it involve removing from the Gospel whatever seems difficult for the modern mentality to accept. Culture is not the measure of the Gospel, but it is Jesus Christ who is the measure of every culture and every human action. No, the new evangelization is not born of the desire for "currying favor with human beings" or "seeking to please people" [Gal 1:10], but of the responsibility for the gift which God has given us in Christ, in which we learn the truth about God and mankind and the possibility for true life.

The new evangelization has, as its point of departure, the certitude that in Christ there are "inscrutable riches" [Eph 3:8] which no culture or era can exhaust, and which we most always bring to people in order to enrich them [Special Assembly for Europe of the Synod of Bishops, *final declaration,* n. 3]. These riches are, first of all, Christ himself, his person, because he himself is our salvation. Drawing near to him in faith and being incorporated into his Body the Church, the men and women of every age and culture can find the answer to those questions, ever ancient yet ever new, with which people face the mystery of existence and which have been indelibly engraved on our hearts since creation and the wound of sin. ✠

 BENIN 1993

FROM 3 TO 5 FEBRUARY 1993 the Pontiff paid a second apostolic visit to the West African nation of Benin. The purpose of his visit was both to encourage the democratic changes that had recently occurred within this country and also to ordain new priests to serve the Church. Late in the evening of his arrival on 3 February he met the bishops of the nation, but in an unprecedented gesture he announced to them, "It is too late for me to be making long speeches; it is better to use the time to read, study, and reflect." He then handed them this text:

Evangelization, which is at the heart of the bishop's ministry, comes through *inculturation of the faith.* This topic is dear to you, and it is the object of your reflection, especially in the perspective of the Special Assembly for Africa of the Synod of Bishops. The Gospel message plays a prophetic and critical role. It is meant to give new life, to sift what is ambiguous or tarnished in ancestral customs as well as in practices recently imported from foreign lands. Everything that is good, noble, and true can be accepted so that the Christian mystery may be expressed according to the African genius. This undertaking of inculteration requires a lot of time, of theological clarity and spiritual discernment. It took time in Europe, the first area outside the Middle East to benefit from the proclamation of the Good News by the Apostles, for the Gospel to help give birth to a Christian culture. It will take time for Africa to do the same.

The Second Vatican Council gave three criteria for discernment in accepting the cultural values of peoples, namely: their ability to contribute to the glory of God the Creator; their ability to show forth the grace of the Savior; and finally their ability to be ordered to Christian life [*Ad gentes,* n. 22].

Founded on the Apostolic and ecclesiastical tradition, inculturation is the great challenge to the Catholic Church in Africa at the threshold of the third millennium. Starting from the Christian lifeblood, it is a question of producing authentically African fruits in union with the particular Churches of the continent and the universal Church. For you, the Pastors of Benin, it is a question of seeing how a Beninese can be a Christian with all his being. ✠

$\mathcal{U}$GANDA 1993

ALTOGETHER POPE JOHN PAUL spent seven days in Africa, 5 to 10 February 1993. His principle reason was to pay homage to the nineteenth-century martyrs of Uganda. On 7 February he first visited the shrine of the Anglican martyrs at Nakiyanja. He then visited the Catholic shrine nearby of Saint Charles Lwanga and his twenty-one companions. This latter group was canonized by Pope Paul VI in 1964. All of these were put to death by Uganda's King Mwanga in 1885 and 1887. In a common act of witness these young men, all pages in the court of the king, refused his immoral advances and suffered the consequences by fire and sword. The Pope's principal reason for coming on this African visit was to assume the title of pilgrim to their shrine. This gesture was intended to encourage preparations for the All-African Synod and to proclaim the act of martyrdom an act of "common witness" in the ecumenical experience of the modern world.

Today, too, my greetings go in a special way to Uganda's lay faithful. I embrace you with love in the Lord Jesus. You are the heirs of the strong and faithful lay leaders with which the Church in Uganda was blessed from the beginning.

"You were darkness once," Saint Paul told the Ephesians, "but now you are light in the Lord" [Eph 5:8].

How eloquent were the words of Pope Paul VI in his homily at the canonization of the Uganda Martyrs!

"Who could foresee," the Pope asked, "that alongside the great historical figures of African martyrs and confessors like Cyprian, Felicity, and Perpetua and the outstanding Augustine, we should one day list the beloved names of Charles Lwanga, Mattias Mulumba Kalemba, and their twenty companions [18 October 1964].

Truly, *the Uganda Martyrs became light in the Lord!* Their sacrifice hastened the rebirth of the Church in Africa. In our own days, *all Africa is being called to the light of Christ!* Africa is being called again to discover her true identity in the light of faith in the Son of God. All that is truly African, all that is true and good and noble in Africa's traditions and cultures, is meant to find its fulfillment in Christ. The Uganda Martyrs show this clearly: *They were the truest of Africans,* worthy heirs of the virtues of their ancestors. In embracing Jesus Christ, they opened the door of faith to their own people [Acts 14:27], so that the glory of the Lord could shine on Uganda, on Africa.

In the first place, I wish to acknowledge the outstanding service provided by your catechists. In recent times some of them, like the martyrs of old, have even been called to give their lives for Christ. The history of the Church in Uganda clearly shows that generations of catechists have offered "a singular and absolutely necessary contribution to the spread of the faith and of the Church" [*Ad gentes,* n. 17] in your country.

How obvious this was even at the dawn of Christianity in Uganda! Despite the fact that they themselves had only recently come to know Christ, your martyrs joyfully shared with others the good news about the One who is "the way and the truth and the life"

[Jn 14:6]. They understood that "faith is strengthened when it is given to others" [*Redemptoris Missio*, n. 2]. ✠

$\mathcal{S}$UDAN 1993

ON 10 FEBRUARY 1993 the Pope visited the city of Khartoum in the Sudan. While there he venerated the memory of Blessed Josephine Bakhita, a Sudanese woman whom he had beatified in 1992. Most important, he addressed the civil war, then still active. He was concerned also for the persecution of Christians, especially missionaries, who in many instances had been expelled from the country. His most direct remarks were focused on the theology of the Cross when he spoke at the Archdiocesan Cathedral of Khartoum.

I am well aware of the sad circumstances of your country, tormented by a civil war that brought untold misery, suffering, and death to the Sudanese people, especially in the south. The life of your communities is deeply affected also by a breakdown in the good relations that should exist between Christians and Muslims. Moreover, you and your fellow Christians are poor in the goods of this world, even to the point of extreme hardship.

With admiration and with intense gratitude to our Heavenly Father for your fidelity, I encourage you to "stand firm in one spirit, with one mind striving side by side for the faith of the gospel" [Phil 1:27]. In my own country I have known something of the horrors of war and of the ways in which the history of the catacombs has been repeated in this century. As the Successor of Peter, in my solicitude for all the Churches, I share the trials and sufferings of our brothers and sisters all over the world. Still, in this part of Africa, I see clearly a particular reproduction of the mystery of Calvary in the lives of the majority of the Christian people. And what answer can I give you? What consolation can I offer you? Brothers and sisters, if there is one message that the Pope wants to leave with you it is this: *Make the Paschal mystery the center of your lives! Gather the People of God to celebrate the mystery of faith.* Nourish yourselves and your communities with the Word of life and the sacraments of our salvation. ✠

LBANIA 1993

ON 25 APRIL 1993, Pope John Paul presided over the ordination ceremony of four new bishops for the nation of Albania. These were Archbishop Frano Illia of Schkodrë, Archbishop Rrok Mirdita of Durrës, Bishop Robert Ashta, C.F.M., of Pult, and Auxiliary Bishop Zef Simoni of Schkodrë. In his homily the Pope referred to the recent history of Albania as a "catacombs in a time of suffering and persecution." The moving part of his discourse was the list of credentials of suffering ascribed to the new prelates.

I greet you, Archbishop Frano Illia of Schkodrë, on the very day on which, twenty-five years ago, you were condemned to death. A sentence which was later commuted to hard labor, which you served for twenty years. I greet your Auxiliary, Bishop Zef Simoni, you also condemned, a year before, on 25 April 1967, to fifteen years' imprisonment. Providence also chose 25 April as the date of your Episcopal ordination. I greet you, Archbishop Rrok K. Mirdita of Durrës-Tiranë, who have so generously agreed to face the challenges and hardships of a demanding, tiring pastoral service. Last of all, I greet you, Bishop Robert Ashta of Pult, to whom the people of this land are also grateful for the sufferings you have borne in the difficult past.

BEFORE THE ORDINATION CEREMONY, the Pontiff spoke words of greeting to the entire nation. He was direct about the events of the Marxist period.

I offer you, the noble Albanian people, my warm and affectionate greeting! Everyone is aware of all the tragic events you have had to face, especially over the last twenty-five years. Years of genuine suffering, whose consequences it will be difficult to erase through the passage of time and which, in any case, Europe and the whole world must not forget. Years of deprivation of the basic liberties of the human person, including freedom of expression, association, and religion, which seriously damaged your social fabric and profoundly affected your behavior and consciences.

The Holy See has always followed with close attention—which often became sorrowful anxiety—your difficult journey during the long years of totalitarian oppression, and was near you through prayer and pastoral concern. And today, I am happy to be able to share with you, a country rich in cultural and spiritual traditions, the joy of your newfound freedom. I am pleased to be able to encourage you in the effort that you have undertaken toward moral and material reconstruction, assuring you of the Church's loyal and constant support.

During such a severe and distressing winter of suffering and trial, "the heroic Church of Albania upset by a long hard persecution, but enriched by the testimony of its martyrs," as I had occasion to recall during my pastoral visit to the Archdiocese of Otranto in Puglia in October 1980, shared completely in the sorrows and hopes of the nation, keeping alive even through the personal sacrifice of numerous members the ancient Christian Tradition, in the belief that it represents an intrinsic part of the authentic Albanian identity that must not be rejected.

Just as she shared in the recent trials, so now the Church wishes to share in the joy and responsibility of the new season of freedom that has just begun. It is her great desire to make a significant contribution to the achievement of Albania's integral progress and its active insertion into the European context, toward which its ancient historical roots naturally lead it. ✠

$\mathscr{S}$PAIN 1993

FROM 12 TO 17 JUNE 1993, Pope John Paul visited Spain for the fourth time, for the specific purpose of celebrating the solemn close of the Forty-fifth International Eucharistic Congress, in Seville. This visit likewise coincided with celebrations honoring the close of the fifth centenary of the evangelization of the New World. While in Spain he canonized Father Enrique de Osso y Cervello. Saint Enrique was a Catalonian by birth, who in the late nineteenth and early twentieth centuries as a diocesan priest established lay and religious families under Carmelite spirituality in order to promote the Gospel. The Pope's two principal themes focused on the Eucharist and promotion of the Gospel. This is from his homily of the Eucharistic Congress, delivered during a time of private adoration in the Seville Cathedral. The date was 12 June.

Yes, dear brothers and sisters, it is important for us to live and teach others how to live the total mystery of the Eucharist: the Sacrament of Sacrifice, of the Banquet, and of the abiding presence of Jesus Christ the Savior. You know well that the various forms of Eucharistic devotion are both an extension of the Sacrifice and of Communion and a preparation for them. Is it necessary to stress once again the deep theological and spiritual motivations which underlie devotion to the Blessed Sacrament outside the celebration of Mass? It is true that the reservation of the Sacrament was begun in order to take Communion to the sick and those absent from the celebration. However, as the *Catechism of the Catholic Church* says, "To deepen faith in the real presence of Christ in the Eucharist, the Church is aware of the meaning of silent adoration of the Lord present under the Eucharistic species" [n. 1379].

"And behold, I am with you always, until the end of the age" [Mt 28:20]. These are the words of the risen Christ before his ascension into heaven. Jesus Christ is truly Emmanuel, God with us, from his incarnation to the end of time. And he is so in a specially intense and close way in the mystery of his abiding presence in the Eucharist. What strength, what consolation, what staunch hope the contemplation of the Eucharistic mystery gives rise to! It is God with us who enables us to share his life and sends us into the world to evangelize it and make it holy!

Eucharist and evangelization was the theme of the Forty-fifth International Eucharistic Congress in Seville. You have reflected on it intensely over the past few days and during its long preparation. The Eucharist really is "the source and culmination of all evangelization" [*Presbyteriorum ordinis,* n. 5]. It is the horizon and the goal of the entire proclamation of Christ's Gospel. We are constantly journeying toward it through the word of Truth, the proclamation of the message of salvation. Thus every liturgical celebration of the Eucharist according to the spirit and the norms of the Church has great evangelizing force. Indeed, the celebration of the Eucharist develops an essential and effective teaching of the Christian mystery: The believing community is summoned and gathered as a family and the People of God, the Body of Christ; it is doubly nourished at the table of the Word and of the sacrificial Banquet of the Eucharist; it is sent as a means of salvation into the world. All this is in praise and thanksgiving to the Father.

Join me in asking Jesus Christ the Lord, who died for our sins and rose for our salvation, that as a result of this Eucharistic Congress the whole church may be strengthened for the new evangelization which the whole world needs: new, also, because of its explicit and deep reference to the Eucharist as the center and source of Christian life, as the seed and requisite of fellowship, justice, and service to all humanity, starting with those who are most needy in body and in spirit. Evangelization through the Eucharist, in the Eucharist, and from the Eucharist: these are three inseparable aspects of how the Church lives the mystery of Christ and fulfills her mission of communicating it to all people. ✠

JAMAICA 1993

ON 9 AUGUST 1993, Pope John Paul II left Rome for Denver, Colorado, to preside at World Youth Day, which was to be held on 15 August, the Feast of Our Lady of the Assumption. On 9 August, however, he landed in Kingston, Jamaica, where he was greeted by the governor-general, Sir Howard Felix Hanlan Cooke, and Archbishop Samuel Carter, S.J., of Kingston, Bishop Edgerton Clarke of Montego Bay, and Bishop Paul Boyle, C.P., of Mandeville. The following day he celebrated Mass in Kingston's National Stadium. Because of his awareness of a majority of single-parent families in the island nation, he addressed his remarks to this issue.

In this regard I wish to say a special word to Christian married couples. In God's plan for the human race, "a man leaves his father and mother and clings to his wife, and the two of them become one body" [Gn 2:24; Mt 19:5]. The family, born of the faithful love of man and woman, is the basic unit of society, a cradle of life and love where God's gift of new life is welcomed, nurtured, and allowed to develop. The future of society is essentially linked to the strength of its families [*Familiaris Consortio*, n. 86].

Christian married couples! The witness of your lives must be ever more clear! Your faithful love must shine forth and stand in contrast to ways of living that are not in accord with the Gospel. Your families must be sanctuaries of love in the midst of the many difficult situations caused by the misuse of God's gift of sexuality. As a people, Jamaicans have known the evils of slavery, a system which stripped human beings of their dignity as images of God, denied people's spiritual worth, and reduced them to mere objects to be used and exploited. But apart from its exploitation of individuals, one of the greatest evils of slavery was its destruction of family bonds. Slavery stole men away from their wives; wives were left alone with the burden of raising children; and children were deprived of the presence of their fathers. The tragic fruits of this evil system are still present in attitudes of sexual irresponsibility. They are painfully obvious in the lives of too many children who miss the love and support of their parents and a healthy home life, and in too many women who struggle, often single-handedly, to provide for their children. Complete liberation from the past of slavery must also involve efforts to heal the deep scars left in the life of society. And in healing and rebuilding family life, Christian married couples have a fundamental witness to offer. As teachers of faith and virtue to their children, Christian parents point the way which the next generation will take. And by their lives of faith, fidelity, openness to life, and reconciling love, Christian families will be the primary evangelizers of other families. ✠

MEXICO 1993

Before reaching Denver, the Pope made a two-day visit to the Yucatán Peninsula of Mexico. There he was greeted by President Ernesto Zedillo. On the same day as his arrival, the Pope visited Uxmal, the home of the Mayan culture. The purpose of the visit was to express his solidarity with the indigenous peoples of Central America and, in particular, with the past and the present plight of Mexican history. The date of this visit was 11 August.

In seeing you, dear brothers and sisters, my heart exalts in thanksgiving to God for the gift of faith which your ancestors cultivated like a great treasure, and which you are seeking to incarnate in your life and pass on to your children. To my lips come the words of Jesus: "I give praise to you, Father, Lord of heaven and earth, for although you have hidden these things from the wise and the learned you have revealed them to the childlike" [Mt 11:25]. This prayer of Christ resounds today with a particular emphasis in Izamal, because God has chosen to reveal the riches of his Kingdom to the pure of heart. Since the very beginning of evangelization, the Catholic Church, faithful to the Spirit of Christ, has been the tireless defender of the Indios, the protector of the values found in their cultures, the promoter of humane treatment in the face of the abuses of the sometimes unscrupulous colonizers who were unable to recognize the indigenous peoples as their brothers and sisters, sons and daughters of their one Father, God. The denunciation of injustices and abuses, made by Bartolomé de Las Casas, Antonio de Montesinos, Vasco de Quiroga, José de Anchieta, Manuel de Nóbrega, Pedro de Cordoba, Bartolomé de Olmedo, Juan del Valle, and so many others, was like an outcry which gave rise to legislation inspired by the recognition of the sacred value of the person and, at the same time, a prophetic witness against the abuses committed during the age of colonization. Those missionaries, whom the Puebla Document calls "intrepid champions of justice and proponents of the Gospel message of peace" [n. 8], were not motivated by earthly ambition or personal interest, but by the urgent call to evangelize their brothers and sisters who did not know Jesus Christ. "The Church," we read in the Santo Domingo Document, "in meeting the native groups, sought from the beginning to accompany them in the struggle for their own survival, teaching them the way of Christ the Savior, from the unjust situation of conquered peoples, invaded and trated like slaves" [n. 245].

With this apostolic visit I want most of all to celebrate your faith, to support your human development, to affirm your cultural and Christian identity. My presence in your midst is also meant to give emphatic support to your right to have room for your cultural, social, and ethnic identity as individuals and groups. ✠

United States 1993

On 12 August 1993 Pope John Paul II arrived at Stapleton International Airport in Denver, where he was greeted by William Clinton, president of the United States, and the Most Reverend Francis Stafford, Archbishop of Denver. The occasion of the visit was the celebration of World Youth Day. After being greeted by the president on behalf of the United States, the Pontiff responded. His message had the future of America's youth in mind.

T he well-being of the world's children and young people must be of immense concern to all who have public responsibilities. In my pastoral visits to the Church in every part of the world I have been deeply moved by the almost universal conditions of difficulty in which young people grow up and live. Too many sufferings are visited upon them by natural calamities, famines, epidemics, by economic and political crises, by the atrocities of wars. And where material conditions are at least adequate, other obstacles arise, not the least of which is the breakdown of family values and stability. In developed countries, a serious moral crisis is already affecting the lives of many young people, leaving them adrift, often without hope and conditioned to look only for instant gratification. Yet everywhere there are young men and women deeply concerned about the world around them, ready to give the best of themselves in service to others and particularly sensitive to life's transcendent meaning.

But how do we help them? Only by instilling a high moral vision can a society ensure that its young people are given the possibility to mature as free and intelligent human beings, endowed with the robust sense of responsibility to the common good, capable of working with others to create a community and a nation with a strong moral fiber. America was built on such a vision, and the American people possess the intelligence and will to meet the challenge of rededicating themselves with renewed vigor to fostering the truths on which this country was founded and by which it grew. Those truths are enshrined in the Declaration of Independence, the Constitution, and the Bill of Rights, and they still today receive a broad consensus among Americans. Those truths sustain values which have led people all over the world to look to America with hope and respect.

To all Americans, without exception, I present this invitation: Let *us pause and reason together* [Is 1:18]. To educate without a value system based on truth is to abandon young people to moral confusion, personal insecurity, and easy manipulation. No country, not even the most powerful, can endure if it deprives its own children of this essential good. Respect for the dignity and worth of every person, integrity and responsibility, as well as understanding, compassion, and solidarity toward others, survive only if they are passed on in families, in schools, and through the communications media.

America has a strong tradition of respect for the individual, for human dignity and human rights. I gladly acknowledged this during my previous visit to the United States in 1987, and I would like to repeat today the hope I expressed on that occasion: "America, you are beautiful and blessed in so many ways . . . but your best beauty and your richest blessing is found in the human person; in each man, woman, and child, and every immigrant, in every native-born son and daughter. . . . The ultimate test of your greatness is the way you treat every human being, but especially the weakest and most defenseless ones. The best traditions of your land presume respect for those who cannot defend themselves. If you want equal justice for all, and true freedom and lasting peace, then, America, defend life! All the great causes that are yours today will have meaning only to the extent that you guarantee the right to life and protect the human person" [*Departure Speech in Detroit,* 19 September 1987].

ON THE EVENING OF 15 AUGUST, Pope John Paul was once again greeted at Stapleton Airport. This time he was welcomed by Vice President Albert Gore and Mrs. Gore. He reflected to them his impressions of his visit—again the theme was youth. These were his departing words before he returned to Rome.

I too, came as a pilgrim, a pilgrim of hope. I have always known that for the Church and for civil society young people constitute the hope of our future. But over the years of my ministry, especially through the celebration of events such as this one, that hope has been confirmed and strengthened again and again. It has been the young people themselves who have taught me to have ever new and ever greater confidence. It is not just that the young people of today are the adults of the future, who will step into our shoes and carry on the human adventure. No, the longing present in every heart for a full and free life that is worthy of the human person is particularly strong in them. Certainly, false answers to this longing abound, and humanity is far from being a happy and harmonious family. But so many young people in all societies refuse to descend into selfishness and superficiality. They refuse to relinquish responsibility. That refusal is a beacon of hope.

For believers, commitment to the spiritual and moral renewal which society needs is a gift of the Spirit of the Lord who fills the whole earth, for it is the Spirit who offers man the light and the strength to measure up to his supreme destiny [*Gaudium et Spes,* n. 10].

This has been particularly evident in the prayer-filled attitude of the young people gathered here. As a result, they go away more committed to the victory of *the culture of life* over *the culture of death.* The culture of life means respect for nature and protection of God's work of creation. In a special way, it means respect for human life from the first moment of conception until its natural end. A genuine culture of life is all the more essential when—as I have written in the social Encyclical *Centesimus Annus*—"human ingenuity seems to be directed more toward limiting, suppressing, or destroying the sources of life—including recourse to abortion, which unfortunately is so widespread in the world—than toward defending and opening up the possibilities of life" [n. 39].

A culture of life means service to the underprivileged, the poor, and the oppressed, because justice and freedom are inseparable and exist only if they exist for everyone. The culture of life means thanking God every day for his gift of life, for our worth and dignity as human beings, and for the friendship and fellowship he offers us as we make our pilgrim way toward our eternal destiny.

Mr. Vice President, I leave the United States with gratitude to God in my heart. Gratitude for what has happened here in the World Youth Day.

America, rise to your responsibilities, which encompass all the energies of your enterprising people. Be faithful to your mission. America, be faithful to your true self. America, land of the free, use thy freedom well. Use it, cherish and support with all your strength and capacity the dignity of every human person. ✠

ℒITHUANIA 1993

FROM 4 SEPTEMBER TO 8 SEPTEMBER 1993 the Pontiff visited Lithuania. This visit was his first to a nation of the former Soviet Union. Upon arrival in the nation, he presided at Vespers in the Vilnius Cathedral of Saint Stanislaus. Here he remembered all those who suffered during the Second World War and throughout the Stalinist era until 1991, when the Church emerged from persecution. He recalled the memory of many who suffered during the Cold War, recalling in particular Archbishop Mecislovas Reinys of Vilnius who died a martyr in the Vladimir prison in Russia. At this service the Pontiff spoke to priests and sisters who bore the burden of the past but who must also provide light toward the future.

I t can happen, however, that precisely from this desire to serve man in his social as well as his private dimension, there can arise situations of tension or suspicion between the Church and representatives of political power. You, the priests of Lithuania, have known this from bitter experience in the recent past. During the period of occupation it was forbidden to preach the Gospel and to engage in social work on behalf of the poor. With the return to democracy, it is to be hoped that relations between Church and state will develop according to criteria of mutual respect, resisting the temptations either of secularism or of clericalism. The state in fact must not intrude upon the autonomy which the constitution and international conventions recognize as rightfully belonging to religion, nor must priests, in the exercise of their mission of evangelization, intervene in party politics or in the direct governance of the nation. Like so many other states in Europe and in the world, your country, too, will be able to draw great advantages from a frank dialogue between Church and state, provided that, on the one hand, the legitimate representatives of the Lithuanian people take care to respect the freedom of the ecclesial community, and the Church's ministers, on the other, refrain from any kind of undue interference in the sphere proper to civic institutions!

Here I also wish to emphasize another aspect of your role as pastors of souls in Lithuania. It is the need to acquire and strengthen the so-called human virtues which the priest must cultivate above all in his own life, so as then to teach them to the people entrusted to his care.

After every significant social upheaval, man bears scars both in his patterns of behavior and in his soul. In moments such as these, it is more important than ever that consecrated persons give vivid testimony to the close interdependence between the theological and the human virtues. It is from the combination of these that a new humanity, reconciled with itself, will arise. Loyalty, honesty, industriousness, order, trust in others, a spirit of service, cordiality, respect, detachment, generosity, a sense of justice and responsibility, balance, serenity, sincerity: these are some of the characteristic traits of the "new man." ✠

ATVIA 1993

POPE JOHN PAUL'S VISIT TO LATVIA focused on the renewal of veneration to Saint Meinhard, patron of the country and apostle to the peoples of Latvia. A monk of Segeberg Abbey in Germany, he evangelized the territory of Latvia and its people. During the Communist era, devotion to him was suppressed.

The Pontiff's visit to Latvia extended from 8 to 10 September 1993. While in that nation he addressed the cultural leaders of the country, again drawing distinctions between capitalism and communism; he defined also the role of the Church. These remarks are from a university address delivered on 9 September 1993.

T he Church's social teaching is not a third way between capitalism and communism. In fact, it is essentially "theology" [*Sollicitudo Rei Socialis*, n. 41], or rather a matter which concerns God's plan for man and is therefore interested in economics or politics, not in order to evaluate their technical and organizational aspects, but to cast light on their inevitable moral implications. Its task is not to draw up a "system" but to indicate the impassable limits and suggest possible ways so that the various political and economic policies formulated in the concrete history of peoples in relationship to an infinite number of variables may be worthy of man and in conformity to the moral law.

Ladies and gentlemen, no doubt we are living in a time of enormous change. Behind us we have bloody, unprecedented tragedies from which we have miraculously escaped, without having arrived at that world of peace for which we all long. We are thus living in a most sensitive period of the history of Europe and the world, troubled by senseless conflicts, against an overall background marked by thousands of contradictions. None of us can foresee the future. But we do know that the world will be what we want it to be. To this joint expression of responsibility, we Christians want to contribute our firm hope, founded on the certainty that man is not alone, for God "so loved the world that he gave his only Son" [Jn 3:16]. This God is our Father and Friend who, despite his seeming silence, became man's traveling companion. ✠

ESTONIA 1993

ON 10 SEPTEMBER 1993 the Pope made a one-day visit in Tallinn, Estonia. The purpose of his visit was to respond to an invitation, which had been extended to him by a group of Estonian Catholics during his visit to Finland in 1989. While in Estonia he praised the integrity of the nation and its fidelity to Christ. At the conclusion of the Mass that he celebrated in Tallinn's municipal square, he made his personal reflections on the Europe of the late twentieth century.

We must look to Providence which has enabled us to experience these changes in Europe which have also led to the independence of the Baltic States: Lithuania, Latvia, and Estonia. From this geographical and historical point, we need to look toward the whole of our continent. The logic of the two great blocs decided upon at Yalta has fallen; and thus countries, peoples, and states have become free and independent, and have regained their sovereignty.

Looking from this point of Europe toward all the European countries, from West to East, from the Atlantic to the Urals, we must reconfirm those fundamental rights which enable individuals, communities, and peoples to live in peace, with respect for one another's rights. The rights of the human person, together with the rights of peoples, constitute the foundation of civilization—human, Christian, democratic, European. . . . We must accept one another, because Christ has accepted us. We must accept one another in our individual relations. These relations, in a sense, come down to respect for the rights of the human person. Mutual acceptance in relations between peoples and states is also expressed in mutual respect for rights between these peoples and these states. Thus the whole order of human coexistence comes down to two orders of rights: the rights of individuals and the rights of peoples.

We have vivid memories of the tragic period of European history in this century, when all were preparing to trample upon the rights of others by force. It was the period of fear, of intimidation, it was the period in which the principle of supremacy of force prevailed. ✠

CROATIA 1994

POPE JOHN PAUL II visited Zagreb in Croatia on 10 and 11 September 1994. The occasion of the visit was the nine hundredth anniversary of the evangelization of Croatia. In his talks the Pontiff recalled the loyalty of Croatia to the Holy See and Croatia's heroes, among whom are Saint Nicholas Tavelic, O.F.M., Saint Leopold Bogdan Mandic, Blessed Marcus Crisismus, and the Servant of God Aloysius Stepinac. The Pope intended to visit the war-torn city of Sarajevo, but to his disappointment the visit was canceled due to threats of violence. In an address upon his arrival, he spoke to the president of the republic, Franjo Tudjman.

Beloved citizens of Zagreb, I am glad to be among you. I have come to celebrate a historic event for the archdiocese with you: the ninth centenary of its creation. All the Pope's journeys always have a pastoral mission. Today's is an apostolic pilgrimage of ecclesial communion, whose purpose is to strengthen the existing bonds between the See of Peter and the Catholic people in Croatia.

Contacts between the Croatian Catholic community and the Apostolic See never weakened. As centuries passed, the Christians of this land who have frequently had to fight "for the holy Cross and the treasure of freedom" on the whole remain faithful to the Gospel and united with the Roman Pontiff, despite persecution and all kinds of adversity.

Mr. President, in your welcome address you mentioned events that have recently involved Croatia. One event of considerable importance occurred in 1992, when the collapse of the Communist regime, the proclamation of sovereignty, and its subsequent international recognition—for the first time in the Croatian nation's history, which is over a thousand years old—led to the exchange of diplomatic representation between Croatia and the Holy See.

Unfortunately, such joy has been clouded by the atrocious suffering caused by a conflict which is still leaving deep wounds in the country. Who does not remember Vukovar, Dubrovnik, Zadar, and so many other Croatian cities and villages smitten by the hurricane of war? Having come to an end in Croatia, the fighting unfortunately spread to neighboring Bosnia and Herzegovina. How much innocent blood has been shed! How many tears have lined the faces of mothers and children, old people and young ones!

Peace, if it is really desired, is always possible! To be able to build it on the foundations of justice and truth, it should first be implored from God.

But prayer must be accompanied by the generous initiative of men of goodwill. We need to promote a peace-loving culture, inspired by sentiments of tolerance and universal solidarity. This culture does not reject a healthy patriotism, but keeps it far from exacerbated nationalism and narrowness. It is able to form great and noble souls, who are well aware that the wounds produced by hatred are not healed with bitterness, but rather with the therapy of patience and the balm of forgiveness. Forgiveness to be asked and granted, with humble and generous magnanimity. ✠

PHILIPPINES 1995

IN 1995 POPE JOHN PAUL VISITED ASIA from 12 to 21 January. The countries visited included the Philippine Islands, Australia, Papua New Guinea, and Sri Lanka. Well into his pontificate the Pope began the custom of attending as many World Youth Days as possible. In 1995 the tenth World Youth Day was held in the Philippines. The Pontiff celebrated the concluding mass on 15 January in Manila's Rizal Park. In his homily he told a million young adults that the third millennium depended upon them. He also spoke of Asian history, but he made his challenge to be that of one between the generations.

Within this commitment of the whole People of God, *what is the role of young people in continuing the Messianic mission of Christ?* What is your part, your role? We have already meditated on this during the World Youth Day and especially last night at the Vigil. Somebody could say, "They danced, they sang, but they meditated!" It was creative meditation of the sending they received from Christ. Meditation can also be done through dancing and through singing, through entertainment. And it was a very entertaining meditation yesterday. Finally, after this meditation, I was able to sleep. And now after sleep I will add one specific challenge and appeal, which involves the healing of a source of immense frustration and suffering in many families all over the world.

Parents and older people sometimes feel that they *have lost contact with you,* and they are upset just as Mary and Joseph felt anguish when they realized that Jesus had stayed behind in Jerusalem. Many elderly parents feel abandoned because of us. Is it true, or no? It should not be true! It should be otherwise! But sometimes it is true. Sometimes you are very critical of the world of adults (and I was also like you) and sometimes they are very critical of you (that is also true). Sometimes you are very critical of the world of adults, and sometimes they are very critical of you. This not something new, and it is not always without a real basis in life. But always remember that you owe your life and upbringing to your parents; remember what your debt is to your parents; the Fourth Commandment expresses in a precise way the demands of justice toward them [*Catechism of the Catholic Church,* n. 2215]. In most cases they have provided for your education at the cost of personal sacrifice. Thanks to them you have been introduced into the cultural and social heritage of your community and country, your homeland. Generally speaking, your parents have been your first teachers in the faith.

Parents therefore have a right to expect from their sons and daughters the mature fruits of their efforts, just as children and young people have the right to expect from their parents the love and care which leads to a healthy development. All that is the Fourth Commandment. The Fourth Commandment is very rich. I suggest that you meditate about the Fourth Commandment of the Decalogue of God. I am asking you to build bridges of dialogue and communication with your parents. No splendid isolation! Communication! Love! Be a healthy influence on society to help to break down the barriers which have been raised between generations! No barriers! No barriers! Communion between generations, between parents and sons and daughters. Communion!

In this atmosphere, Jesus can say, "I send you!" It begins in the family home, where Jesus says first, "I send you." And to the parents he says, "I send your son. I send your daughter. I say to them, 'Follow me!'" All that requires the right atmosphere to complete the image of the social life in the Philippines and everywhere. And it is also this spiritual environment in which our sending is realized. "As the Father sent me," says Christ, "I am sending you." ✠

*P*APUA NEW GUINEA 1995

The purpose of Pope John Paul's visit to Papua, New Guinea, from 16 to 18 January 1995 was the Beatification of Mr. Peter To Rot, a lay catechist who was put to death for his faith by the Japanese on 17 July 1945. During the Japanese occupation, when all priests had been arrested, he alone kept the Catholic community together. He defied the Japanese order that all Christian couples should revert to the old practice of polygamy. Accused of conducting church services secretly, he suffered imprisonment for his fidelity. Executed without trial, he received a lethal injection from a Japanese doctor and died by convulsions. In his homily of Beatification the Pontiff praised him as a layman, as the father of a family, and as a minister of the Gospel, as a martyr.

In God's saving plan, "Suffering, more than anything else, makes present in the history of humanity the powers of the Redemption" [*Salvifici doloris,* n. 27]. Just as the Lord Jesus saved his people by loving them "to the end" (Jn 13:1), "even death on a cross" (Phil 2:8), so also he continues to invite each disciple to suffer for the Kingdom of God. When united with the redemptive Passion of Christ, human suffering becomes an instrument of spiritual maturity and a magnificent school of evangelical love.

Blessed Peter understood the value of suffering. Inspired by his faith in Christ, he was a devoted husband, a loving father, and a dedicated catechist known for his kindness, gentleness, and compassion. Daily Mass and Holy Communion and frequent visits to our Lord in the Blessed Sacrament sustained him, gave him courage to counsel the disheartened, encouraged to persevere until death. In order to be an effective evangelizer, Peter To Rot studied hard and sought advice from wise and holy "big men." Most of all he prayed—for himself, for his family, for his people, for the Church. His witness to the Gospel inspired others, in very difficult situations, because he lived his Christian life so purely and joyfully. Without being aware of it, he was preparing throughout his life for his greatest offering: by dying daily to himself, he walked with his Lord on the road which leads to Calvary [Mt 10:38–39].

During times of persecution the faith of individuals and communities is "tested by fire" [1 Pt 1:7]. But Christ tells us that there is no reason to be afraid. Those persecuted for their faith will be more eloquent than ever: *"It is not you who will be speaking; the spirit of your father will be speaking in you"* [Mt 10:20]. So it was for blessed Peter To Rot. When the village of Rakunai was occupied during the Second World War, and after the heroic missionary priests were imprisoned, he assumed responsibility for the spiritual life of the villagers. Not only did he continue to instruct the faithful and visit the sick, he also baptized, assisted at marriages, and led people in prayer.

On the day of his death, blessed Peter asked his wife to bring him his catechist crucifix. It accompanied him to the end. Condemned without trial, he suffered his martyrdom calmly. Following in the footsteps of his Master, the "Lamb of God, who takes away the sin of the world" [Jn 1:29], he too was *"led like a lamb to the slaughter"* [Is 53:7]. And yet this "grain of wheat" which fell silently into the earth [Jn 12:24] has produced a harvest of blessings for the Church in Papua, New Guinea! ✠

$\mathscr{A}$ustralia 1995

From 18 to 20 January 1995 Pope John Paul made a brief visit to the island continent of Australia; this was his second visit. He came to declare Mary MacKillop (1842–1909) Blessed. The foundress of a religious order of women known as the Sisters of Saint Joseph of the Sacred Heart of Jesus, she was known as Sister Mary of the Cross. In her lifetime this woman undertook educational and social service to the poorest of the poor of Australia. She was made to suffer much, even by members of the Church: she was accused of disobedience and then unjustly excommunicated. Still she remained faithful. Her beatification process was stretched out across the entire twentieth century—even after death she seemed to be a victim of injustice. When he landed at the Kingsford-Smith Airport in Sidney on 18 January, the Pope spoke of the significance of the life of Mary MacKillop for contemporary Australia.

Although my visit this time will be brief, I am certain that it will be an intense experience of prayer, dialogue, and shared joy, as was my previous visit in 1986. At that time I was able to travel to every state and territory in Australia. I remember the vastness of the land, its majestic features and natural beauty, your modern cities, the rich variety of your people and impressive signs of their energy and enterprise. From the original inhabitants to the most recent immigrants, in the young and the old, among parents with their families, I was privileged to discover the most precious of your national treasures: the Australian people themselves, with their creativity and determination.

The abundant fruits which this heritage can produce when illuminated by a deep faith in God are evident in the example of an outstanding Australian woman: Mother Mary MacKillop. Mary MacKillop embodied all that is best in your nation and in its people: genuine openness to others, hospitality to strangers, generosity to the needy, justice to those unfairly treated, perseverance in the face of adversity, kindness and support to the suffering. I pray that her example will inspire many Australians to take new pride in their Christian heritage and to work for a better society for all. This they will do by acting with courage and commitment wherever there is poverty or injustice, wherever innocent life is threatened or human dignity degraded.

In the years since my last visit much has changed in the world, and much has changed in Australia. On the international level, the fall of totalitarianism based on ideology, and the lessening of political and military tensions between blocs, are undoubtedly the most striking events. Yet, the benefits which could be expected from such enormous transformations have not always been forthcoming, and new sources of tension and conflict have appeared. Like many other developed countries, Australia, too, has faced economic and social challenges, to which it is responding. But many people, especially the poor and disadvantaged, still need society's help.

There exists a cultural and spiritual crisis which leaves many, especially young people, confused regarding the meaning of their lives and the values which would give sense and direction to their efforts. At the very heart of modern culture there is a growing sense of the need for moral and spiritual renewal: the need for a new attitude, one in which people will have more importance than things, and human dignity will take precedence over material gain.

Dear Australian friends, your own Mary MacKillop offers a key to such a renewal: she was a woman of courage who placed the spiritual and material well-being of others ahead of any personal ambition or convenience. The honor which the Church will give to Mother Mary MacKillop by declaring her among the blessed is in a sense an honor given to Australia and its people. It is also an invitation, an invitation to the whole of society to show genuine love and concern for all who are weighed down by life's burdens. I dare to say that your response will greatly determine the kind of society you will pass on to future generations in this land of great promise. ✠

$\mathscr{S}$RI LANKA 1995

Pope John Paul beatified Father Joseph Vaz (1651–1711) in Colombo, Sri Lanka, on 21 January 1995. This was the purpose of his visit. Blessed Joseph Vaz was a priest from Goa who, after establishing an oratory in his native land, was moved by missionary zeal to help establish the Church in Ceylon. While there he suffered persecution and imprisonment, but lost nothing of his zeal. He is the first to be beatified in Sri Lanka. Before the ceremony of beatification the Pontiff met with Buddhist, Hindu, Muslim, Anglican, Protestant, and Catholic leaders at an interfaith gathering. The meeting was important for its address to past sources of civil unrest. It was held at the Bandaranaike Memorial International Conference Hall. Here the Pope stressed again the value of interreligious dialogue.

Especially since the Second Vatican Council, the Catholic Church has been fully committed to *pursuing the path of dialogue and cooperation with the members of other religions.* Interreligious dialogue is a precious means by which the followers of the various religions discover shared points of contact in the spiritual life, while acknowledging the differences which exist between them. The Church respects the freedom of individuals to seek the truth and to embrace it according to the dictates of conscience, and in this light she firmly rejects proselytism and the use of unethical means to gain conversions.

The Catholic community hopes that through a continuing "dialogue of life" all believers will cooperate willingly in order to defend and promote moral values, social justice, liberty, and peace. Like many modern societies, *Sri Lanka is facing the spiritual threat represented by the growth of a materialistic outlook,* which is more concerned with "having" than with "being." Experience makes it clear that mere technological progress does not satisfy man's inner yearning for truth and communion. Deeper spiritual needs have to be met if individuals, families, and society itself are not to fall into a serious crisis of values.

There is ample room for cooperation among the followers of the various religions in meeting this serious challenge.

For this reason, I appeal to you and encourage you, as the religious leaders of the Sri Lankan people, to consider the concerns which unite believers, rather than the things which divide them. The safeguarding of Sri Lanka's spiritual heritage calls for strenuous efforts on the part of everyone to proclaim before the world the sacredness of human life, to defend the inalienable dignity and rights of every individual, to strengthen the family as the primary unit of society and the place where children learn humanity, generosity, and love, and to encourage respect for the natural environment. Interreligious cooperation is also a powerful force for promoting ethically upright socioeconomic and political standards. Democracy itself benefits greatly from the religiously motivated commitment of believers to the common good. ✠

*C*ZECHOSLOVAKIA 1995

FROM 20 TO 21 MAY 1995, Pope John Paul II visited the Czech Republic. On Sunday, 21 May, he celebrated the canonization ceremonies for two new saints: Jan Sarkander and Zdislava of Lemberk.

Saint Zdislava, who lived in the thirteenth century, was a countess of Northern Bohemia. Upon the death of her husband she lived as a Dominican tertiary and a hermit. Renowned for her piety, she was also known as an animator of family life. Saint Jan Sarkander was a priest of Moravia who died a martyr's death in the seventeenth century. This visit obviously had great pastoral overtones, as the Czech Republic was experiencing a second Prague Spring. A separation had occurred between the Czech Republic and the Slovak Republic, and the Pontiff sought to encourage a rebirth of Church life and the fostering of vocations. His words to the president of the republic, Václav Havel, were very focused upon the times.

Your presence, Mr. President, is a visible sign of the new historical reality which has come to pass in such a short space of time. Thanks to your personal commitment, and to the natural gifts of industriousness, moderation, and strength of character of your fellow citizens, the Czech Republic has won for itself a position of great respect in the European and international communities.

When I visited you for the first time, the Church was coming out of the catacombs, and after great sufferings, persecutions, and deprivations; it was only a short time since all the bishops, residential or auxiliary, had been restored to their dioceses, some of which had for a long time been without a Pastor.

As was the case five years ago, I am convinced that the soul of Prague and the Czech Republic will resound together in the meetings which we shall have today and throughout my stay in your beloved nation. The precious values of faith, spirituality, history, culture, and art which it enjoys undoubtedly have the power and strength to unite all of you in a great family, despite the differences between you, differences which on the other hand make even more interesting the spiritual panorama of this nation. Conscious of this rich reality, I wish all of you even greater civil, moral, and social progress.

ON THIS SAME OCCASION POPE JOHN PAUL addressed the question of Christian unity both in an address and in a very pointed letter to Dr. Pavel Smetana, an official of the Czech Evangelical Church of the Brethren and president of the Ecumenical Council of Churches. In an attitude of humility, the Pontiff sought reconciliation for Church divisions which began in this region even before the Reformation.

On several occasions I have visited countries where memories remain strong of conflicts between Catholics and Protestants. I have always made urgent appeals for the members of the various Churches and ecclesial communities, and especially the members of the Catholic Church, not to allow past injustices to determine present relations. I am deeply convinced, especially as we approach the third millennium of the Christian era, that this is a time of grace, a time to ask pardon and to offer pardon, to look beyond the sufferings of the past and to work together to bear clear witness to the

Gospel of Jesus Christ "so that the world may believe" [Jn 17:21]. It is a time for the Church "to express profound regret for the weakness of so many of her sons and daughters who sullied her face, preventing her from mirroring the image of the Crucified Lord, the supreme witness of patient love and humble meekness" [*Tertio Millennio Adveniente*, n. 35]. ✠

$\mathscr{P}$OLAND 1995

ON 22 MAY 1995, before returning to Rome, the Pope visited his native land once again. He made a personal visit to the city of Bielsko-Biala, the birthplace of his father. The Pontiff's brother had also worked there as a physician, and died during an outbreak of scarlet fever in 1937. Pope John Paul visited his brother's grave. On 22 May, he also spoke with representatives of the Lutheran community and then celebrated Mass in honor of the newly canonized saint, Jan Sarkander. The liturgy was conducted in Skoczow, the birthplace of the martyr. After greeting the president of the Republic of Poland, Lech Walesa, he addressed the issue of a creeping secularism, that was becoming more evident in post-Marxist Poland.

Today our homeland is facing many difficult social, economic, and political problems. They must be solved with wisdom and perseverance. Most important of all, however, remains the problem of a just moral order. This order is the foundation of every individual's life and of the life of every society. For this reason, today Poland urgently and primarily needs men and women of conscience!

To be a person of conscience means first of all obeying one's own conscience in every situation and not silencing its inner voice, even if it is sometimes severe and demanding. It means working for what is good and increasing it within and around oneself, and never giving in to evil, in the spirit of Saint Paul's words: "Do not be overcome by evil, but overcome evil with good" [Rom 12:21]. To be a person of conscience means being demanding with oneself, getting up again after falling, being ever converted anew. To be a person of conscience means working to build up the kingdom of God, the kingdom of truth and life, of justice, love, and peace—in our families, in the communities in which we live, and throughout our homeland. It also means courageously assuming public affairs; it means being concerned for the common good and not closing our eyes to the misery and need of our neighbor, in a spirit of Gospel solidarity: "Bear one another's burdens" [Gal 6:2]. I remember saying these words in Gdańsk during my visit to Zaspa in 1987.

Our twentieth century has been a period in which human consciences have been particularly violated in the name of totalitarian ideologies; millions of people were forced to act against their deepest convictions. Central and Eastern Europe has had unusually painful experiences in this respect. We recall this period when consciences were suppressed, when human dignity was despised, when so many innocent people suffered for deciding to remain faithful to their convictions. We recall the outstanding role taken in those difficult times by the Church in defending the rights of conscience, and not only for the benefit of believers.

In those years we often ask ourselves: Can history swim against the tide of conscience? At what price can it do so? I ask again: At what price? . . . This price is unfortunately the deep wounds in the nation's moral fiber, open wounds which still need a long time to heal. ✠

ℬELGIUM 1995

ON 4 JUNE 1995, Pope John Paul visited Belgium, where he beatified Father Damien de Veuster, a member of the Congregation of the Sacred Hearts. Through the reports of Robert Louis Stevenson, Father Damien became famous for his heroic work among the lepers of Molokai in Hawaii. Father Damien himself died of the disease in 1889.

Belgium has long been noted as a mission-sending nation. Throughout the last century, the memory of Father Damien has stood as a symbol of the total commitment necessary for evangelization. In an age of materialism and religious inertia, Pope John Paul recalled his memory through the act of beatification. The occasion was Pentecost Sunday.

The Church gives thanks to the Holy Spirit for Father Damien, since it is the Spirit who inspired him with the desire to devote himself unreservedly to lepers on the islands of the Pacific, particularly on Molokai. Today, through me, the Church acknowledges and confirms the value of Father Damien's example along the path of holiness, praising God for having guided him to the end of his life on an often-difficult journey. She joyfully contemplates what God can achieve through human weakness, for "it is he who gives us holiness and it is man who receives it" [Origen, *Homilies on Samuel,* I, 11:11].

Father Damien displayed a particular form of holiness in his ministry; he was at once a priest, religious, and missionary. With these three qualities, he revealed the face of Christ, showing the path of salvation, teaching the Gospel and working tirelessly for development. He organized religious, social, and fraternal life on Molokai, at the time an island of banishment from society; with him everyone had a place, each one was recognized and loved by his brothers and sisters.

On this Day of Pentecost we ask the assistance of the Holy Spirit for ourselves and for all men, so that we can let him take hold of us. We are certain that he imposes nothing unattainable on us, but that sometimes by steep paths he leads our being and our existence to their perfection. This celebration is also an appeal to deepen our spiritual life, whether we are sick or healthy, regardless of our social status. Dear brothers and sisters of Belgium, each of you is called to holiness: Put your talents at the service of Christ, the Church, and your brothers and sisters; let yourselves be humbly and patiently molded by the Spirit! Holiness is not perfection according to the human criteria; it is not reserved for a small number of exceptional persons. It is for everyone; it is the Lord who brings us to holiness when we are willing to collaborate in the salvation of the world for the glory of God, despite our sin and our sometimes rebellious tempera-ment. In your daily life, you are called to make choices that "occa-sionally demand uncommon sacrifices" [*Veritatis Splendor,* n. 102]. This is the price of true happiness. The apostle of the lepers is witness to that.

Today's celebration is also a call to solidarity. While Damien was among the sick he could say in his heart, "Our Lord will give me the graces I need to carry my cross and follow him, even to our special Calvary at Kalawao." The certainty that the only things that count are love and the gift of self was his inspiration and the source of his hap-piness. The apostle of the lepers is a shining example of how the love of God does not take us away from the world. Far from it: the love of Christ makes us love our brothers and sisters even to the point of giv-ing up our lives for them. ✠

Slovakia 1995

Pope John Paul II made a pastoral visit to the Slovak Republic from 30 June to 3 July 1995. The purpose of his visit was to canon-ize three martyrs of the sixteenth and early seventeenth centuries. Two of these, Saint Stefan Pongracz and Melchior Grodziecky, were Jesuits. The third, Saint Marek Krizin, was a canon of Esztergom. One was from Croatia, one was from Hungary, and one was from Poland. They found their unity in serving the Slovak people in the time of the great Reformation. Because they were martyrs, they represent a cer-tain spirit of fidelity for which the Catholic Church in Slovakia has been noted in the time of the Cold War. The Pontiff was seeking unity in Eastern Europe by this liturgical gesture.

M artyrdom unites us with all those believers in Christ, both
in the East and in the West, with whom we still await the
attainment of full ecclesial communion.

I wish therefore to express my joy at having been able to add
these new names today to the *martyrologium* of the Church in Slovakia, and I am confident that this act will serve to encourage all the
sister Churches, especially those of Central and Eastern Europe.

The three new saints belonged to three different nations, but
they shared the same faith and, sustained by that faith, they were
united also in facing death. May their example renew in their fellow
citizens of today a commitment to mutual understanding, and may
it strengthen especially between Slovaks and the Hungarian minority
the bonds of friendship and cooperation! Only on the foundation of
mutual respect for the rights and duties of majorities and minorities
can a pluralistic and democratic state endure and flourish.

On 2 July, Pope John Paul reiterated the theme of unity in Eastern
Europe, speaking directly to the tragedy of oppression during the
Marxist period of Czechoslovakia. In particular, the Pontiff recalled
the special suffering of Byzantine-rite Catholics and the martyrdom
of their Pastors as the government at Prague sought to oppress the
identity of the Greek tradition.

D uring my visit to Slovakia, especially in this eastern part of the
country, I have been able to observe at close hand the particular characteristics of this area's religious life and traditions. Here West meets East: the Latin rite meets the Eastern rite. In
an almost tangible way we experience clear signs of the heritage and
message of Saints Cyril and Methodius, the Apostles of the Slavs and
copatrons of Europe.

The holy brothers of Thessalonica, through their work of evangelization, developed a model of Church life that combines the canonical, liturgical, theological, and spiritual wealth of the Eastern tradition
with the principle of the one, holy, catholic, and apostolic Church, in
communion with the Bishop of Rome.

Throughout history there have been times when it seemed too
difficult to maintain this model which linked the diversity of traditions

with the requirement of unity which Christ willed for his Church. But your very presence is an eloquent witness of how, down the centuries and in spite of difficulties, it is possible to remain faithful to the original model established by Cyril and Methodius while still preserving communion with the universal Church and with the See of Rome which, by God's will, constitutes its center.

Be proud of this most ancient tradition of yours and cultivate unity among yourselves. Protect that unity from every seed of discord and of division; the union of mind and hearts, which takes concrete form in practical cooperation, is your strength.

Everyone still remembers the tragic situation of the recent past, when the forces of ideology, opposed to freedom and human dignity, condemned your ecclesial community to destruction. But God "has put down the mighty from their thrones and exalted those of low degree" [Lk 1:52], because they were sharers in the love of Christ.

"Blessed are they who believed that there would be a fulfillment of what was spoken to them from the Lord" [Lk 1:45]. The Greek Catholic community emerged from this trial renewed and strengthened. Thanks also to the witness and the blood of many martyrs. The faith of a great number of laypeople, of men and women religious, of priests and Pastors, is living proof of this. One need only think of the sufferings of Bishop Vasil Hopko and the martyrdom of Bishop Pavol Gojdic. On the threshold of the third Christian millennium, this is the precious contribution which your community has made to the treasury of the Church and in particular to the cause of ecumenism.

You, brothers and sisters of the Greek Catholic rite, have preserved your liturgy for centuries; you have accumulated a manifold spiritual patrimony which distinguishes your Church and which finds expression in sacred buildings, icons, chants, and devotions. Be grateful to God for the wealth bestowed on you and remain faithful to the gifts he has given you!

I have often heard this invitation from Slovak pilgrims who come to Rome: "Holy Father, come and see the Tatra Mountains from their southern side too!" Today this wish of yours and mine has come true. The Tatras, our common Tatras, which are so close to Poland, enclose a multitude of small lakes called *"plesa."* Their crystal-clear waters reflect the majestic grandeur of the mountain peaks. This countryside, unique amid the diversity of creation, speaks to us of the beauty and goodness of the Creator.

From the southern slopes of the Tatra Mountains to the plains of Zemplin, Greek Catholic communities have lived for centuries side by side with their brothers and sisters of the Latin rite; they too have been called to represent, like the little *plesa* lakes, the shining, transparent generosity of God. It is the Lord himself who enriches the Church with a variety of forms and traditions. Thus, wherever Byzantine-rite Catholics find themselves among those of another rite, it is everyone's task to ensure that these "lakes" do not shrink, or even disappear.

Dear young people, to you is entrusted this heritage which your forebears zealously and courageously preserved. Rediscover your roots! They are the Christian roots which brought values in civilization to the whole of Europe, both east and west. Your Christian roots draw strength from the witness of your forebears, who were able to remain tenaciously faithful to Christ, despite the difficulties and challenges which they had to face down the centuries. ✠

CAMEROON 1995

FROM 14 TO 16 SEPTEMBER 1995, Pope John Paul II visited the African nation of Cameroon, before moving on to South Africa and Kenya. At the invitation of the entire African hierarchy, he came to participate in the second phase of the African Synod, which directly addressed the question of inculturation. In his homily to the bishops assembled at Yaoundé, the capital of Cameroon, the Pontiff outlined the scope of the Synod. He did so, however, for the sake of the Church of all Africa.

I n accordance with the decisions taken with your Cardinals, we are meeting in three chosen places in Africa to make known the results of the Synod's work. We also desire to give thanks to God for the maturity shown by the African Churches in this work, and to gather its fruit in joy. It was not only the work of the Bishops, your Pastors, but also the work of all the communities and their lay faithful. It was here in Africa that the whole preparatory phase of the Synod took place. Many laypeople actively participated. It is here also among the People of God of the Churches in Africa that we want to conclude this great work.

The African Synod, which during this week is taking place on your continent, wishes to present you with a final document, the result of its work. Among the topics highlighted, that of "inculturation" deserves special attention, for it is linked to the proclamation of the Good News to the peoples and nations of your continent as well as to their entrance into life according to the Gospel. Nations take life from their culture. As has already been said, the Gospel is inscribed in cultures and renews them. This is how individuals and peoples of Africa experience it, and this is the reason why they seek to stress this topic.

Today, then, we must deepen the very concept of inculturation. The parable of the vine and the branches, narrated by Saint John [Jn 15:1–11], can help us in a special way. Culture is no more than the act of cultivating. In this parable, the Heavenly Father is rightly presented as the vine grower. He tended it. He cultivated this vine of humanity by sending his Son. He sent him not only as the bearer of a message of salvation. He sent him as a graft that was to enable the branches to become firmly attached to God's vine. And this is why the Son of God, true God consubstantial with the Father, became man. He became man in order that the human race might be grafted on to him and, in this way, have new life. The purpose was constantly and gradually a noble humanity in all peoples, whatever their race or the color of their skin. ✠

SOUTH AFRICA 1995

ON 16 SEPTEMBER 1995, Pope John Paul II landed at Johannesburg International Airport in order to take up again the themes of the African Synod. He was met by President Nelson Mandela. In an address to the nation, he spoke to the circumstances of the time. His words were directed to the president and reflect significant change in South Africa's policy.

Today my journey brings me to South Africa, to the new South Africa, a nation firmly set on the course of reconciliation and harmony among all its citizens. At the beginning of my visit, I wish to pay tribute to you, Mr. President, who after being a silent and suffering "witness" of your people's yearning for true liberation now shoulder the burden of inspiring and challenging everyone to succeed in the task of national reconciliation and reconstruction. I remember our meeting at the Vatican in June 1990, shortly after your release from prison. In your kind words of welcome today I recognize the same spirit which sustained you then in the ideal of achieving a better life for the peoples of the nation. To you and to former President F. W. de Klerk, joint recipients of the 1993 Nobel Peace Prize, we must all be grateful that you acted with wisdom and courage. And let us commend to God in our prayers all those who have worked and suffered and continue to strive for that day when everyone's dignity will be fully acknowledged, respected, and safeguarded throughout this land and all over this continent.

South Africa refers to itself as a "rainbow nation," indicating the diversity of races, ethnic groups, languages, cultures, and religions which characterize it. And you have the extremely rich concept of UBUNTU [fellowship] to guide you, according to the saying that "people are made people through other people." Certainly, the Government of National Unity's commitment to bring all the citizens of this land together in a united, fair, and more prosperous society is shared by South Africa's religious leaders, Christian, Jewish, Islamic, Hindu, and Traditional, all of whom I greet with cordial esteem. By insisting on the things which unite, all believers can "build together," using their spiritual resources to keep alive the flame of hope on the horizon of humanity's march toward a brighter future.

ON 17 SEPTEMBER, Pope John Paul presided at another Synodal Assembly, during which he celebrated Mass. In his homily he addressed the women of Africa.

The prophet Isaiah exclaims: "Open up, clear the way, remove all obstacles from the way of my people" [Is 57:14]. The Synod for Africa addresses this call and this encouragement to all the peoples of this continent. In a special way, this call and encouragement goes out to the *women of Africa.* The Synod gave ample space to the special burdens which lie on you, to the specific injustices which you undergo, to the violence and crimes committed against you. The Church in Africa deplores whatever deprives you of your rights and the respect due to you [*Ecclesia in Africa,* n. 121].

The Church knows that you, the women of Africa, have an irreplaceable part to play in humanizing society. You are more sensitive to the implications of justice and the demands of peace because you are closer to the mystery of life and the wonder of its transmission. The Church therefore appeals to you in a special way to *respect, protect, love, and serve life, every human life, from conception to natural death!* As mothers, you bring your children into life; you educate them for life. Every shedding of blood is a wound to your unique genius. With all your strength you tend to defend the life that was conceived in you, the life that is the object of your great love. History shows that wars are made above all by men. It has always been so, and it is still so today.

What can you do to change this situation? No one can teach as you can the reality of respect for every human being. *By educating in respect and love, you teach peace and serve peace,* in your families and in your countries and in the world. ✠

KENYA 1995

ON 19 SEPTEMBER, Pope John Paul II celebrated the concluding ceremony of the Special Assembly of African bishops in a suburb of Nairobi, Kenya. The Pope selected a theme for his talk: "Agents and Means of Evangelization."

As the Successor of Peter, I have ardently looked forward to coming once more to Africa, to encourage you to make the Synod's findings the goal and direction of your ecclesial life toward the great jubilee of the year 2000.

The Document itself, however, is only an instrument and a beginning. What counts is the effective renewal of the Church's members and their ever more generous ministry and service. The Church exists to continue the mission of the Son in the power of the Holy Spirit, and to bring the good news of salvation to the human family. But the Church herself, the community of her members, must be thoroughly evangelized, in order to possess the grace and vitality to proclaim and bear witness to the Gospel of the Crucified and Risen Lord. In God's plan, the Church is not a means to be used for some common enterprise, no matter how noble and useful. Rather, the Church as she comes to us from the loving hand of the Father is the sign and the instrument of the human family's communion with God himself and of its own deepest unity. If Africa is fragmented and divided, the Church as the Family of God must be a model of unity for society. If Africa is hurt by poverty, corruption, injustice, and violence, the Church must be a healing, reconciling, forgiving, and supporting community. Love is the binding force of this community, in which none are so poor that they have nothing to give, and none are so rich that they have nothing to receive. Love of God and love for every human being, especially the poor and defenseless, is the motivating force of the evangelizing mission to which you are being called. Love impels Christ's followers to carry his light and his healing to the ends of the earth, and therefore to every corner of Africa.

In a special way the fruits of the Synod are entrusted to families, to families striving to live their Christian vocation to the fullest, for "the home is the first school of Christian life and a school for human enrichment." Precisely because of the strength of Africa's family traditions, the Synod fathers saw the Church as the Family of God as the guiding idea for the evangelization of this continent. And it is precisely in the family and through the family that the important question of the inculturation of the faith can be properly fostered in the everyday reality of the people's experience. The African family's warmth of relations, its members' care for one another, especially for children and for the elderly, the solidarity that bonds it to the wider community, and its intense love and respect for life conceived and born is the rich soil in which the Gospel seed can bring forth a splendid flowering of the spirit of the Beatitudes. When traditional family values are purified, elevated, and transformed by their encounter with the Gospel of life, the universal Catholic community rediscovers essential dimensions of Christian love and brotherhood, which in more secularized societies are seriously threatened by exaggerated individualism. ✠

United States 1995

On 5 October 1995, the Pontiff addressed the United Nations General Assembly. This was the second day of his four-day visit to the United States. The occasion was the fiftieth anniversary of the establishment of the United Nations. The Secretary-General on the occasion was Dr. Boutros Boutros-Ghali. Here the Pope spoke to the post–Cold War era. Within these times, the specific needs of a variety of ethnic peoples emerged. Throughout his talk, the tone of his respect for the work of the UN is clear and resounding.

Ladies and gentlemen! On the threshold of a new millennium we are witnessing an extraordinary global acceleration of that quest for freedom which is one of the great dynamics of human history. This phenomenon is not limited to any one part of the world, nor is it the expression of any single culture. Men and women throughout the world, even when threatened by violence, have taken the risk of freedom, asking to be given a place in social, political, and economic life which is commensurate with their dignity as free human beings. This universal longing for freedom is truly one of the distinguishing marks of our time.

The quest for freedom in the second half of the twentieth century has engaged not only individuals, but nations as well. Fifty years after the end of the Second World War, it is important to remember that that war was fought because of violations to the rights of nations. Many of those nations suffered grievously for no other reason than that they were deemed "other." Terrible crimes were committed in the names of lethal doctrines which taught the "inferiority" of some nations and cultures. In a certain sense, the United Nations Organization was born of a conviction that such doctrines were antithetical to peace; and the Charter's commitment to "save succeeding generations from the scourge of war" [Preamble] surely implied a moral commitment to defend every nation and culture from unjust and violent aggression.

Unfortunately, even after the end of the Second World War, the rights of nations continue to be violated. To take but one set of examples, the Baltic States and extensive territories in Ukraine and Belarus were absorbed into the Soviet Union, as had already happened to Armenia, Azerbaijan, and Georgia in the Caucasus. At the same time the so-called "People's Democracies" of Central and Eastern Europe effectively lost their sovereignty and were required to submit to the will dominating the entire bloc. The result of this artificial division of Europe was the "Cold War," a situation of international tension in which the threat of nuclear holocaust hung over humanity. It was only when freedom was restored to the nations of Central and Eastern Europe that the promise of the peace which should have come with the end of the war began to be realized for many of the victims of that conflict.

The Universal Declaration of Human Rights, adopted in 1948, spoke eloquently of the rights of persons; but *no similar international agreement has adequately addressed the rights of nations*. This situation must be carefully pondered, for it raises urgent questions about justice and freedom in the world today.

Ladies and gentlemen! Freedom is the measure of man's dignity and greatness. Living the freedom sought by individuals and peoples is a great challenge to man's spiritual growth and to the moral vitality of nations. The basic question which we must all face today is the responsible use of freedom, in both its personal and social dimensions. Our reflection must turn then to the question of the moral structure of freedom, which is the inner architecture of the culture of freedom.

Freedom is not simply the absence of tyranny or oppression. Nor is freedom the license to do whatever we like. Freedom has an inner "logic" which distinguishes it and ennobles it: freedom is ordered to the truth, and is fulfilled in man's quest for truth and in man's living in the truth. Detached from the truth about the human person, freedom deteriorates into license in the lives of individuals and, in political life, it becomes the caprice of the most powerful and the arrogance of power. Far from being a limitation upon freedom or a threat to it, reference to the truth about the human person—a truth universally knowable through the moral order written on the hearts of all—is, in fact, the guarantor of freedom's future.

DURING HIS VISIT TO THE UNITED STATES, Pope John Paul celebrated Mass in Newark, New Jersey; New York City; Brooklyn; and Baltimore, Maryland. In Baltimore, where he was the guest of William Cardinal Keeler, Archbishop of America's senior metropolitan See, the Pontiff spoke of Church history in the United States, the enthusiasm and creativity with which American Catholics have undertaken tasks of evangelization and education. But he also spoke pastorally to those afflicted by confusion and internal distress.

Today some Catholics are tempted to discouragement or disillusionment, like the prophet Habakkuk in the first reading. They are tempted to cry out to the Lord in a different way:

Why does God not intervene when violence threatens his people; why does God not let us see misery and ruin; why does he let us see ruin and misery; why does God permit evil? Like the prophet Habakkuk, and like the thirsty Israelites in the desert at Meribah and Massah, our trust can falter; we can lose patience with God. In the drama of history, we can find our dependence upon God burdensome rather than liberating. We, too, can "harden our hearts."

And yet, the prophet gives us an answer to our impatience: "If God delays, wait for him; he will surely come, he will not be late" (Hb 2:3). A Polish proverb expresses the same conviction in another way: "God takes his time, but he is just." Our waiting for God is never in vain. Every moment is our opportunity to model ourselves on Jesus Christ—to allow the power of the Gospel to transform our personal lives and our service to others according to the spirit of the Beatitudes. "Bear your share of the hardship which the Gospel entails," writes Paul to Timothy in today's second reading (2 Tm 1:8). This is no idle exhortation to endurance. No, it is an invitation to enter more deeply into the Christian vocation which belongs to us all by baptism. There is no evil to be faced that Christ does not face with us. There is no enemy that Christ has not already conquered. There is no cross to bear that Christ has not already borne for us and does not now bear with us. And on the far side of every cross we find the newness of life in the Holy Spirit, that new life which will reach its fulfillment in the Resurrection. This is our faith. This is our witness before the world. ✠

GUATEMALA 1996

ON 5 FEBRUARY 1996, the Pontiff arrived at La Aurora International Airport, Guatemala, for a three-day visit. There he was greeted by Alvaro Arzú Irigoyen, president of the republic. He noted that there were many positive changes in the region of Central America. At the same time, he spoke with sadness of all the tragedies of the region in the past three and half decades. As on the previous visit, he first outlined the scope of his presence in the region.

On every possible occasion I have not hesitated to ask that all the necessary efforts be made to halt the din of war and that hearts be moved to ways of greater justice. Although the path to peace has been arduous and not free from problems, today we can glimpse on the horizon the joyous moment of the signing of the agreements that will put an end to recent history of war and violence over the past thirty-five years. This, together with natural disasters—I recall that the twentieth anniversary [of the earthquake] which caused more than twenty thousand victims falls precisely at this time, has hindered the desired progress and well-being that the children of Guatemala expect from the fertile and fruitful land Providence has given them. . . . I would like to raise my voice once more to say: "True peace is urgently needed." A peace that is God's gift and the fruit of dialogue, of the spirit of reconciliation, of serious commitment to integral development and solidarity with every level of society, and especially with respect for the dignity of each person. ✠

Nicaragua 1996

On 7 February, Pope John Paul arrived in Nicaragua for a one-day visit. His previous visit had not been a happy one, with controversy regarding his presence and the efforts made to drown out his voice during the outdoor Mass. This occasion found another atmosphere altogether. After celebrating Mass in Managua, he departed with words for the president, Violeta Barrios de Chamorro.

I would like this papal visit to be a lasting memory, a happy memory. I wished to reach all of your hearts, to speak to you in the name of Jesus Christ and to remind you of the way which, by leading to him, also leads to the happiness of individuals and of society.

This second pastoral visit has enabled me to perceive the new and positive changes that have occurred in your country. However, some dangers and evils still persist that affect many levels of the population. After the civil war and the temptation of totalitarian systems, the terrible scourges of poverty and ignorance have yet to be overcome. They are evident in the high number of unemployed persons, in the families who live in situations of extreme deprivation, in the children and young people who receive no adequate education.

It is the responsibility of government authorities to deal with these situations, but also of all sectors of society and of each citizen. A joint, coordinated effort transcending special or partisan interests is required of all, in order to advance toward moral and spiritual, human and social progress based on education in authentic values, which can make Nicaragua prominent among all the nations of the continent. ✠

El SALVADOR 1996

THE PONTIFF ARRIVED IN EL SALVADOR on 8 February and was greeted by President and Mrs. Armando Calderón. During his stay, he again visited the tomb of the late Archbishop Oscar Romero. When he celebrated Mass at the Twenty-first Century esplanade in San Salvador, he spoke of the necessary components of an optimistic future.

Thanks be to God circumstances have changed. Now that *your nation,* like most of her neighboring nations in Central America, has overcome in part these conflicting ideologies, *she is enjoying a more favorable atmosphere of greater civil harmony.* It is the appropriate moment to reinforce the peace process. This is the only way to build a new society with that Christian spirit which, also beyond all human aspirations but with the certainty that it corresponds to God's will, we call the "civilization of love." This could become reality if an appropriate pedagogy of forgiveness were developed. This is urgently needed, since the conflicts were so violent and the effects so destructive.

Precisely because *evil is still lodged in many hearts, and sin* is the ultimate cause of personal and social disorder, of all selfishness and oppression, of violence and revenge, it is necessary for Christians to engage in fostering the task of teaching peace by practicing forgiveness. Thus they will make themselves worthy of Christ's Beatitudes. "Blessed are the peacemakers, for they shall be called sons of God" [Mt 5:9].

The Gospel words we have heard are demanding beyond human logic, but capable of bringing about that revolution of love which starts by opening the heart to forgiveness and mercy: "You have heard that it was said, 'You shall love your neighbor and hate your enemy.' But I say to you, love your enemies, and pray for those who persecute you" [Mt 5:43–44].

These words invite us to conversion if a certain contrast can be perceived between what the Gospel proposes to us and our own sentiments; this is because these words come from heaven and not from earth. They are proclaimed by Christ, who fulfilled them perfectly by his example and has granted us the gift of his Spirit to be able to love our enemies, do good to those who hate us, pray for those who persecute and slander us. In fact, Christ himself by his example, by his death and Resurrection, is the measure of forgiveness that we receive from God so that we may also be able to forgive totally. It is he who proclaims peace to us on Easter morning so that we may share in a world renewed by love. He fills us with his Spirit, so that we may be able to forgive everyone.

Forgiving one's enemies, as the martyrs of all ages have done, is the decisive truth and authentic expression of the radical nature of Christian love.

This is the source of the *wisdom of peace,* as we have heard in the exhortation of the Apostle James. There is a worldly wisdom which he calls "earthly, unspiritual, devilish" [Jas 3:15]. It stems from worldly instincts and causes the division of hearts, which always comes from the evil one and serves personal interest. But the wisdom that comes from above is "first pure, then peaceable, gentle, open to reason, full of mercy and good fruits, without uncertainty or insincerity" [Jas 3:17]. It is as if God has set you before two roads to choose the future of your nation: *the way of death* or *the way of life;* an existence ruled by the world's vain wisdom that destroys harmony, or soundly guided by the wisdom that comes from above and builds the civilization of love.

Build a future of hope with the wisdom of peace. ✠

VENEZUELA 1996

FROM 9 TO 11 FEBRUARY, the Pope made a pastoral visit to the South American nation of Venezuela. He was greeted by President Rafael Caldera Rodríguez and also by the entire hierarchy of the nation. The Pope continued to address the religious atmosphere of Latin America. The elements of religious culture constituted his theme. This address was delivered to distinguished representatives of Venezuela's cultural, social, political, and economic spheres. It was delivered on 10 February at the Teresa Carreño Theater in Caracas.

The Church's proclamation and acceptance of the Gospel helps Christians to be new men [Col 3:10], who can work together to build a new society, based on justice, dialogue, and service, capable of meeting the challenges of the future. In this task it is necessary to start by constantly promoting a more dignified view of man, which respects the truth about man as God's image [Gn 1:27] and as the way for the Church [*Redemptor Hominis,* n. 14]. Therefore a contribution is made to elevating society, since "the social nature of man shows that there is an interdependence between personal betterment and the improvement of society" [*Gaudium et Spes,* n. 25]. In this way a plan for true human advancement which strives for the true liberation of the full human is prepared [*Evangelii Nuntiandi,* nn. 29–39].

The necessary "changes of mentality, behavior and structures" [*Centesimus Annus,* n. 60] will encourage a culture of solidarity to prevail over the wish for domination or for a selfish life, and an economy of participation instead of a system for the accumulation of possessions, which causes a great gap not only between the different states but also between citizens of the same country.

Among the subjects that require special attention for building a really new and dynamic society, the family and life must definitively be singled out. Indeed, society's future passes through the family [*Familiaris Consortio,* n. 51]. In addition: "The well-being of the individual person and of both human and Christian society is closely bound up with the healthy state of conjugal and family life. Hence Christians today are overjoyed, and so too are all who esteem conjugal and family life highly, to witness the various ways to which progress is being made in fostering those partnerships of love" [*Gaudium et Spes,* n. 47]. Urgent attention must also be paid to children who, having been born outside of the family institution or having been abandoned, are growing up without parental care or guidance and have difficulty in integrating themselves into society, scarred as they are by grave emotional and material deficiencies. They are exposed, as a result of their lack of education and instruction, to the risk, for example, of early delinquency, violence, drugs, and child prostitution. ✠

TUNISIA 1996

ON 14 APRIL 1996 Pope John Paul made a one-day pastoral visit to the diocese of Tunis. His opening remarks at the Cathedral of St. Vincent de Paul and St. Olive indicated his sensitivity to the Catholic communities of the entire Middle East. The bishops of Algeria, Morocco, and Libya had come to greet the Pope with delegations representing the people of their dioceses. His host was Archbishop Fouad Twal, leader of the Roman Catholic community of Tunis. During this visit the Pope placed great emphasis on dialogue. He also stressed the history of the land, which possessed both a rich Christian and a Muslim culture. This is particularly seen in his address to the leaders of the nation at the Presidential Palace in Carthage. He began by speaking of social awareness.

C oncern for the most underprivileged is not the responsibility of the public authorities alone; it must be everyone's concern. The Church in Tunisia also hopes, in her own capacity, to contribute to meeting new needs. Her institutions in the area of social assistance, which promote development, education, and health care, are intended for all Tunisians. They are places for fruitful cooperation between Muslims and Christians, so that they together may contribute to the common good.

I must admit that I am moved by coming to this country which calls to mind the glorious pages of Christianity's history. Who can forget the names of Cyprian, Tertullian, or Augustine? I remembered them this morning as I prayed with the Christian community. But how could we fail to mention with equal admiration the contribution made by Arab civilization and the role of its thinkers, especially in the transmission of knowledge, or again, in the writings of the great Tunisian philosopher Ibn Khaldūn, a forerunner in the area of historical and sociological thought?

The works produced by the great minds of this century, Christian and Muslim alike, are a rich heritage that deserves to be better known. I would also like to recall particularly in this context the importance of cultural exchanges between people strongly marked by both Christianity and Islam. These exchanges must be fostered and sustained, for as I said last year during my visit to the United Nations Organization, culture "is a way of giving expression to the transcendent dimension of human life. The heart of all culture is its approach to the greatest of all mysteries: the mystery of God" [*L'Osservatore Romano*, English edition, 11 October 1995, p. 9]. But it is also a paradoxical fact of our contemporary world that at a time when communication is getting easier and faster, our level of mutual knowledge is in danger of remaining superficial. ✠

LOVENIA 1996

From 17 to 19 May 1996, Pope John Paul II made a pastoral journey to Slovenia, stopping in the cities of Ljubljana, Postojna, and Maribor. In the course of the visit he announced the future beatification of the Servant of God, Venerable Anton Martin Slomsek, a Slovenian hero of the faith. Recalling years of suffering under a Marxist regime, he addressed the Church of Slovenia as a representation of the Upper Room. He foresaw a new outpouring of the Holy Spirit upon a Church which is being reborn. After his visit with the president of Slovenia, Milan Kučan, the Pope focused the history of the faith in the need for a renewal of the clerical life. On 17 May, he summoned clergy, religious, and lay faithful to a prayer vigil at the Cathedral of Ljubljana. There he reiterated a theme of Slovenia as "symbolic of the Cenacle at Jerusalem," waiting for the Holy Spirit and, once receiving Him, running everywhere to tell the Good News, with joy.

Dear brothers and sisters, we too are gathered in prayer together with our Heavenly Mother to ask the Lord to renew the outpouring of the Holy Spirit. The Church in Slovenia, as in all the countries of the world, needs the divine power of the Spirit in order to continue the work of the new evangelization. Mary, implore this great gift for the whole ecclesial community, and especially for bishops, priests, and consecrated persons, that they will be able to fulfill their mission in the service of the Gospel!

During the trials to which the Slovenian people have been subjected down the ages, the Pastors of the Church have not failed to make their presence felt, proclaiming the Gospel of life and defending the dignity and the inalienable rights of every human being. This has happened with even greater courage in recent years, during fascism, Nazism, and communism. How can we forget the heroic example of the fearless devotion of bishops, priests, and religious, who with deep faith and divine Providence have shared the faith of the people of God? And how can we fail to mention the activity of many priests and consecrated persons in culture, education, science, and the economy, in addition to the religious and humanitarian fields? Standing out among the many shining examples is the remarkable figure of a Pastor totally dedicated to serving his flock, the Venerable Servant of God Anton Martin Slomsek, whose canonical process is successfully nearing its conclusion.

Dear priests and consecrated persons, society expects constant spiritual support from you. It has needed your consistent Gospel witness. Approach all with a great and free heart in order to lead your brothers and sisters kindly, but firmly, to live fully their vocation as children of the one heavenly Father who desires that all be saved [1 Tm 2:4].

Your people are going through a time of radical change: while they are seeking gradually to free themselves from the negative consequences of the totalitarian ideology by which they have been strongly conditioned, they are striving with every effort to build a more fraternal and democratic society. However, it is still necessary to be particularly alert to preventing the acceptance of another equally dangerous ideology, that of unbridled liberalism, from filling the void left by the previous one. These are years of transition, and your word, together with an example, is indispensable, as was the guidance of Moses, who, with firm trust in God, succeeded in leading the chosen people in the difficult passage from slavery to true freedom [Ex 14:15–31].

I commend this task to you in the certainty that, with God's help, you will be able to carry it through to completion. In this way you will also make an essential contribution to the civil and spiritual rebirth of the beloved Slovenian nation, instilling trust and optimism in the present efforts for the material and moral rebuilding of your country. Be concerned above all to prepare the new generations for the responsibilities that await them. ✠

GERMANY 1996

THE HOLY FATHER'S THIRD PASTORAL VISIT to Germany was conducted between 21 and 23 June 1996. During this time, he met with the local churches of Paderborn and Berlin. The occasion of his presence in Germany was multifold. He beatified two priests who had opposed the Nazi regime during the Second World War. These were Karl Leisner and Bernard Lichtenberg. Both died as a result of their imprisonment. Father Leisner had been ordained in secret, while a prisoner in Dachau Concentration Camp, and had only celebrated one Mass by the time of his death on August 12, 1945. Father Lichtenberg, who had outspokenly defended the rights of German Jews, died in a cattle car in 1943 while on his way to prison in Dachau. The Pope referred to the Second World War and fascism as the epitome of "the culture of death."

The Pope also announced the convening of a Second European Synod of Bishops, in preparation for the jubilee year of 2000. Finally, he addressed the need for "common witness" by Catholics and Protestants alike, in a new ecumenical age which has evangelization as its goal and which sets spiritual values ahead of material values. In an ecumenical Liturgy of the Word at Paderborn on 22 June, he praised the heroism of Protestants and Catholics alike, singling out among others Edith Stein, Alfred Delp, Dietrich Bonhoeffer, and Helmuth Count Moltke.

B ernard Lichtenberg, provost of the Berlin Cathedral, and Karl Leisner, a deacon who was ordained a priest while a prisoner in the Dachau Concentration Camp. Tomorrow, in Berlin, I will proclaim these men blessed. However, they were not alone. Already nine years ago I was able to beatify, here in your country, Sister Teresa Benedicta of the Cross, better known as Edith Stein, and Father Rupert Mayer. Their martyrdom too was a witness to Christ and a sign of resistance to the demonic powers of a world far removed from God.

These four blesseds represent the many Catholic women and men who, at the cost of numerous sacrifices, rejected the despotism imposed by national socialism and opposed the ideology of the brownshirts. They are therefore part of the resistance the whole Church put up against that system which scorned God and man. Finally, they also represent the many persons who by their resistance and their sacrifice were able to keep alive in mankind faith in the goodness in man and in a different and better Germany. Our own century too has a rich martyrology [Apostolic Letter *Tertio Millenio Adveniente,* n. 37]. Let us make sure that all these testimonies of true greatness of spirit and holiness are not forgotten.

A martyrology is not just a record of facts. It is an exhortation. Martyrdom in our century too is an exhortation. Was not the work of the Second Vatican Council a result of this? And the World Day of Prayer for Peace? And the many apostolic initiatives, such as the World Youth Days?

Through martyrdom, which represents the experiences of our century, the Church has gained a better understanding of herself.

As families you must also form an evangelizing community, in which the Gospel is welcomed and put into practice, where prayer is learned and practiced together, where all its members, through words, deeds, and the love they have for each other, bear witness to the Good News of the Redemption. "One body and one Spirit, just as you were called to the one hope that belongs to your call, one Lord, one faith, one baptism, one God and Father of us all, who is above all and through all and in all" [Eph 4:4–6].

This "unity of the Spirit" [Eph 4:3] is not a dream, a mere idea, but a visible reality in the community of the Church. The "one hope" [Eph 4:4] can be experienced in the *"communio"* of the one Church. A glance at the history of the People of God shows us how important it is to bear visible witness to this "unity of the Spirit" and this common "hope." ✠

Hungary 1996

On 6 and 7 September 1996, Pope John Paul made his second pastoral visit to Hungary. During this time he celebrated the one thousandth anniversary of the Benedictine Archabbey of Pannonhalma. This monastic foundation dedicated to Saint Martin is the oldest of Hungary. Here the Pope again acknowledged the contribution of the Sons and Daughters of Saint Benedict to the culture of Europe. On 7 September, at a special Mass at Ipari Park in the diocese of Győr, he spoke words of encouragement to the personal and national insecurities expressed by the faithful in Hungary in the post-Communist era.

Over the course of the centuries, your country has many times had to start over again; this was true also for the Christian community. This has happened most recently in 1989. It is against this background that I would like to express my appreciation to the bishops of the Church in Hungary for the work which they have done in the past five years. Dear brothers in the Episcopate, you preserved the unity of the Church and gave fresh impetus, in the context of your refound freedom, to missionary activity in every area of Christian life. You have encountered great difficulties but have not lost hope! In the spiritual reconstruction of your country you can count on religious orders and congregations which are being renewed, as well as on Catholic teachers and committed laypeople.

Dear brothers and sisters! Do not be discouraged by economic and social difficulties, by unemployment, by widespread poverty, by the decline of moral values in the generation which grew up without religion! The temptation of letting go, passively accepting the situation, is great indeed. Saint Paul described the pagans as those "who have no hope" (1 Thes 4:13). We Christians, on the other hand, draw life from the presence of Christ. Christ is our hope! We are never alone! We are the sheep of Christ the Good Shepherd, who is always with us.

You have shining examples to look to even when dark clouds gather overhead. First of all, the martyrs and witnesses of the faith in the past forty years bear testimony to the light of Christ. I am thinking of Bishop Vilmos Apor, who in this very city offered his life for those entrusted to him; I am thinking of Cardinal József Mindszenty and his formidable resistance to the dictatorship, with the consequent long *"Via Crucis"* which he had to travel. I am thinking of the doctor to the poor László Batthyany Strattman, a true hero of charity; I am thinking of the priests, the men and women religious, and the many lay Christians who gave their lives for Jesus. Let us pay homage to all who, in the past decades, suffered persecution rather than deny their faith!

To reveal to others the Father, his mercy and his love—this was for Jesus the most important task. At the end of the twentieth century, how great is the need to know Christ, his person, his life, his teaching! ✠

FRANCE 1996

FROM 19 TO 22 SEPTEMBER 1996, Pope John Paul II returned to France in order to commemorate the fifteenth centenary of the baptism of Clovis, king of the Franks, and the conversion of France to Christianity. At the same time, he commemorated the sixteenth centenary of the death of Saint Martin of Tours, Apostle of France and the first saint of the Catholic Church who was not a martyr. He also commemorated the martyrs of the Vendée, who were guillotined in the French Revolution. Among these he mentioned Blessed Peter René Rogue.

In a reference to contemporary martyrdom, he cited the recent execution of the seven Trappists at Notre-Dame de l'Atlas. Several of these were of the French Abbey of Belle Fontaine. This was in an address to the consecrated religious of northern and western France. All in all, he visited the cities of Reims, Sainte-Anne-d'Auray in Brittany, Tours, and Saint-Laurent-sur-Sevre. At the shrine of Saint Anne, on 20 September, he incited the pilgrims to that shrine to be missionaries to their own country. He recalled religious and lay saints alike who form part of the rich tradition of missionary France. Among these were Saint John Eudes, Blessed Jeanne Jugan, and Saint Louis de Montfort.

D ear young people, my friends, do not be afraid to respond generously to Christ's invitation to follow him! In the priestly or religious vocation, you will find the richness and the joy of giving yourselves for the service of God and your brothers and sisters. Your dioceses have a long missionary tradition. Do not let it die out. So many men and women await the witness of light and hope!

We bless the God of the covenant because your country owes much to the message of the Gospel in the history of its communities and its culture. We hope that the Church in France, continuing her journey in the footsteps of her father in faith, proud of her centuries-old tradition, will continue to shine with a salutary radiance in the history of peoples and nations. The witness to the Gospel is not a human achievement, but a service of God and of neighbor. Clearly expressing what is at the heart of missionary activity, St Thérèse of Lisieux wrote: "To love is to give one's all and to give one's self." You, too, go forth to proclaim the Gospel to your brothers and sisters! With all people of goodwill, build the civilization of love! Walking without hesitation in the footsteps of Christ, Savior of the world, witness to the love of God offered to all mankind. ✠

Sarajevo 1997

On 12 and 13 April 1997, Pope John Paul II made a long-awaited visit to the city of Sarajevo. In the midst of a war-torn country, he pleaded for reconciliation and for a cessation to all hostilities. He asked that Croats, Muslims, and Serbs come together in one family and claim together the heritage of a common land. In the course of his visit, the Pontiff publicly encouraged Cardinal Vinko Puljic, the hierarchy, the clergy, and seminarians, and especially the Franciscan Friars, to be instruments of healing in an atmosphere where hatred is tangible to the world. He addressed this international tragedy in the persons of the three-man presidency of the region: Alija Izetbegovic, Momčilo Krajisnik, and Kresimir Zubak. He made this speech shortly before his departure from the nation.

The tensions which can develop between individuals and ethnic groups as an inheritance from the past and as a consequence of close proximity and diversity ought to find in religious values reasons for moderation and restraint, indeed for understanding, with a view to constructive cooperation. I have had occasion to affirm—and I say it again here today—that Sarajevo, a city at the crossroads of the tensions between cultures, religions, and different peoples, can be considered the city symbolizing our century. Precisely here the First World War began in 1914; here the violence of the Second World War was unleashed in all its fury; here, finally, in the closing decade of the century, its people have experienced amidst destruction and death interminable years of fear and anguish. Now, after so much suffering, Bosnia and Herzegovina are finally committed to building peace. This is not an easy undertaking, as the experience of the months since the end of the conflict have shown. Nevertheless, with the help of the international community, peace is possible, indeed peace is necessary. From a historical perspective, Sarajevo and the whole of Bosnia and Herzegovina, if they succeed in peace, can become at the end of this century an example of coexistence and diversity for many nations experiencing this same difficulty in Europe and elsewhere in the world.

The method which must be rigorously followed in solving the problems which arise along the arduous path is the method of dialogue, inspired by listening to the other side and mutual respect. The method which, despite cases of resistance, is being increasingly acknowledged, requires of those taking part frankness, courage, patience, and perseverance. The effort required by face-to-face encounter will be richly rewarded. It will slowly become possible for the wounds inflicted by the recent terrible war to heal; and real hope for a more worthy future for all the peoples, who together live in this territory, will become possible. ✠

*C*ZECHOSLOVAKIA 1997

From 25 to 27 April 1997, Pope John Paul visited the Czech Republic in order to celebrate the one thousandth anniversary of the martyrdom of Saint Adalbert, Bishop of Prague. He was executed by pagan Prussians, and he is honored as the cornerstone of the history of the Czech, Slovak, and Polish nations. In commemorating him, the Pontiff spoke strongly not of history, but of present-day morality, condemning indifference and hedonism within those regions. His address was to the bishops of all three nations.

In the society of his time, both civil and ecclesiastical, Saint Adalbert faced enormously serious challenges and undertook a significant work, which, even if it did not bear visible fruits, eventually produced effects which still endure today.

The challenges lying before you today, dear bishops, are no less demanding than those of that time. I think in the first place of religious indifference which, as I had occasion to reaffirm in my apostolic letter *Tertio Millenio Adveniente,* leads many people to live as if God did not exist, or to be content with a vague religiosity, incapable of adequately responding to the problem of truth and the duty of consistency [n. 36]. Forty years of systematic repression of the Church, the elimination of her pastors, bishops, and priests, the intimidation of individuals and families, weigh heavily upon the present generation. This can be seen particularly in the area of family morality, as was shown by some statistical data gathered on the occasion of the International Year of the Family. Nearly a half of the marriages end in divorce or separation, especially in Bohemia. The practice of abortion, permitted by laws inherited from the past regime, is showing signs of a slight decrease, yet the number of abortions remains among the highest in the world. As a result, there has been a considerable decrease in the birth rate. For some years now, the number of deaths has exceeded the number of births.

Another challenge to the proclamation of the Gospel is hedonism, which has invaded these lands from neighboring countries and contributed to a growing crisis of values in everyday life, in family structure, and even in people's outlook on the meaning of life. The spread of pornography, prostitution, and pedophilia is also symptomatic of a situation of grave social malaise.

The family must be at the center of your concern as Pastors. As the "domestic church," the family is the firmest guarantee for the desired renewal as we approach the third millennium. I express my appreciation for the numerous programs and the various family centers which have sprung up in every part of the country in order to help provide concrete assistance to children, young people in difficulty, and unwed mothers. The family is also critical for the training of young people. The Europe of the year 2000 needs generous, enthusiastic, and pure young people capable of shaping the future. ✠

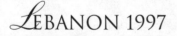EBANON 1997

FOR MORE THAN TWO DECADES the nation of Lebanon has been plagued by civil war and external intervention. Not only does the nation bear the scars of war, but the population has declined, as many Lebanese citizens have migrated to other countries. Because Lebanon is considered one of the Holy Lands, the Catholic bishops were assembled in Synod in Rome in 1995 to discuss that nation's religious and social problems. With this visit from 10 to 11 May 1997, the Pontiff solemnly and publicly concluded its decisions by signing a document of accord two years after the Synod.

Today I greet Lebanon. For a long time I have wanted to come among you, and for many reasons! I arrive in your country only today, to conclude the special Assembly for Lebanon of the Synod of Bishops. Almost two years ago the Synodal Assembly conducted its work in Rome. But the solemn part of it, the publication of the Post-Synodal document, is taking place now, here in Lebanon. These circumstances enable me to be in your land for the first time, and to tell you of the love that the Church and Apostolic See have for your nation, for all Lebanese: for the Catholics of the different rites—Maronite, Melkite, Armenian, Chaldean, Syrian, Latin; for the faithful belonging to the other Christian Churches; as well as for the Muslims and the Druze who believe in the one God.

At this exceptional Assembly we wish to declare before the world the importance of Lebanon, its historical mission accomplished down through the centuries: a country of many religious faiths, Lebanon has shown that these different faiths can live together in peace, brotherhood, and cooperation; it has shown that people can respect the rights of every individual to religious freedom, that they are united in love for this homeland which has matured over the centuries, preserving the spiritual heritage of their forebears, notably of the monk Saint Maron.

We are here in the region where the feet of Christ, the Savior of the world, trod two thousand years ago. The Holy Scriptures teach us that Jesus went to preach beyond the borders of the Palestine of that time, that he visited also the territory of the ten cities of the Decapolis—Tyre and Sidon in particular—and that he worked miracles there. Men and women of Lebanon, the Son of God himself was the first to preach the Good News to your ancestors. This is an extraordinary privilege. Speaking of Tyre and Sidon, I cannot forget to mention the great sufferings experienced by their peoples. Today I ask Jesus to put an end to these sufferings and implore from him just and lasting peace in the Middle East, with respect for everyone's rights and aspirations.

People often spoke of the "martyr Lebanon," especially during the period of war which afflicted your country more than ten years ago. In this historical context, the words of Saint Peter can well be applied to all who have suffered in this land. The Apostle writes: "In so far as you share in Christ's sufferings, rejoice because the Spirit of God rests upon you, and that is the Spirit of glory" [1 Pt 4:13–14]. I am mindful that we are gathered near the historic heart of Beirut, Martyrs' Square: but you have also called it Freedom Square and Unity Square. I am certain that the sufferings of the past years will not be in vain; they will strengthen your freedom and unity.

IN ANOTHER SPEECH, to the civic leadership of the nation, the Pontiff explained the scope of the visit as viewed by a world audience.

On 12 June 1991 I announced the convening of the Special Assembly for Lebanon of the Synod of Bishops. After many stages of reflection and sharing within the Catholic Church in Lebanon, the Assembly met in November and December 1995. Today I have come among you for the solemn phase of the Synodal Assembly. To Catholics, to the Christians of other Churches and ecclesial communities, and to all people of goodwill, I am bringing the results of the bishops' work enriched by cordial dialogues with the fraternal delegates—the Post-Synodal Apostolic Exhortation, *A New Hope for Lebanon.* This document, which I shall sign this evening in the presence of the young people, is not a conclusion or the final point in the journey which has been begun. Quite the opposite: It is an invitation to all Lebanese to begin with confidence a new page in their history. It is the contribution of the universal Church to the greater unity of the Catholic Church in Lebanon, to the overcoming of divisions between the different Churches, and to the development of the country, in which all Lebanese are called to take part.

THAT EVENING THE PONTIFF SIGNED the Synodal Document in the Basilica of Our Lady of Lebanon. There he addressed the nation's young people. As he signed the text, he spoke to the theme "Hope Never Disappoints."

So, are you willing to follow Christ? If you are willing to follow Christ and to let yourselves by seized by him, he will show you that the mystery of his death and Resurrection is the key par excellence to understanding the Christian life and human life. In fact, in every life there are times when God seems to be silent, like Holy Thursday night, times of distress like Good Friday when God seems to abandon those he loves; times of light like the dawn of Easter morning which saw the definitive victory of life over death. After the example of Christ, who put his life in the Father's hands, it is by putting your trust in God that you will achieve great things. For if we rely only on ourselves, our projects all too often reveal individual and partisan interests. But everything can change when one relies first of all on the Lord, who comes to transform, purify, and bring peace to one's inner self. The changes to which you aspire in your land first call for a change of heart.

Indeed, it is your task to pull down the walls built up during the painful periods of your nation's history; do not build new walls in your country. On the contrary, it is your task to build bridges between people, between families, and between the different communities. In your daily life, may you achieve works of reconciliation in order to pass from mistrust to trust! It is also your task to see that every Lebanese, especially every young person, can take part in social life in your common home. Thus a new brotherhood will be born and solid bonds woven in order to build up Lebanon, since the principal and decisive weapon is love. By drawing on intimate life with the Lord, the source of love and peace, you in turn will be artisans of peace and love. In this way, the Apostle says, we will be recognized as his disciples.

You are the treasure of Lebanon, you who hunger for peace and brotherhood and wish to commit yourselves every day to this land to which you are deeply attached. ✠

Poland 1997

From 31 May through 10 June 1997, Pope John Paul made his sixth visit to Poland. During this visit he first closed a Eucharistic Congress in the city of Wroclaw. Throughout his visit he constantly made reference to the Eucharistic theme, as also to the theme of European unity based on a sound spirituality. He again visited the shrine of Our Lady of Jasna Góra. On 7 June he spoke movingly at the shrine of the Divine Mercy in Kraków. On this entire visit he revealed much of his personal spirituality and his longtime admiration for Blessed Faustina Kawalska (1905–38), of the Congregation of the Sisters of Our Lady of Mercy.

Here I have come to this shrine as a pilgrim to take part in the unending hymn in honor of Divine Mercy. The Psalmist of the Lord had intoned it, expressing what every generation preserved and will continue to preserve as a most precious fruit of faith. There is nothing that man needs more than Divine Mercy—that love which is benevolent, which is compassionate, which raises man above his weakness to the infinite heights of the holiness of God. In this place we become particularly aware of this. From here, in fact, went out the message of Divine Mercy that Christ himself chose to pass on to our generation through Blessed Faustina. And it is a message that is clear and understandable for everyone. Anyone can come here, look at this picture of the Merciful Jesus, his Heart radiating grace, and hear in the depths of his own soul what Blessed Faustina heard: *"Fear nothing. I am with you always"* [Diary, Q. II]. And if this person responds with a sincere heart, "Jesus, I trust in you!" he will find comfort in all his anxieties and fears. In this dialogue of abandonment, there is established between man and Christ a special bond that sets love free. And "there is no fear in love; perfect love casts out fear" [1 Jn 4:18].

The Church rereads the message of mercy in order to bring with greater effectiveness to this generation at the end of the millennium and to future generations the light of hope.

The message of Divine Mercy has always been near and dear to me. It is as if history had inscribed it in the tragic experience of the Second World War. In those difficult years it was a particular support and an inexhaustible source of hope, not only for the people of Kraków, but for the entire nation. This was also my personal experience, which I took with me to the See of Peter and which in a sense forms the image of this pontificate. I give thanks to Divine Providence that I have been enabled to contribute personally to the fulfillment of Christ's will, through the institution of the Feast of Divine Mercy. Here, near the relics of Blessed Faustina Kowalska, I give thanks also for the gift of her beatification. I pray unceasingly that God will have "mercy on us and the whole world" [Chaplet].

WHILE IN POLAND, the Pope continued to single out Polish men and women who were heroes of the faith. On 6 June, in the diocese of Zakopane, he beatified two nuns. One was Sister Maria Bernardina Jablonska (1878–1940), a former Superior General of the Albertine Franciscan community. She distinguished herself by her work among the very poor. The other, Sister Maria Karlowska (1878–1940), was the foundress of the Polish Good Shepherd Sisters, a religious order dedicated to the rehabilitation of prostitutes and the care of those suffering from sexually transmitted diseases. Both women were dedicated to the Sacred Heart. Of them the Pope said, "the Heart of Jesus became the source of strength for the two women whom the Church is raising today to the glory of the altars."

On 10 June, in the city of Krosno, the Pope canonized Saint John of Dukla, a Bernardine Franciscan priest of the fifteenth century who was associated with the theological faculty at Kraków. Saint John of Dukla epitomized in his life the intense evangelical activity of the Franciscan Friars who helped intensify the faith of Poland. The canonization process of this holy Franciscan was interrupted by the partition of Poland in the eighteenth century and the ensuing political troubles. He was beatified in 1733 by Pope Clement XII. On 8 June, Pope John Paul canonized Saint Hedwig (also known as Saint Jadwiga). Throughout his many visits to Poland and in the course of his references to his homeland and his home diocese, the Pope continually made references to her with deep affection. She was the foundress of the Jagiellonian University, the Pope's alma mater. Formerly a princess of Anjou, she was born in Hungary in 1374 and died as queen of Poland and Lithuania in 1399. Through astute administrative skills, she contributed to the spiritual, cultural, and pastoral life of Poland and Lithuania. This canonization was the fulfillment of expectations and hopes expressed by the Pope's immediate predecessors from the leadership of Poland.

How happy the Primate of the Millennium, the Servant of God Cardinal Stefan Wyszyński, would have been today if he had been able to share with us in the great day of Hedwig's canonization! She was close to his heart as she was to the great Metropolitans of Kraków, to the Cardinal Prince Adam Stefan Sapieha, and the whole Polish Episcopate. Everyone thought that the canonization of Queen Hedwig would have been the culmination of the Millennium of the Baptism of Poland. Her canonization would also have been his fulfillment because, through the efforts of Queen Hedwig, the Poles, baptized in the tenth century, four centuries later undertook the apostolic mission and contributed to the evangelization and baptism of their neighbors. Hedwig knew that her mission was to bring the Gospel to her Lithuanian brothers and sisters. She accomplished this with the help of her consort, King Wladyslaw Jagiello.

And we today, listening to the words of the Apostles, wish to tell you, our Holy Queen, that you, as few others, had grasped this teaching of Christ and the Apostles. Often you would kneel at the feet of the Crucified One at Wawel (Castle) to learn this generous love from Christ himself. And learn it you did. You showed by your life that the greatest thing is love.

It is from him, the Christ of Wawel, the black Crucifix to which the people of Kraków go every year on pilgrimage on Good Friday, that you learned, Queen Hedwig, to give your life for the brethren. Your deep wisdom and your intense activity flowed from contemplation, from your personal bond with the Crucified One. Here *Contemplatio et Vita Activa* found the right balance. Thus you never lost the "better part," the presence of Christ. Today we wish to kneel with you, Hedwig, at the feet of the Crucified One of Wawel, to hear the echo of that lesson of love which you listen to. We wish to learn from you how to put that lesson into practice in our time. ✠

RANCE 1997

From 21 to 24 August 1997 Pope John Paul spent his time in Paris, where he celebrated the twelfth World Youth Day. His most important address occurred during the Sacred Liturgy of 24 August, when he delivered the homily at the concluding Mass. His theme was "resting in the Lord." Throughout this "youth experience," the Holy Father spoke of "the presence of God in Christ."

The few lines of the Gospel of John [Jn 1:36–39] which we have just heard sum up the program of World Youth Day: It is an exchange of questions, and then an answer which is also an appeal. In presenting this encounter with Jesus, today's liturgy wants to show that which counts most in your lives. As the Successor of Peter, I too have come to invite you to ask Christ: "Where are you staying?" If you ask him this question sincerely, you will be able to hear his response and receive from him the courage and strength to carry it out. The question is born of a quest. Men and women seek God. Young people realize in the depths of their being that this quest is the inner law of their lives. Human beings seek their way in the visible world and, through the visible world, they seek the unseen world at every stage of their spiritual journey. Each of us can repeat the words of the Psalmist: "Your face, Lord, do I seek; hide not your face from me" [Psalm 27(26):8–9]. We all have our personal history and an innate desire to see God—a desire which makes itself felt at the same time as we discover the created world. This world is wonderful and rich: it sets before us countless treasures; it enchants us; it attracts both our reason and our will. But in the end it does not satisfy our spirit. Man realizes that this world, with all its many riches, is superficial and precarious; in a sense, it is destined for death. Nowadays we are more aware of the fragility of our earth, too often degraded by the hand of man himself, to whom the Creator entrusted it.

As regards man himself, each person comes into the world, is born from a mother's womb, grows, and matures. We discover our vocation and develop our personality throughout our years of activity; then the moment comes when we must leave this world. The longer we live, the more we realize how precarious life is, and the more we wonder about immortality: What exists beyond the frontiers of death? Then, from the depths of our being, there arises the same question asked of the One who conquered death: "Rabbi, where are you staying?" Teacher, you who love and respect the human person, you who have shared in human suffering, you who illumine the mystery of human existence, help us to discover the true meaning of our life and vocation! "Your face, Lord, do I seek; hide not your face from me" [Ps 27 (26):8–9].

Dear young people, your journey does not end here. Time does not come to a halt. Go forth now along the roads of the world, along the pathways of humanity, while remaining ever united in Christ's Church!

Continue to contemplate God's glory and God's love, and you will receive the enlightenment needed to build "the civilization of love," to help our brothers and sisters, to see the world transfigured by God's eternal wisdom and love.

IN THE COURSE OF HIS CELEBRATIONS FOR WORLD YOUTH DAY, Pope John Paul II beatified Frédéric Ozanam (1813–53), the father of a family who founded the Saint Vincent de Paul Society, an organization of lay men and women dedicated to the destitute of nineteenth-century France. In remembering Frédéric Ozanam, whose love for the poor was equaled by his love of study, the Pontiff connected the themes of culture and service. The Beatification ceremonies were conducted at Notre-Dame Cathedral on 22 August 1997.

Frédéric Ozanam loved everyone who was deprived. From his youth, he became aware that it was not enough to speak about charity and the mission of the Church in the world; rather, what was needed was an effective commitment of Christians in the service of the poor. He had the same intuition as Saint Vincent: "Let us love God, my brothers, let us love God, but let it be through the work of our hands, let it be by the sweat of our brow" [Saint Vincent de Paul, XI, 40]. In order to show this concretely, at age twenty, with a group of friends, he created the Conferences of Saint Vincent de Paul, which aimed at helping the very poor, in a spirit of service and sharing. These Conferences rapidly spread beyond France to all the European countries and to the world. I myself, as a student before the Second World War, was a member of one of them. From then on, the love of those in extreme need, of those with no one to care for them, became the center of Frédéric Ozanam's life and concerns. Speaking of these men and women, he writes: "We must fall at their feet and say to them, like the Apostle: *'Tu es Dominus meus.'* You are our masters and we are your servants; you are for us the sacred images of the God whom we do not see and, not knowing how to love him in another way, we love him through you" [*To Louis Janmot*].

He observed the real situation of the poor and sought to be more and more effective in helping them in their human development. He understood that charity must lead to efforts to remedy injustice. Charity and justice go together. He had the clear-sighted courage to seek a front-line social and political commitment in a troubled time in the life of his country, for no society can accept indigence as if it were a simple fatality without damaging its honor. So it is that we can see in him a precursor of the social doctrine of the Church which Pope Leo XIII would develop some years later in the encyclical *Rerum Novarum*. ✠

BRAZIL 1997

From 2 to 5 October 1997, Pope John Paul II traveled to Brazil to attend the second World Meeting with Families. On 3 October, he spoke to the bishops and the delegates of the assembly in a special theological meeting in Rio de Janeiro. His talk summarized the sacramentality of Marriage and the inner working of grace in the family as a community. The subject of the family has been a perennial topic during all the papal visits. This talk could be considered the climax of the development of this theme.

The family is not an accessory, an extrinsic structure to man, hindering his development and his inner dynamism. "For by his innermost nature man is a social being; and if he does not enter into relations with others he can neither live nor develop his gifts" [*Gaudium et Spes*, n.12]. The family, far from being an obstacle to the person's development and growth, is the privileged place for the growth of the personal and social potential inscribed in his being.

The family, founded on love and enlivened by it, is the place where every person is called to experience, appropriate, and participate in that love without which man could not live and his whole life would be deprived of meaning [*Redemptoris Missio*, n. 10; *Familiaris Consortio*, n. 18].

Today the darkness that affects the very concept of man directly and primarily attacks the reality and expressions which are conatural to it. Person and family are correlated in esteem and in the acknowledgment of their own dignity, as well as the attacks against them and attempts to destroy them. God's greatness and wisdom are manifest in his works. Today it seems that God's enemies, rather than directly attacking the Author of creation, prefer to strike him through his creatures. Man is the culmination, the apex of his visible works. *"Gloria enim dei vivens homo, vita autem hominis visio dei"* [Saint Irenaeus, *Adv. haer.* 4, 20, 7].

Among the truths obscured in man's heart because of increasing secularization and the prevailing hedonism, all those concerning the family are particularly affected. Today, the basic struggle for human dignity is centered on the family and life. In the first place, the elements of equality in the spouse's dignity, and their necessary diversity and sexual complementarity in the conjugal relationship, are neither recognized nor respected. Even marital fidelity and the respect for life in every phase of its existence are subverted by a culture that denies the transcendence of man, created in God's image and likeness. While the disintegrating forces of evil succeed in separating marriage from its mission to human life, they strike at humanity, depriving it of one of the essential guarantees of its future. ✠

*C*UBA 1998

ON 21 JANUARY 1998 Pope John Paul began a five-day pastoral visit to Cuba, commencing at the airport in Havana. The trip was considered historical, in that it marked a breakthrough in the strained relations between the Holy See and the Communist government of Fidel Castro. The president of Cuba, Fidel Castro himself, visited the Vatican in 1997 to prepare for the occasion. The Cardinal Archbishop of San Cristóbal de La Habana, Jaime Lucas Ortega y Alamino, extended the invitation on behalf of the Cuban hierarchy.

This papal visit gave Cuba worldwide television exposure. The Pope took this occasion to develop his own topics of evangelization and the meaning of the Church. Also, however, he disclosed the rich Cuban Christian culture which has remained unnoticed for so long. Apart from his native Poland, this is his only other turn preaching in a Marxist environment: commentators call it one of his more significant visits.

During his five-day visit the Pontiff spoke of education, the family, the goals of youth, religious freedom, and Cuban piety. This visit, the first of 1998, occurs in the twentieth year of Pope John Paul's apostolic ministry. The inaugural address bears the same Christological character as his very first papal discourse:

In fulfilling my ministry, I have not ceased to proclaim *the truth concerning Jesus Christ,* the One who has revealed the truth about man, his mission to the world, the greatness of his destiny, and his inviolable dignity. In this respect, *the service of man is the path of the Church.* I am here today to share with you my profound conviction that the message of the Gospel leads to love, commitment, self-sacrifice, and forgiveness; a people that follows this path is a people with hope for a better future. Therefore, from the very first moment of my presence among you, I wish to say with the same force as at the beginning of my pontificate: "Do not be afraid to open your hearts to Christ." Allow him to come into your lives, into your families, into society. In this way all things will be made new. The Church repeats this appeal, calling everyone together without exception, individuals, families, peoples, so that by *faithfully following Jesus Christ all may find the full meaning of their lives,* commit themselves to serving their neighbor, and transform the bonds of family, work, and friendship. This will always redound to the benefit of the nation and of society.

ON FRIDAY, 23 JANUARY, Pope John Paul visited the University of Havana and addressed the faculty and representatives of the student body. In particular, he emphasized the contribution of the Servant of God, Father Felix Varela (1788–1853) to the philosophy and political development of the Americas. After praying for a short while before Father Varela's tomb, he spoke these words about the premier academic representative of Cuban culture:

A preeminent son of this land is *Father Felix Varela y Morales,* considered by many to be *the foundation stone of the Cuban national identity.* He is, in his own person, the best synthesis one could find of Christian faith and Cuban culture. An exemplary priest of Havana and an undeniable patriot, Father Varela was an outstanding thinker, who in nineteenth-century Cuba renewed the method and content of teaching in philosophy, law, science, and theology. To generations of Cubans, he taught that to assume full responsibility for our existence we must first learn the difficult art of thinking in a right way and with our own mind. He was the first to speak of independence in these lands. He also spoke of democracy, judging it to be the political project best in keeping with human nature, while at the same time underscoring its demands. Among these demands, he stressed two in particular: first, that *people must be educated for freedom and responsibility,* with a personally assimilated ethical code which includes the best of the heritage of civilization and enduring transcendental values, so that they may be able to undertake decisive tasks in service of the community; and second, that *human relationships, like the form of society as a whole, must give people suitable opportunities to perform,* with proper respect and solidarity, *their historic role giving substance to the rule of law,* which is the essential guarantee of every form of human concourse claiming to be democratic.

Father Varela realized that, in his time, independence was an as yet unattainable ideal. He therefore devoted himself to *training people, men and women of conscience,* who were neither high-handed with the weak nor weak with the powerful. From his exile in New York, he used a range of means to pursue his goal: personal letters, the press, and what might be judged his finest work, *Letters to Elpidio concerning impiety, superstition, and fanaticism in relation to society,* a true monument of moral teaching, his precious legacy to the young people of Cuba. In the last thirty years of his life, far from his teaching post in Havana, he continued to teach from afar and so gave birth to a school of thought, a vision of human society, and an attitude toward one's own country which even today should illumine all Cubans.

The entire life of Father Varela was *inspired by a profound Christian spirituality.* This was his deep driving force, the wellspring of his virtues, the root of his commitment to the Church and to Cuba: *to seek the glory of God in all things.* This led him to believe in the power of little things, in the creative force of seeds of truth, in the appropriateness of changes being made step by step toward great and authentic reforms. When he came to the end of his journey, moments before he closed his eyes to the light of this world and opened them to the Light which never ends, he fulfilled the promise which he had always made: "Guided by the torch of faith, I go to the tomb, on the edge of which I hope, with God's grace, to make with my last breath a profession of my firm belief and a fervent prayer for the good of my country" [*Letters to Elpidio,* vol. 1, letter 6, p. 182].

This is the heritage which Father Varela left. The good of his country still needs the undying light which is Christ. *Christ* is the way which leads man to the fullness of life, *the way which leads to a society which is more just, more free, more human, more caring.* The love for Christ and for Cuba which illumined Father Varela's life is part of the indestructible root of Cuban culture.

On the day before his departure from Cuba, Pope John Paul visited the city of Santiago de Cuba in order to venerate Our Lady of Charity of El Cobre. Here, a small image of Mary, found in Cuban water around 1605, has been housed since that time. The sanctuary is both a Cuban expression of Marian piety and an inspiration for the laborers in the nearby copper mines. In the nineteenth century, Our Lady of Cobre represented the Cuban independence movement. In his homily, the Holy Father identified the image of Mary with the evangelical mission of the Church:

During this celebration we will crown the image of Our Lady of Charity of El Cobre. From her shrine, not far from here, the Queen and Mother of all Cubans regardless of race, political allegiance, or ideology guides and sustains, as in times past, the steps of her sons and daughters toward our heavenly homeland, and she encourages them to live in such a way that *in society those authentic moral values may reign* which constitute the rich spiritual heritage received from your forebears. With gratitude, we turn to her, as did her cousin Elizabeth, and say: *"Blessed is she who believed that there would be a fulfillment of what was spoken to her by the Lord"* [Lk 1:45]. In these words lies the secret of the true happiness of individuals and peoples: to believe and proclaim that the Lord has done marvelous things for us and that his mercy is from generation to generation on those who are faithful to him. This conviction is the force which inspires men and women to commit themselves selflessly, even at the cost of sacrifice, to the service of others.

Mary's example of readiness to serve shows us the path to take. With her, the Church fulfills her own vocation and mission, proclaiming Jesus Christ and exhorting us to do what she says, building a universal brotherhood in which every person can call God "Father."

Like the Virgin Mary, *the Church is Mother and Teacher in the following of Christ,* who is light for the nations and the *dispenser of divine mercy.* As the community of all the baptized, the Church is likewise *the place of forgiveness, peace, and reconciliation,* opening her arms to all people so that she might proclaim to them the true God. By serving the faith of the men and women of this beloved people, the Church helps them to advance on the path of goodness. The evangelizing efforts being carried out in different places, for example, the missions in districts and towns which have no churches, must be sustained and promoted so that they may increase and serve not only Catholics but *the whole Cuban people, so that everyone may come to know and love Jesus Christ.* History teaches that without faith virtue disappears, moral values are dulled, truth no longer shines forth, life loses its transcendent meaning, and even service of the nation can cease to be inspired by solid motivations. In this respect, Antonio Maceo, the great patriot, said: "He who loves not God loves not his country."

The Pope concluded his remarks with his own prayer to Our Lady of Cobre:

> *Our Lady of Charity of El Cobre,*
> *Patroness of Cuba!*
> *Hail Mary, full of grace!*
> *You are the beloved Daughter of the*
> *Father,*
> *the Mother of Christ, our God,*
> *the living Temple of the Holy Spirit.*
> *Your name, O Virgin of Charity,*
> *evokes thoughts of the God who is*
> *Love,*
> *recalls the new commandment given*
> *by Jesus,*
> *invokes the Holy Spirit:*
> *love poured into our hearts,*
> *fire of charity sent on Pentecost over*
> *the Church,*
> *gift of the total freedom of the sons*
> *and daughters of God.*
> *Blessed are you among women*
> *and blessed is the fruit of your*
> *womb, Jesus!*
> *You came to visit our people*
> *and wished to remain with us*
> *as Mother and Lady of Cuba,*
> *throughout its pilgrimage*
> *along the paths of history.*
> *Your name and image are sculpted*
> *in the mind and heart of every*
> *Cuban,*

both within and outside the country,
as a sign of hope and focus
of fraternal communion.
Holy Mary, Mother of God and
Mother of us all!
Pray for us before your Son Jesus
Christ,
intercede for us with your maternal
heart,
filled with the Spirit's charity.
Increase our faith, enliven our hope,
augment and strengthen love in us.
Shelter our families,
protect young people and
little children,
comfort the suffering.
Be the Mother of the faithful and of
the Shepherds of the Church,
the model and star of the new
evangelization.
Mother of reconciliation!
Gather together your people
scattered throughout the world.
Make the Cuban nation a home
of brothers and sisters
so that this people will open wide
its mind, its heart, and its life
to Christ,
the sole Savior and Redeemer,
who lives and reigns with the Father
and the Holy Spirit,
for ever and ever.
Amen.

AMONG THE MANY THEMES reiterated by Pope John Paul during his visitations is that of the theology of the Cross. In a short discourse at a leprosarium at El Rincón outside of Havana, the Pope spoke to an audience of Daughters of Charity of Saint Vincent de Paul, as well as the medical staff and all the patients, at the Shrine of Saint Lazarus. Besides direct reference to physical suffering, the Pontiff spoke of the personal pain of isolation and persecution. While other remarks during this visit speak in political terms and of religious freedom, his most important remarks refer to that sustenance which comes from the memory of the Crucified Christ.

C hrist responds neither directly nor abstractly to human questioning about the meaning of suffering. Human beings come to know his saving response insofar as they share in the sufferings of Christ. The response which comes from this sharing is before all else a call. It is a vocation. Christ does not explain in some abstract way the reasons for suffering, but says first of all: "Follow me." "Come, *with your suffering share in this work of salvation of the world,* which is realized through my suffering, by means of my Cross." This is the true meaning and value of suffering, of the pain which is physical, moral, and spiritual. This is the Good News which I wish to pass to you. To our human questioning, the Lord responds with a call, with a special vocation which is grounded in love. Christ comes to us not with explanations and reasons which might either anesthetize or alienate us. Instead, he comes to us saying: "Come with me. Follow me on the way of the Cross. The Cross is suffering." "Whoever wants to be a follower of mine, let him deny himself, take up his Cross, and follow me" [Lk 9:23]. Jesus Christ has taken the lead on the way of the Cross. He has suffered first. He does not drive us toward suffering but shares it with us, wanting us to have life and to have it in abundance [see Jn 10:10].

Suffering is transformed when we experience in ourselves the closeness and solidarity of the living God: "I know that my Redeemer lives, and at the last . . . I shall see God my Savior" [Jb 19:25–26]. With this assurance comes inner peace, and from this a spiritual joy, quiet and deep, springing from the "Gospel of suffering," which understands the grandeur and dignity of human beings who suffer with a generous spirit and offer their pain "as a living sacrifice, holy and acceptable to God" [Rom 12:1]. This is why those who suffer are no burden to others, but with their suffering contribute to the salvation of all.

Suffering is not only physical. There is also suffering of the soul, such as we see in those who are isolated, persecuted, imprisoned for various offenses or for reasons of conscience, for ideas which though dissident are nonetheless peaceful. These prisoners of conscience suffer an isolation and a penalty for something for which their own conscience does not condemn them. What they want is to participate actively in life with the opportunity to speak their mind with respect and tolerance. I encourage efforts to reinsert prisoners into society. This is a gesture of high humanity and a seed of reconciliation, a gesture which honors the authority promoting it and strengthens social harmony in the country. To all of you who are detained, to your families who suffer the pain of separation and long for your return, I send my heartfelt greeting, urging you not to succumb to pessimism or discouragement.

Dear brothers and sisters, Cubans need this interior strength, the deep peace and joy which spring from the "Gospel of suffering." Let this be your generous offering so that Cuba "may see God face to face," that Cuba may walk in the light of his face toward the eternal and universal kingdom, that all Cubans, from the very depths of their being, may say: "I know that my Redeemer lives" [Jb 19:25–26]. This Redeemer is none other than Jesus Christ our Lord.

The Christian dimension of suffering reaches beyond its deeper meaning and its redemptive character. Pain is a call to love, which means that it ought to engender solidarity, self-giving, generosity in those who suffer and in those called to accompany and aid them in their distress. The parable of the good Samaritan [see Lk 10:29ff.], which puts before us the Gospel of solidarity with our suffering neighbor, "has become one of the essential elements of moral culture and of universally human civilization" [*Salvifici doloris,* n. 29]. In effect, Jesus in this parable teaches us that our neighbor is anyone we meet on our way who is wounded and in need of help. He must be helped in an appropriate way in the evil that has befallen him, and we must care for him until he is fully recovered. Families, schools, and other educational institutions, even if only for humanitarian motives, need to work perseveringly to awaken and refine this sensitivity to the suffering neighbor, whom the Samaritan of the Gospel symbolizes. The eloquence of the parable of the good Samaritan, as of the entire

Gospel, is in real terms this: Human beings must feel personally called to witness to love in the midst of suffering. "Institutions are very important, indeed indispensable; but no institution can of itself substitute for the human heart, human understanding, human love, human initiative, when it is a question of going to meet the suffering of another" [ibid., n. 29]. ✠

NIGERIA 1998

DURING A THREE-DAY VISIT TO NIGERIA (21 to 23 March 1998), Pope John Paul II beatified Father Cyprian Michael Tansi, O.C.S.O. The Beatification ceremony of this Trappist priest came after the African Synod, during which the future of the Church in Africa was discussed by the African hierarchy. Father Cyprian was born in 1903 and died in 1964. A convert to Catholicism, he first became a diocesan priest in 1937, and in 1950 entered the Trappist Abbey of Mount St. Bernard in England. His bishop, Charles Herrey, encouraged his formation as a Trappist with the hope that he would eventually open a contemplative foundation in Nigeria. Father Cyprian died before that hope could be fulfilled.

His personal life recalls the development of the Church in Nigeria in the first half of this century. His contemplative vocation highlights the need for serenity in the midst of chaos. His evangelical spirit reflects the missionary activity now undertaken by the Church in Nigeria. His sense of reconciliation addresses the political uncertainty of the Nigerian government and economy.

Blessed Cyprian Michael Tansi is a prime example of the fruits of holiness which have grown and matured in the Church in Nigeria since the Gospel was first preached in this land. He received the gift of faith through the efforts of the missionaries, and taking the Christian way of life as his own, he made it truly African and Nigerian. So too the Nigerians of today—young and old alike—are called to reap the spiritual fruits which have been planted among them and are now ready for the harvest. In this regard, I wish to thank and to encourage the Church in Nigeria for her missionary work in Nigeria, in Africa, and beyond. Father Tansi's witness to the Gospel and to Christian charity is a spiritual gift which this local Church now offers to the universal Church.

Reconciliation necessarily involves solidarity. The effect of solidarity is peace. And the fruits of peace are joy and unity in families, cooperation and development in society, truth and justice in the life of the nation. May all this be Nigeria's bright future! ✠

USTRIA 1998

From 19 to 21 June 1998, Pope John Paul made a third pastoral visit to Austria. He came at the invitation of Christophe Cardinal Schönborn, O.P., Archbishop of Vienna, on behalf of the hierarchy of Austria.

Amid declining Church attendance and a certain cynicism expressed in the secular press, the Pope reminded Austria of its key position in a new Europe which recognizes East and West as partners in the faith. He beatified three religious personalities to illustrate fidelity, Catholic culture, and inclusiveness in the ministry. The Pope had already spoken of the importance of Austria to the future of Europe, because of its history, culture, and geographic location. He also referred to it as key in restoring fervor, according to the "new evangelization"! Greeting President Thomas Klestil and Chancellor Viktor Klima, the Pontiff spoke of the anthropology of faith:

Thus *the concept of man created in the image and likeness of God is not a museum piece, but represents the keystone of contemporary Europe, in which the many building stones of various* cultures, peoples, and religions can be held together for the construction of the new building. Without this standard, *the European house under construction* is in danger of collapse and cannot last.

With these sentiments, I extend my gaze across these countries' borders to *the whole of Europe,* to all the nations on our continent with their history, from the Atlantic to the Urals, from the North Sea to the Mediterranean. Austria, in particular, has shared in Europe's fortunes, exercising a decisive influence. It shows in an exemplary way how many ethnic groups in the limited space can live together in fruitful tension, working creatively to build *unity in diversity.* In the national territory today, small in comparison to other countries, the charac-teristics of the Celts and Romans, Germans, Hungarians, and Slavs have put down roots, and these characteristics are still alive in the population. Thus Austria is becoming *the mirror and model of a united Europe* which does not want to marginalize anyone, but to make room for all.

TO EMPHASIZE AUSTRIA'S CATHOLIC CULTURE, the Pontiff beatified three Austrians. The ceremony was conducted in the Heldenplaty of Vienna (Heroes' Square) on 21 June.

Blessed Maria Restituta Kafka (Helena, 1894–1943) was a nurse and entered the Congregation of the Franciscan Sisters of Christian Charity in 1914. She worked as a nurse for the poor and oppressed until she took a stand against the occupation of Hitler in Austria. Sis-ter Restituta was arrested for hanging images of the crucifix through-out her order's hospital, despite being ordered to remove them by the Nazis. She was sentenced to death, but was offered freedom if she left her religious congregation. She refused. Sentenced to death by beheading, she tended to the other prisoners until her execution in March of 1943. The Pope's words underscore her devotion to the Cross:

Looking at Blessed Sister Restituta, we can see to what heights of inner maturity a person can be led by the divine hand. She risked her life for her *witness to the Cross*. And she kept the cross in her heart, bearing witness to it once again before being led to ex-ecution, when she asked the prison chaplain to "make the sign of the Cross on my forehead."

Many things can be taken from us Christians. But we will not let the Cross, as a sign of salvation, be taken from us. We will not let it be removed from public life! We will listen to the voice of our conscience, which says: "We must obey God rather than men" [Acts 5:29].

BLESSED JAKOB KERN (Franz Alexander,1897–1924) left the seminary in 1915 when he was drafted for the First World War. While serving his country, he sustained serious injury in battle. Barely recovered, he returned to seminary in Vienna, but was recalled to uniform. When the war was over, he entered the Norbertine Abbey at Geras. He felt a personal call to make reparation for a Norbertine priest who had left the Church. With papal dispensation, he was ordained a priest in 1922 without making final vows. Even though his war injuries worsened, Father Jakob showed zeal and kindness to all. He died the day his solemn profession was scheduled to take place, 20 October 1924. The Pope recognized his unwavering fidelity.

B lessed Jakob Kern stands before us as a *witness of fidelity to the priesthood.* At the beginning, it was a childhood desire that he expressed in imitating the priest at the altar. Later this desire matured. The purification of pain revealed the profound meaning of his priestly vocation: to unite his own life with the sacrifice of Christ on the Cross and to offer it vicariously for the salvation of others.

BLESSED ANTON MARIA SCHWARTZ (1852–1929) was ordained in 1875. In 1879 he was appointed chaplain to the Daughters of Charity Hospital in Vienna-Sechshaus. Through his contact with suffering workers and apprentices, Father Schwartz decided to found the Congregation of Religious Workers of Saint Joseph Calasanz. By appealing to the business community's Christian faith, Blessed Anton was able to protect apprentices from abuse, namely, allowing them to observe the Sabbath. Father Schwartz defended workers' rights to organize before the publication of Leo XIII's Encyclical *Rerum Novarum.* In 1908, Father Schwartz withdrew from public activity amid the controversy. In obedience, he remained publicly silent until his death in 1929. Later, the Pope would follow up this beatification with an apostolic letter to the whole Church "On the Holiness of Sunday":

Father Schwartz] leaves us a message: Do all you can to protect Sunday! Show that it cannot be a work day because it is celebrated as *the Lord's day*! Above all, support young people who are *unemployed*! Those who give today's young people an opportunity to earn their living help make it possible for tomorrow's adults to pass the meaning of life on to their children. I know that there are no easy solutions. This is why I repeat the words which guided Blessed Father Schwartz in his many efforts: *"We must pray more!"* ✠

CROATIA 1998

The beatification of Aloysius Cardinal Stepinac of Zagreb during Pope John Paul's visit to Croatia (2 to 4 October 1998) was considered controversial. After the Second World War, the government of Josip Broz Tito condemned Archbishop Stepinac as an anti-Semite and a fascist collaborator. In 1946, when Archbishop Stepinac protested the government's arrest and execution of clergy, he was put on trial for treason. During that trial, the Archbishop defended the unity of the Catholic Church within Yugoslavia and the unity of the entire Church with Rome. Found guilty of the charge of treason, he was sentenced to sixteen years of hard labor. Because of poor health, he was confined to house arrest, and died in 1960. It is believed he was slowly poisoned. In 1953, Pope Pius XII named Aloysius Stepinac a Cardinal and awarded him the Red Hat in absentia. The following sentences are excerpts from Pope John Paul's homily of October 3 at the national shrine Marija Bistrica on the occasion of the Beatification of the Servant of God Aloysius Cardinal Stepinac:

Blessed Alojzije [Aloysius] Stepinac did not shed his blood in the strict sense of the word. His death was caused by the long suffering he endured: the last fifteen years of his life were a continual succession of trials, amid which he courageously endangered his own life in order to bear witness to the Gospel and the unity of the Church. In the words of the Psalmist, he put his very life in God's hands [see Ps 16 [15]:5].

Very little time separates us from the life and death of Cardinal Stepinac: barely thirty-eight years. We all know the context of this death. Many present here today can testify from direct experience how much the sufferings of Christ abounded in those years among the people of Croatia and those of so many other nations of the continent. Today, reflecting on the words of the Apostle, we wish to express the heartfelt hope that, after the time of trial, the comfort of the Crucified and Risen Christ may abound in all who dwell in this land.

"Father, glorify your name!" [Jn 12:28]. In his human and spiritual journey, Blessed Alojzije Stepinac gave his people a sort of compass to serve as an orientation. And these were its cardinal points: faith in God, respect for man, love toward all even to the offer of forgiveness, and unity with the Church guided by the Successor of Peter. He knew well that no bargains can be made with truth, because truth is not negotiable. Thus he faced suffering rather than betray his conscience and not abide by the promise given to Christ and the Church.

In this courageous witness he was not alone. He had at his side other courageous souls who, in order to preserve the unity of the Church and defend her freedom, agreed to pay with him a heavy price in imprisonment, mistreatment, and even bloodshed. To these generous souls—bishops, priests, men and women religious, and lay faithful—we offer today our admiration and gratitude. Let us listen to their urgent call for forgiveness and reconciliation. To forgive and to be reconciled means to purify one's memory of hatred, rancor, the desire for revenge; it means acknowledging as a brother even those who have wronged us; it means not being overcome by evil but overcoming evil with good [see Rom 12:21]. ✠

MÉXICO 1999

On 22 January 1999 Mexican President Ernesto Zedillo Ponce de Leon and Cardinal Norberto Rivera Carrera, Archbishop of Mexico City and Primate of All Mexico, welcomed Pope John Paul II at the Benito Juarez International Airport in Mexico City. The Pontiff remained in Mexico four days, 22 January to 26 January. The goal of his visit was to present his Apostolic Exhortation, *Ecclesia in America,* to representatives of all the Episcopal Conferences of North, Central, South America and the Caribbean. This document was his response to the Synod of the Americas, held in Rome from mid-November to mid-December 1997. The theme for that Synod had been chosen earlier by the Pope himself and was enunciated in the *lineamenta* (the preparations) for that gathering in 1996. Thus, the Special Assembly for the Synod of the Americas labeled itself "Encounter with the Living Jesus Christ: The Way to Conversion, Communion and Solidarity in America."

Earlier, in 1992, in Santo Domingo, while celebrating the five hundredth anniversary of the first evangelization of the Americas, he publicly foresaw such an assembly and underscored the need in terms of the "new evangelization." In an Apostolic letter of 10 November 1994, *Tertio Millennio Adveniente,* he announced the convocation of the Special Assembly of the Synod. The major goals given to that Synod by the Holy Father were the fostering of a "new evangelization," the increment of pastoral solidarity among the local churches of the Americas, and the examination of problems of both social justice and international economic activity. All of this was taken up by the Synod membership in light of two realities. The first is that the Church in America enjoys its own peculiar structure—it is not European-centered and there are distinctive North-South divisions. Secondly, the Synod expressed hope in the future as the world crosses the threshhold into the twenty-first century, which celebrates the "fullness of time," i.e., the birth of Jesus Christ, the Son of God who is both Lord and Messiah. On 23 January 1999 Pope John Paul signed the Synod Document. Two days later, on 25 January, the Pontiff addressed the challenges and the joys of the century to come. He did this in the Azteca Stadium before "representatives of all the generations of the century." His theme again was the urgency, even the immediacy, of the "new evangelization." He concluded his talk with a special appeal to the young people who were present.

The last five centuries have left a decisive mark on the identity and destiny of the continent: five hundred years of shared history, interwoven with the indigenous peoples and those who came from Europe, later joined by those from Africa and Asia. Together with the characteristic phenomenon of intermingling it became evident that all races have equal dignity and a right to their own culture. Throughout this long and complex process, Christ has been constantly present on the American people's journey, giving them his Mother, the Blessed Virgin Mary as their own Mother, whom you love so deeply.

As suggested by the motto Mexico has chosen to welcome the Pope for the fourth time, "A Millennium Is Born: Let Us Reaffirm Our Faith," the forthcoming new era must lead to a strengthening of America's faith in Jesus Christ.

Four generations are present here and I ask them: Is it true that the world we live in is both great and fragile, sublime and sometimes confused? Is this world advanced in some respects but backwards in so many others? Yet this world, our world, needs Christ, the Lord of history, who sheds light on the mystery of man and guides him by his Gospel in the search for solutions to the chief problems of our time [see *Gaudium et Spes,* n. 10]. Since some of the powerful have turned their backs on Christ, the century now ending is impotently witnessing the death from starvation of thousands of human beings, although paradoxically agricultural and industrial production are on the rise; it no longer promotes moral values, which have been gradually eroded by phenomena such as drugs, corruption, unbridled consumerism, and wide-spread hedonism; defenseless, it beholds the growing gap between poor, indebted countries and others which are powerful and affluent; it continues to ignore the intrinsic perversion and terrible consequences of the "culture of death"; it promotes ecology, but ignores the fact that any attack on nature is deeply rooted in moral disorder and man's contempt for man.

America, land of Christ and Mary! You have an important role in building the new world that the Second Vatican Council wanted to promote. You must be committed to making the truth prevail over the many forms of deceit, so that good may triumph over evil, justice over injustice, honesty over corruption. Accept without reservation the Council's vision of the human being created by God and redeemed by Jesus Christ. In this way, you will attain the full truth of moral values despite the illusion of temporary, precarious, and subjective certitudes.

Christians of the twenty-first century also have an inexhaustible source of inspiration in the ecclesial communities of the early centuries. Those who lived with Jesus or listened directly to the Apostles' testimony felt their lives transformed and flooded with a new light. However, they had to live their faith in an indifferent and even hostile world. To make the truth of the Gospel penetrate, to transform the numerous convictions and customs that denigrated human dignity, required huge sacrifices, firm perseverance, and great creativity. Only with unshakeable faith in Christ constantly nourished by prayer, by listening to God's word, and by regular participation in the Eucharist were the first Christian generations able to overcome those difficulties and make human history fruitful with the newness of the Gospel, even many times by shedding their blood. In the new era now unfolding, the era of informatics and powerful means of communication, on the verge of an increasingly fluid globalization of economic and social relations, dear young people, you and your contemporaries face the challenge of opening the minds and hearts of humanity to the newness of Christ and the graciousness of God. Only in this way can we avoid the risk of a world and a history without soul, overproud of its technological achievements but lacking hope and deep meaning.

You young people of Mexico and America must ensure that the world, which will be in your hands one day, is oriented to God and that its political, scientific, financial, and cultural institutions are put at the authentic service of the human being, without racial of social distinction. Thanks to you, our future society must know, by the joy which comes from fully living your Christian faith, that in God alone can the human heart find peace and complete happiness. As good Christians, you must also be exemplary citizens capable of working together with people of goodwill to transform nations and regions with the power of Jesus' truth and a hope that never wavers in the face of adversity. Try to put St. Paul's advice into practice: "Do not be overcome by evil, but overcome evil with good" [Rom 12:21]. ✠

*U*NITED STATES 1999

ON 26 AND 27 JANUARY, POPE JOHN PAUL II visited the United States with a short sojourn in St. Louis, Missouri, where he was greeted by President and Mrs. William Clinton and the Most Reverend Justin Rigali, Archbishop of St. Louis. Here he continued and expanded the theme of the Synod for the Americas in terms of the "new evangelization," the phrase he coined in Haiti in 1983. In the discourse to the youth of North America shortly after his arrival, he developed the theme of "apostolic formation" for all the faithful. He had concluded his visit to Mexico with the challenge to tomorrow's generation to become "evangelizers." In St. Louis he spoke about the implications of the call to Christ and of genuine discipleship.

This is the time of your "training" of your physical, intellectual, emotional, and spiritual development. But this does not mean that you can put off until later your meeting with Christ and your sharing in the Church's mission. Even though you are young, "the time for action is now!" Jesus does not have "contempt for your youth." He does not set you aside for a later time when you will be older and your training will be complete. Your training will never be finished. *Christians are always in training.* You are ready for what Christ wants of you now. He wants you, all of you, *to be the light of the world, as only young people can be light. It is time to let your light shine!*

You are children of the light [see Jn 12:36]. *You belong to Christ, and he has called you by name. But you will get to know him truly and personally only through prayer. What is needed is that you talk to him, and listen to him. Today we are living in an age of instant communications. But do you realize what a unique form of communication prayer is?* Prayer enables us to meet God at the most profound level of our being. It connects us to God, the living God: Father, Son, and Holy Spirit, in a constant exchange of love. Through prayer you will learn to become the light of the world, *because in prayer you become one with the source of our true light, Jesus himself.*

Each of you has a special mission in life, and you are each called to be a disciple of Christ. Many of you will serve God in the vocation of Christian married life; some of you will serve him as dedicated single persons; some as priests and religious. But *all of you must be the light of the world.* To those of you who think that Christ may be inviting you to follow him in the priesthood or the consecrated life I make this personal appeal: I ask you to open your hearts generously to him; do not delay your response. The Lord will help you to know his will; he will help you to follow your vocation courageously.

On the horizon of this city stands the Gateway Arch, which often catches the sunlight in its different colors and hues. In a similar way, in a thousand ways, you must *reflect the light of Christ through your lives of prayer and joyful service to others.* With the help of Mary, the Mother of Jesus, the young people of America will do this magnificently! Remember: *Christ is calling you; the Church needs you; the Pope believes in you and he expects great things of you!*

ON WEDNESDAY, 27 JANUARY, prior to his departure from St. Louis, the Pope celebrated a votive Mass of the Sacred Heart of Jesus at the Trans World Dome in St. Louis. In his homily he spoke of the "seriousness" of the "new evangelization." In this way he outlined the ethical dimension of proclaiming the *Good News.*

Today, American Catholics are seriously challenged to *know and cherish this immense heritage of holiness and service.* Out of that heritage you must draw inspiration and strength for the *new evangelization* so urgently needed at the approach of the third Christian millennium. In the holiness and service of St. Louis's own St. Philippine Duchesne, and of countless faithful priests, religious, and laity since the Church's earliest days in this area, Catholic life has appeared in all its rich and varied splendour. *Nothing less is asked of you today.*

As the "new evangelization" unfolds, it must include a special emphasis on the *family and the renewal of Christian marriage.* In their primary mission of communicating love to each other, of being cocreators with God of family life, and of transmitting the love of God to their children, parents must know that they are fully supported by the Church and by society. The new evangelization must bring a fuller appreciation of *the family as the primary and most vital foundation of society,* the first school of social virtue and solidarity [see *Familiaris consortio,* n. 42]. *As the family goes, so goes the nation!*

The new evangelization must also bring out the truth that "the Gospel of God's love for man, the Gospel of the dignity of the person, and the Gospel of life are a single, and indivisible Gospel" [*Evangelium Vitae,* n. 2]. As believers, how can we fail to see that abortion, euthanasia, and assisted suicide are a terrible rejection of God's gift of life and love? And as believers, how can we fail to feel the duty to surround the sick and those in distress with the warmth of our affection and the support that will help them always to embrace life? The new evangelization calls for *followers of Christ who are unconditionally pro-life* who will proclaim, celebrate, and serve the Gospel of life in every situation. A sign of hope is the *increasing recognition that the dignity of human life must never be taken away,* even in the case of someone who has done great evil. Modern society has the means of protecting itself, without definitively denying criminals the chance to reform [see *Evangelium Vitae,* n. 27]. I renew the appeal I made most recently at Christmas for a consensus to end the death penalty, which is both cruel and unnecessary.

As the new millennium approaches, there remains another great challenge facing this community of St. Louis, east and west of the Mississippi, and not St. Louis alone, but the whole country: to *put an end to every form of racism,* a plague which your bishops have called one of the most persistent and destructive evils of the nation.

The Great Jubilee of the Year 2000 will begin with the opening of the Holy Door in St. Peter's Basilica in Rome: This is a powerful symbol of the Church, *open to every one who feels a need for the love and mercy of the Heart of Christ.* In the Gospel Jesus says: "I am the door; whoever enters through me will be saved, and will come in and go out and find pasture" [see Jn 10:9]. Our Christian life can be seen as a great *pilgrimage to the house of the Father,* which passes through the door that is Jesus Christ. The key to that door is repentance and conversion. The strength to pass through that door comes from our faith and hope and love. For many Catholics, an important part of the journey must be to rediscover the belonging to the Church, *to cherish the Church* as the Lord has given her to us, *as Mother and Teacher.*

WITH THIS VISIT TO MEXICO CITY AND ST. LOUIS, Pope John Paul deepened the mission that first brought him to the Americas and to the Latin American Episcopal Conference Assembly in Medellin twenty years earlier. There he developed a theme of a "common witness" to the Gospel, inherent in a model of "evangelization" outlined by his predecessor Pope Paul VI in 1975. Since 1983, the Pontiff has engaged in the clarification of his own evangelical model, known as the "new evangelization." This phrase connotes a special urgency, innovation, and courage, which is a challenge to the materialism of the times. In this sense, Pope John Paul has directly addressed his own age. Through his person and his office, he has also affected that age, especially through the discourses and activities of his unprecedented travels. ✠

ROMANIA 1999

FROM 7 TO 9 MAY 1999 Pope John Paul II visited Bucharest, Romania. This was the first pontifical visit of John Paul II to a country where the majority of Christians are Orthodox. In the history of Orthodox-Roman Catholic relations, the visit to Romania was a genuine milestone. During his visit, the Pope was hosted by Emil Constantinescu, president of the country, and by the Orthodox Patriarch Teoctist, as well as the Holy Synod of the Orthdox Church. Most remarkable was the size of the crowds who lined the streets to get a glimpse of the Bishop of Rome. On 8 May, the Pope and Patriarch signed a joint declaration regarding the political situation in Yugoslavia. In the course of his addresses Pope John Paul highlighted many issues from the recent history of Romania, including the Communist regime, which persecuted all Christians intensely. It is to be noted that the Greek Catholic Church, to which Romania's Roman Catholics belong, endured a severe loss of clergy and laity alike. However, that dramatic witness was indeed an ecumenical event. "The experience of martyrdom joined Christians of different denominations in Romania. The Orthodox, Catholics, and Protestants gave a united witness to Christ by the sacrifice of their lives. From the heroism of these martyrs springs an encouragement to harmony and reconciliation in order to overcome the divisions which still exist" (general audience at Rome, 12 May). Among the most significant of the addresses was the discourse delivered to the Patriarch Teoctist and the Holy Synod of the Orthodox Church on 8 May.

A culture inherited from ancient Rome, which has been patiently built up in a tradition of holiness beginning in the countless cells of monks and nuns who devoted their time to singing God's praises and, like Moses, to holding up their arms in prayer so that the peaceful battle of faith might be won for the benefit of the peoples of this land. The Gospel message thus reached the worktable of intellectuals, many of whom contributed through their charism to fostering its assimilation by the new generation of Romanians, starting out to build their future.

Your Beatitude, I have come here as a pilgrim to express the whole Catholic Church's affectionate closeness to you in the efforts of the bishops, clergy, and faithful of the Romanian Orthodox Church as one millennium ends and another emerges on the horizon. I am close to you and support you with esteem and admiration in the program of ecclesial renewal which the Holy Synod has undertaken in such essential areas as theological and catechetical formation, to make the Christian soul, which is one with your history, flourish anew. In this work of renewal blessed by God, know, Your Beatitude, that Catholics are at the side of their Orthodox brethren in prayer and in their willingness to help in any useful way. The one Gospel is waiting to be proclaimed by everyone together, in love and in mutual esteem. How many fields are opening before us in a task which involves us all, with mutual respect and in the shared desire to be useful to mankind for whom the Son of God gave his life! Common witness is a powerful means of evangelization. Division, on the other hand, shows the victory of darkness over light.

Your Beatitude, both of us in our personal histories have seen chains and experienced the oppression of an ideology that wanted to eradicate faith in Christ the Lord from the souls of our people. But the gates of hell did not prevail against the Church, Bride of the Lamb. It is he, the Lamb, sacrificed and glorious, who sustains us in distress and who now allows us to sing the song of regained freedom. It is he whom one of your contemporary theologians called "the restorer of man," the one who heals the sick and raises them up after their long subjection to the heavy burden of slavery. After so many years of violence and the repression of freedom, the Church can pour the balm of grace on man's wounds and heal him in Christ's name, saying, as Peter said to the man lame from birth: "I have no silver and gold, but I give you what I have: In the name of Jesus Christ of Nazareth, walk" (Acts 3:6). The Church does not tire of urging and imploring the men and women of our time to stand up, to set out again for the Father, to be reconciled with God. This is the first act of charity humanity expects of us: the proclamation of the Gospel and rebirth in the sacraments, which are then prolonged in serving our brothers and sisters.

Your Beatitude, dear brother bishops, our meeting is taking place on the day when the Byzantine liturgy celebrates the feast of the holy Apostle and Evangelist John the Theologian. Who better than he, who was intensely loved by the Master, can communicate to us this living experience of love? This is what seems in his letters to be the synthesis of his life, the word which in old age, when what is superfluous disappears, stayed with him to mark his personal experience: "God is Love." This is what he contemplated as he lay his head on Jesus' heart and raised his eyes to his pierced side, from which flowed the water of baptism and the blood of the Eucharist. This experience of God's love not only invites us, but I would say gently obliges us to love, the true and only synthesis of the Christ faith. "Love is patient and kind; love is not jealous or boastful; it is not arrogant or rude.

Love does not insist on its own way; it is not irritable or resentful; it does not rejoice at wrong, but rejoices in the right. Love bears all things, believes all things, hopes all things, endures all things" (1 Cor 13:4–7). These are the words of the Apostle Paul to a community tormented by conflicts and tensions. These words are valid for all times. We know well that today these words are addressed first of all to us. They do not serve to reproach the other for his error but to unmask our own, the error of each one of us. We have known conflict, recrimination, inner reticence, and closure to one another. Yet, we are both witnesses that despite these divisions, at the moment of great trial when our churches seemed shaken to their very foundations, here, too, in this land of Romania, the martyrs and confessors knew how to glorify God's name with one heart and one soul. It is precisely by reflecting on the marvelous work of the spirit, incomprehensible to human logic, that our weakness finds its strength and our hearts gain new courage and confidence amid the difficulties of the present situation.

I am pleased that in practical terms, it has been possible to begin a fraternal dialogue here in Romania on the problems which still divide us. The Greek Catholic Church of Romania suffered violent repression in recent decades, and her rights were scorned and violated. Her children suffered greatly, some even bearing the supreme witness of bloodshed. The end of persecution brought freedom, but the problem of ecclesial structures still awaits a definitive solution. May dialogue be the way to heal the wounds that are still open and to resolve the difficulties which still exist. The victory of love will not only be an example for the Churches but for all society. I pray God, the Father of Mercies and Source of Peace, that love, accepted and given, will be the sign by which Christians are recognized as faithful to their Lord. Your Beatitude, dear brothers in the Episcopate, let us restore visible unity to the Church or this world will be deprived of a witness that only the disciples of God's Son, who died and rose out of love, can offer it so that it may be promoted to open itself to faith (Jn 17:2). And what can encourage the people of today to believe in him, if we continue to tear the seamless garment of the Church, if we do not succeed in receiving the miracle of unity from God by working to remove the obstacles which prevent its full manifestation? Who will forgive us for this lack of witness? I have sought unity with all my strength, and I will continue to do all I can until the end to make it one of the priority concerns of the Churches and of those who govern them in the apostolic ministry.

Your land is strewn with monasteries. From St. Nicodemus of Tismana, buried in the mountains and forests, beats the heart of ceaseless prayer, of the invocation of the holy name of Jesus . . . the convents, the churches covered with frescoes, the icons, liturgical ornaments and manuscripts are not only the jewels of your culture but also a moving testimony of Christian faith, of a lived Christian faith. This artistic heritage, born of the prayer of monks and nuns, of artisans and peasants inspired by the beauty of the Byzantine liturgy, is a particularly significant contribution to the dialogue between East and West, as well as the rebirth of brotherhood which the Holy Spirit is enkindling in us on the threshhold of the new millennium. Your land of Romania, between *latinas* and Byzantium, can become the land of encounter and communion. It is crossed by the mighty, majestic Danube, which bathes the regions of the East and West. May Romania, like this river, know how to build relations of understanding and communion between different peoples, thus helping to strengthen the civilization of love in Europe and the world! ✠

ℐFTERWORD

As a young man, Karol Wojtyla expressed an interest in drama, philosophy, and literature. All three of these endeavors have a common basis in language. The skills of the young man who was to become Pope John Paul II were finely honed when he learned the discipline of Polish letters at the Jagiellonian University in Kracøw in 1938. In his autobiography *Gift and Mystery* (New York: Doubleday, 1996), he writes:

> As for my studies, I would like to point out that my choice of Polish language and letters was determined by a clear inclination toward literature. Right from the beginning of the first year, however, I found myself attracted to *the study of the language itself*. We study the descriptive grammar of modern Polish as well as the historical evolution of the language, with a special interest in its ancient Slavic roots. This opened up completely new horizons for me; it introduced me to *the mystery of language itself* [p.7].

The Pope's language skills were apparent from the very inception of his pontificate, when he addressed the crowd in St. Peter's Square moments after his election. He spoke with an unanticipated fluency. On the morning of his inaugural Mass, 22 October 1978, he greeted the world in a multiplicity of languages. His interest in language is very apparent in the style of his Encyclicals, Apostolic letters, and other exhortations; most noteworthy was the Encyclical *Dives in Misericordia* (30 November 1980). It was filled with footnotes, some of which contained scholarly references to the biblical use of Hebrew and Greek words.

This commitment to language likewise is apparent in the many discourses which he delivered on his eighty-five apostolic journeys. These trips provided him with a large audience and many varying occasions to use his language skills. Very often he relied on Polish, French, German, Spanish,

325

English, and of course Italian for a primary text. But he also made use of his familiarity with Japanese, Korean, Hungarian, Portuguese. His charisma, however, rests not in the number of languages he knows or how well he knows them. Instead there is a special power contained in his use of chosen words which convey a theme.

In the texts which we have examined from every one of his travels outside of Italy, four themes predominate. "Solidarity" is the first that comes to mind, because of its identity with the Polish labor movement and the disappearance of the Marxist empire in Eastern Europe which it anticipated. Solidarity, however, has a deeper connotation. It refers to a sense of communion, of human community, that is, an existential bonding between persons that grows out of a fundamental need and a concrete expression of fidelity from the deepest level. Another concept, heard most often in the African speeches, is "inculturation," the adaptation of the Gospel from a parent culture, which conveys the Good News to a society which receives and translates vividly the content of the Word. In 1983, the Pontiff coined a phrase during his visit to Haiti which originally applied to the Americas and specifically Latin America. This was the term "new evangelization," a reinvigorated creativity and commitment to expressing the invitation of the Holy Spirit in Christ. In particular the phrase cut through the glamour of materialism and calls out those who witness the deeper dimension of life. Finally the Pontiff spoke of a new Christian humanism which embodies references to culture as the conveyor of human identity and to dignity which is the privilege and indeed the right of every human being. His references to history, to personalities, and to creative expressions of the self all underscore his profound commitment to supporting, sustaining, and expressing the significance of each human life.

The Pope is no longer the young man who went from Wadowice to #10 Tyniecka Street in Kraców to study philosophy and Polish belle lettres. His wartime experiences, the death of his father, and the "rhapsodic theater" events of those years gave way to a priestly vocation in which he encountered the person of Jesus Christ.

This led him to the field of theology, which is also the study of words and the profound concepts which they convey. Ultimately he became a professor of that subject. In one of his more profound discourses, he reveals the significance of his background, his talent, and his personal inclination against the background of his vocation. In 1991 he addressed philosophers and theologians in a large seminar organized by the Catholic University of Lublin. He was again back home among colleagues, and he spoke eloquently of certain words and their significance in human history. He speaks of *Boho-slowie,* the Slavic word for theology, and of *Martyrion,* the Greek word for witness. He then weaves the logic of his presentation of Jesus, the "Faithful Witness," as the ultimate witness to the mystery of God. But witness is likewise a very profound word. A witness does not merely tell the event, a witness is also a part of the event and is therefore credible. By his use of words, the Pope's talks are essentially an invitation to all his listeners, and to his readers, to likewise become witnesses of Christ, who is the ultimate event.

JEROME M. VEREB, C.P.

ᴀCKNOWLEDGMENTS

THE EDITORS WISH TO ACKNOWLEDGE with gratitude the translations of the papal speeches, all of which came from the English edition of *L'Osservatore Romano*. We have also relied on *L'Osservatore Romano*'s translations of biblical texts. The biblical references contained here are in conformity with the Roman Catholic edition of the Revised Standard Version of the Bible.

Special thanks are due to Benjamin Tinker, who greatly assisted with the research and the structure of this book. Thanks also to Father James Dunfee of the Steubenville diocese for his help in highlighting texts and to Margaret Hoenig, Drew Bosee, and Francis Griffin, who helped with transcription of passages from the papal speeches.

Research assistance came from Father Dominic Papa, C.P., Director of the Passionist Preaching Apostolate. Father Paul Joseph Fullam, C.P., opened a great store of information through the Passionist Library in Jamaica, New York. Margaret Rose Vereb and Loretta Vereb also provided research assistance. Father Xavier Hayes, C.P., gave the initial inspiration with his own well-organized resource material.

Thanks, too, to the Very Reverend Jack Douglas, C.P., Rector, and to the community at Immaculate Conception Monastery in Jamaica, New York, where most of this book was put together. Finally, sincere thanks to the Very Reverend Terry Kristofak, C.P., Provincial Superior of the Eastern Province of the Passionists, for his support and assistance.

JEROME M. VEREB, C.P.